THE STORY OF GLIDING

Gordon Beaton
Kingskettle.
Fife

January 1984.

THE STORY OF
GLIDING

Second Edition

ANN WELCH

JOHN MURRAY
Fifty Albemarle Street London

Published by John Murray (Publishers) Ltd
50 Albemarle Street, London w1x 4bd

British Library Cataloguing in Publication Data
Welch, Ann
The story of gliding – 2nd ed.
1. Gliding and soaring – History
I. Title
797.5'5' 0904   GV764
ISBN 0 7195-3659-6

Printed and bound in Great Britain at
The Camelot Press Ltd, Southampton

To *BASIL MEADS*

CONTENTS

CONTENTS

ILLUSTRATIONS

LINE DRAWINGS (*by the author*)

ACKNOWLEDGEMENTS

The author would like to acknowledge and thank the following for their help in providing the plates: 1a, F. E. Wrightson & Associates, York; 2a, 10b, 42b, Anthony C. Elworthy; 2b, 9c, 9e, 11a–b, 11d, 13a–c, Dr A. E. Slater; 2c, 9d, 11e, 22a, 25b, 26b, 30a, 30d, 31a, 32a, c, d, e, 37c, 39b, c, e, 40a–c, 43a–d, 44a–c, the Author; 3, 4, *Aerokurier*; 5a, F. P. Raynham; 5b, Gordon England; 6a–b, 7a–b, Associated Newspapers Group Ltd; 8a–b, Alex Stöcker, W. Berlin; 9b, Von Fritz Krauskopf; 9f, Hermann Eckert, Eisenach; 10a, J. Jay Hirz; 11c, Central News, London; 11f, 17a–b, 19a, 21a, 28b, 29a, Charles E. Brown, Surrey; 12a–b, Sport & General Ltd, London; 20a, Heimgartner, Zürich; 22b, H. C. N. Goodhart; 23a, P.A.-Reuter, London; 23b, Rolu Photo, Paris; 24a, 27d, 37b, Bernard J. Koszewski; 26a, 27b, 38, Philip Wills; 27a, 35a, All-American Engineering Co, Wilmington; 31b, Udo Hans Wolter; 32b, *Daily Telegraph*; 33a, Research Station, St Auban; 33b, 36, Mannering & Donaldson, Christchurch; 34a–b, R. Georgeson, 39a, S. A. Aldott; 39d, Moss Potter; 41a, Adolf Seiler; 41c, Dr Anne Stolle; 42a, Uveges.

The names of the photographers of all other plates are unknown to the Author, including plates 14a–19c, which were found at Imperial College, London.

INTRODUCTION

This book is not intended to be a history of gliding, but a story about some of the people who wanted to fly in the same manner as the birds—on their own wings, using the energy of the sun and the wind.

Gliding did not, of course, start as a sport but as a stepping-stone in man's quest for flight. Lilienthal believed that much could be learnt from copying the birds and kept his gliders light enough to be foot-launched like the hang-gliders of today. The Wright brothers had no real interest in gliding. They wanted to develop powered flight, and although their first aircraft were gliders they were designed to carry the pilot and eventually an engine. By accepting the penalty of more weight, and launch complications, they could work directly towards the aeroplane.

Once the aeroplane was invented, running on your own feet with frail contraptions was of no further consequence, except to a very small number of individuals who still longed to fly as the birds did. It was from these few, wandering in the hills with their flimsy hang-gliders in the early 1900s, that led to the elegant and sophisticated fibreglass birds of today.

It is not only the aircraft that have changed over the years. To begin with the objective was to achieve controlled flight, and the sense of purpose needed was so demanding that it could be sustained by only a highly dedicated few. But when the first hang-glider pilots got together in the Rhön mountains they attracted like minds, and together they built better gliders. The objective now was not merely to fly—that was no longer a problem—but to soar; if the birds could do it there must be some way a glider could stay high in the sky.

Hill soaring, and later cloud and then thermal soaring, not only brought people together but welded them into an élite group, almost a sect; it did not matter that outsiders looked on gliding as an odd sort of flying—although sometimes tinged with an envious glance—the pilots themselves simply knew that their brand of flying was the finest. In England, in the '30s, this 'same species' feeling soon manifested itself among pilots in that national feature, the club. But gliding clubs were no strongholds of tradition; they were enterprising self-help groups which became almost a way of life.

This enthusiastic approach to flying, where every soaring flight was still a voyage of exploration, lasted almost into the '60s. There were competitions, of course, because gliding is a form of flying which lends itself to really satisfying contests, but these still retained an element of the unexpected and even the unknown. With gliders still made of wood some entrants arrived with brilliant new aircraft still in the course of construction, and feverish hammering would continue all night.

But it was competitions, or rather the concentration and prestige that was heaped upon them, that shifted the emphasis from the exploratory, migratory soaring of the birds to the closed-circuit racing of the car, the horse or the sailing dinghy. As gliders became heavier and faster, so as to be able to compete at higher speeds, they became less able to slope soar, be hand- or bungey-launched from hills, or to be afforded by young pilots. And so the simple delights, such as circling with a buzzard, or just wandering high above a cloud-dappled landscape, became harder to obtain. At the same time much of the identity of purpose in soaring dispersed. Gliding became specialised, polarised by its top pilots into a demand for more performance at almost any price.

A few glider pilots stayed out of the mainstream and flew solely for the simple pleasure of being in the air, often in a carefully restored vintage glider. Others added a little engine, a paradox that gave them the independence to fly as they wished. Then in the late '60s the new hang-glider appeared, bringing with its crude and rustling sail a long-overdue opportunity to fly in an unsophisticated, unregulated way. The demand, unsatisfied by current gliding or any other existing form of flying was enormous. In less than a decade there were 60,000 hang-glider pilots in the world and as many hang-gliders. These pilots, as their forebears had done, became an élite pioneering group.

Now there is gliding and soaring at each, extreme, end of the spectrum. There is the expensive fibreglass glider with its fantastic performance and the computerised thinking required of its pilot. At the other end there is the simple soft-wing, achieving its effective performance largely from its ability to be flown slowly with good physical co-ordination.

What is needed now is for these two magnificent means of soaring to find a link, so that there will no longer be a gulf between them. There is need for a new light simple glider to be pioneered, and a need to accept that there is delight for some pilots in every variety of soaring.

In the first edition (1965) the measurements were given in feet and inches and weights in pounds, etc. In order to minimise alterations to the existing text and drawings, the same units have been continued. However, in the new glider data table at the end of the book all units are metric.

I am most grateful for the generous help given to me, in the reading and checking of the manuscript, the loan of photographs and for agreement to reproduce excerpts from other publications. I am especially indebted to George Benson, Hugh Bergel, Paul Bikle, Terence Boughton, Peter Brooks, Charles E. Brown, Max Gasnier, Dick Georgeson, Nick Goodhart, Tony Goodhart, T. Heimgartner, Frau E. Hirth, Gordon Hookings, Frank Irving, Bernard Koszewski, Bill Kronfeld, Eric Nessler, Dick Schreder, Doc Slater, Philip Wills; to the Editors of *Gliding, The Sailplane and Glider, Sailplane and Gliding*, and *Soaring*; and not least to my publisher.

Part I

TO FLY LIKE THE BIRDS

Chapter One

MYTHS OR MADNESS

It is probably true to say that man has wanted to fly ever since he first saw a bird; but how much has he wanted to? Whereas 2,500 years have gone by since he showed himself capable of logical engineering thought, it is only just on a century since he first clambered uncertainly into the air on his own wings. For several hundred years before that, human gliding flight was possible, but dilatoriness and lack of enterprise in getting airborne has indicated that flying was clearly not one of mankind's more serious desires.

Three thousand years ago, the Chinese flew kites which were fundamentally sound aircraft, requiring speed through the air to maintain themselves just as aeroplanes do. Some of their kites were shaped like birds, and some were even big enough to carry people. The Chinese understood at what point on the kite the string should be attached to make it fly well, or climb steeply. If, instead of holding the kite at an angle to the wind so that it went up, they had removed the string, weighted the nose suitably, and launched it off a cliff so that it glided down, it would have flown just as effectively as the aircraft of the 19th-century experimenters. But flying kites high in the bright sky was fun, and merely throwing a beautifully worked kite down into a valley was senseless. With its competitions and its craftsmanship, kite-flying was sufficient in itself.

As the art moved slowly over the centuries from China to India, and then to Europe, it must have stimulated the thoughts of many hundreds of people. But the kite did not become translated into a glider. Perhaps it was because kites were captive, and so did not fill the imagination with thoughts of flying as a means of travel. But even if going anywhere in

3

them was impossible, the most surprising thing is that they do not even appear to have been used as observation platforms. In 2,000 years there is no record of a kite having been used to watch out for invading fleets, spy into besieged castles, or even to make signals. The first occasion on which these simple flying machines were used other than for pleasure was probably the Franco-Prussian war of 1870.

It was much the same with balloons. Since primeval times the smoke of fires had risen into the air, but not until the 18th century did people learn how to make practical hot-air balloons.

Enough knowledge to build an artificial bird existed at the time of the Armada in 1588. Leonardo da Vinci had started thinking about aerodynamics, and defined the difference between soaring and flapping (or powered) flight. Among the ship and coach builders adequate knowledge of structures existed, but da Vinci never actually built an aircraft and no shipwright wanted to fly.

It is strange, this dream of flight, which no one succeeded in turning into reality. Even in the age of the great navigations, when there was a flowering of the whole civilised world into the realms of exploration, nothing happened. People were prepared to go out to find new worlds, even though many still thought that the lands did not exist and that the earth was flat. The determination to discover was so strong that they were not deterred. In the heat of this vast activity better ships were built, new navigating instruments designed, and new skills learnt. But not one-hundredth, or even one-thousandth part of all the energy in this age of new things was spent on trying to fly.

It would be interesting to try to discover whether this disinterest was due to a huge feeling of material impossibility, or to a mental prohibition, which involved religious principles or fear of black magic, or whether there was just a natural inborn instinct for man to stay connected to the good earth. Whatever it was, it was sufficiently strong to delay the possibility of gliding or soaring flight by some 300 years (and powered

4

flight by fifty or so). Perhaps the key to this puzzle lies in the lateness with which the art of the simple experiment appeared. To us this often seems the obvious way of investigating how to overcome a problem, but the concept is comparatively recent. By the 16th century, not a great deal of experimental activity would have been needed to produce an artificial bird which was sufficiently near the right basic principles to have given some indication of the way ahead: it was quite within the scope of people living at the time. But there was no passionate desire to get into the air. Even today, among some, there still lingers a sort of unconscious guiltiness, even a dislike of flying.

There were, of course, a few prospective aviators throughout history. They attempted to fly for nearly every reason possible —except the right one, and their efforts showed an almost complete lack of logical thought. If we are to believe the legend, they started with the well known and dutiful son, Icarus, the wax of whose wings melted as he neared the sun. Imprisoned with his father, a 'cunning artificer', the pair naturally wanted to escape, and made some wings using wax as the rather improbable adhesive. Whether they both flew, or whether Daedalus slipped out while his son sacrificed himself, will never be known. In the excitement of seeing the unlucky Icarus hurtling towards the sea from the ramparts, shedding feathers in all directions, the guards could easily have missed a creeping figure.

Escape seems to have been one of the main motives of early attempts at flight, one of the most successful being that of the Chinese Emperor Shun, who as a boy escaped from captivity by 'donning the work clothes of a bird'. Presumably no one actually saw him in the act, otherwise he is likely to have been recaptured. There is, however, some mythological evidence that the boy, who could have been small and skinny, used a couple of large reed hats, which are known to have been anything up to three feet in diameter, as wings, and in the few seconds of his descent became the unknowing inventor of the parachute.

There are many more accounts of attempts to fly, almost

all fatal. Men dressed in feathers, and shrouds stiffened with withy wands, continued to hurtle from towers, and people believed that witches really could get airborne on that most unsuitable device—the broomstick.

Possibly the first account of anyone who approached the problem of real flying with any likelihood of success was an Italian mathematician from Perugia, called Danti. He is said to have constructed a flying machine in about 1490, and flown over Perugia, as well as, according to legend, Lake Trasimeno. Although there is no evidence, it is possible that Danti knew of da Vinci's work, which was taking place less than 50 miles away, and had even seen some of his drawings. In any case he knew that it was necessary to have wings proportionate to the weight of the operator. This was an improvement on the designers of cherubs, who had divine faith in the power of the ridiculous little pink wings that adorned the plump bodies of their creations. The hissing supposedly made by Danti's device in flight led some to believe that it may possibly have been an ornithopter with flapping wings, but the noise was probably not dissimilar to the sound made by a primitive high-drag glider. The mention of iron stays to the wings lends strength to this theory.

The type of glider which someone of Danti's time was most likely to have built would have consisted of wings only, which the operator would fix to his upper body and arms, and from which he would hang when in the air, like a basic hang-glider. Legend says that Danti made flights over the lake; if he made them at all, he may have deliberately chosen this location in order to end in the water, and avoid having to run on landing. There are more windless days in Central Italy than in many parts of Europe, and so his arrival speed on to hard ground could have been inconveniently high. The one flight for which there seems to be real evidence is the flight over Perugia itself. Watched by a crowd of people, one of the iron wing stays unfortunately collapsed, and he severely injured himself falling onto the roof of St Marius's church.

If he did fly, and there is reason to believe that he probably made more than one serious attempt, Danti was the first glider pilot.

Time went on, and a few more adventurers experimented. They did themselves no good at all, until about 150 years later, when John Wilkins (1614–72), Bishop of Chester, applied the glimmerings of modern scientific thought to the problem. His main contribution, as well as sorting out ideas into a rational form, was to realise that flying was not a pursuit in which success could be expected first time. He advocated the flyer, having made and attached his wings, not to take the usual spectacular leap from a high tower, but to run along the ground, endeavouring to extend the length of flight. He wrote that it was possible to 'step constantly ten yards at a time', which although not up to the same level of audience appeal, was clearly more profitable for the operator. One can visualise clearly the public image created by some white winged figure taking flying leaps across a field in the hoped for privacy of moonlight.

In Italy, at this time, a Neapolitan called Borelli, ignorant of da Vinci's works, produced a conclusion which although negative, contributed in the long term to the sum of useful knowledge. He concluded that, because a man's pectoral muscles are a much smaller proportion of his total weight than are a bird's, 'it is impossible that men should be able to fly craftily by their own strength'. Thus Borelli could have saved much useless work on ornithopters if his writings had been available, and accepted.

During the great ballooning era of the 18th century nothing was done towards heavier-than-air flight. The problems were by now sufficiently well understood to have reduced the leaping-off-a-tower fraternity to almost nil, but no one person really knew enough to get going. Not only did insufficient background knowledge exist for the inventor to draw on, but there was no usable source of power, and none in prospect. Gunpowder was seriously considered as a possibility, but its success in a structurally unsound aircraft covered in feathers would have been problematical.

7

Flight without power was possible; birds with still wings soared above the cliffs, the waves and the deserts, flaunting their simple superiority to any human who cared to look. But not until the beginning of the 19th century did men start to give sufficient calculating thought to the problem for progress to be made. Sir George Cayley (1773–1857), of Scarborough, improved the foundations of aeronautical knowledge to such an extent that the way became open, not only to more thinkers, but for the first practical experiments by ordinary people. Cayley did what the Chinese could have done; he weighted the nose of a paper kite and flew it as a glider. He found that 'if pointed downward in an angle of about 18°, it would proceed uniformly in a right line for ever with a velocity of 15 feet per second. It was very pretty to see it sail down a steep hill, and it gave the idea that a larger instrument would be a better and safer conveyance down the Alps than even the surefooted mule, let him meditate his track ever so intently.'

FIG. 1. Cayley's 1809 model glider.

During his long life, Cayley experimented with aerofoil sections mounted on whirling arms, learnt how to obtain lateral stability by setting the wings at a dihedral angle, and longitudinal stability with a tailplane. He realised the importance of streamlining, and made and flew many models. By 1850 he was building full-sized aircraft, one of which had carried a boy; in 1853 he produced a man-carrying aircraft. It had a large wing composed of a sail attached to a wooden framework, which took up its aerofoil section only in an airflow, as does the rogallo hang-glider of today. Control was intended to be achieved by deflections of a small cruciform sail on the end of a long lever operated by the pilot, who sat sideways inside a wooden fuselage. The intention was correct but the skill required to get it right was consider-able, and not at the time possessed by the 'pilot'. Because Cayley was nearly eighty years old he felt unable to attempt the flying himself so ordered his startled coachman on board, and had the aircraft launched over a small valley in Brompton Dale. The flight was brief, and in the silence which followed the crumpling noises, the coachman could be heard with-drawing his labour in no uncertain terms.

Chapter Two

THE LONELY MEN

A Frenchman, Jean-Marie le Bris, was sailing the Southern Ocean at the time of Cayley's great work in the early years of the 19th century. For a long time he had been interested in the idea of flying; but he knew nothing about it, nor of experiments that others had made. From his ship, however, he could watch the long-winged albatross, one of the finest soaring birds in the world. He saw it fly hour after hour without effort, using the wind blowing over the wave ridges to stay airborne. The beauty of its flight had stimulated more men than le Bris. What did the bird possess that allowed it this beautiful sweeping flight? Was it the power contained in the creature or its feathers, or in the air alone, or in the air which was disturbed by the waves? Le Bris wanted to find out, so one day, risking the ridicule of his fellow sailors, he fixed the wings of a dead albatross in the flying position, and holding it against the wind that streamed past his ship was delighted to find that the heavy body tended to lift, and became convinced that he could reproduce this ability to fly in a man-made device.

As soon as he had obtained enough money to afford to take some time off, he returned to France to build an artificial albatross, starting work near Douarnenez. His first bird had a span of 50 ft and a length of 25 ft, almost the exact measurements of today's Standard class glider; the weight, however, was only 110 pounds instead of 450 pounds. The fuselage, which was huge, he shaped like a canoe, and in the cockpit installed two levers which were continuations of the wing spars; with these he proposed to flap the huge wings, still not having fathomed the way in which the albatross flew.

The great ship was at last finished in the autumn of 1856, and le Bris took it to the empty beaches nearby, followed, as can be imagined, by a crowd of spectators. To obtain flying speed, he intended to use a horse to pull a trolley on which the albatross was mounted. When all was prepared, le Bris climbed up on to the trolley and stood in the cockpit grasping the levers. The glider-bird was attached to the trolley by a

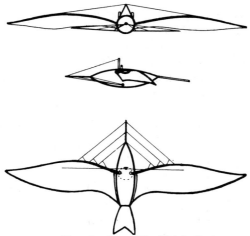

Fig. 2. Sketch-plan of Le Bris' albatross

long tether rolled up on a drum, the end of which was fixed near the coachman who would drive the horse. The whole equipage was faced into the wind.

It must have been a magnificent moment. The sea wind blowing across the great flat sands; the watchers, curious or fearful, standing close together for moral comfort; the coach-man (clearly a hazardous occupation in those days) concerned only with the technicalities of driving his precious horse, and le Bris upright in his winged canoe, thinking of his dream to fly.

He gave the order to advance.

The horse broke into a trot, the trolley ran faster and faster on its hard wheels. At last le Bris decided that the moment had

11

arrived when his vast albatross, shaking and vibrating, had enough speed to fly. Inclining his wings to the wind so that they would provide the greatest lift, he released the cords holding the aircraft to the trolley. Silently the great albatross started to rise, kiting on the strong sea wind. Overcome by astonishment the crowd stared as the rope tethering the bird to the trolley slowly unreeled; it rose higher and higher, and higher, until it was far above their heads, like a bird of prey ready to pounce. At this dramatic moment in history the rope caught round the neck of the unfortunate coachman; continuing to unreel, it took him inexorably aloft. It is a commonplace in aviation that an accident never takes place as the result of a single cause, and at this instant in time a situation unusually pregnant with total disaster existed. But quite remarkably everyone lived to tell the tale. The horse, deprived of the coachman's professional patter, slowed down instead of galloping into the sea, the half-stalled albatross, poised at 300 ft, sank or glided back to the ground—clearly its flapping wings had never flapped. The strength of the sea wind and the softness of the sand took care of the coachman's downfall, and the albatross, still with le Bris upright, touched down, swung round and carried out the first ground loop in history. The fate of the trolley is not known.

Encouraged by his success le Bris decided to continue, but using a different launching system, consisting of a great gallows from which the albatross hung like a pendulum. Standing in his canoe facing the wind he got it oscillating like a swing; at the moment he reckoned the speed was enough to fly, he released the albatross; unfortunately, the glider was still stalled, and it pitched nose down, hitting the ground before le Bris had gained control of any sort. The pilot was taken from the debris with a broken leg, cuts and bruises.

This did not discourage the remarkable inventor, and two years later he built a new albatross. It was better than the first, slightly bigger, stronger, and at the same time lighter. Everything looked hopeful but unfortunately, although the aircraft made a few short flights without the pilot on board, le Bris was continuously troubled by impatient spectators, and at the mercy of unsuitable weather and launching methods which did not prove as satisfactory as he hoped.

Le Bris volunteered for the army in the 1870 war, and the next year joined the police, which unfortunately resulted in his assassination.

At the same time that le Bris was experimenting at Douarnenez, another Frenchman, Louis Mouillard, was working on the possibilities of flight at the other end of France. Born and living in Lyon, Mouillard was fascinated by the flight of birds, and not only observed them with care, but recorded in great detail their vital statistics, weight, changes in wing plan when flying slow and fast, as well as the wind speeds in which they would fly. He discovered that only high aspect-ratio birds, those with long narrow wings like the albatross, would fly when the wind was strong, and that eagles would stay on the ground if it exceeded 26 m.p.h.

About 1860 Mouillard moved to Algeria, which he found to be a fascinating place for continuing his work. In the heat of the day the gold-blue haze of the sky seemed filled with soaring vultures. Each morning as the sun grew strong they would appear silently and seemingly from nowhere, circling endlessly on their still wings, rising higher with the power of the sun until they vanished into its glare. Almost since the beginning of calculable time these birds had followed the same pattern of flight, waiting to devour the wreckage of life. Mouillard watched them for hours until his eyes were dazzled; from the dancing heat of the sand he watched them and longed to fly. He worked out how big the wings should be to carry his weight, and in considerable detail the shape of the craft he would have to make. But he did not know or understand how a bird actually flew, whether feathers were necessary, or that a minimum airspeed was needed to support the wings. Then there was the problem of materials. This was much greater than is often realised, since no one else needed to use materials which were both light and strong. Ship builders, for example, obtained greater strength simply by using heavier scantlings. There was the difficulty of fixing the members together; nailing bamboo is impossible, glues were unreliable, and lashings too flexible. Mouillard was very able, but he found the problems of building a flying machine accumulating the more he thought about them, so he was forced to curtail his dream, and to tackle the problem a little bit at a time. He started by building himself simple wings, crude affairs which fitted on to his shoulders, and from which his body would hang down in flight. There was no fuselage and no tail: he would first just try to find out how a wing worked, and how it could best be made.

With his first efforts Mouillard achieved a flying leap of 15 seconds, in which he travelled 50 yards. This success was tempered by an almost desperate complication, when Mouillard found that his experiments would be subject to the uncompromising derision of his family and his neighbours. After the first one or two leaps made against a background of shrieks of scorn and ribald barracking he attempted to fly only when he could get rid of everyone, having to go to enormous lengths to find excuses for doing so. On one of his secret flights he was caught by an unexpected gust, and flung heavily on to rocky ground. As he lay recovering his breath and feeling for broken limbs, he must have wondered whether it was all worth while. This setback, combined with some illness which afflicted him and the sheer size of his lonely problem, proved too much, and for some time he gave up any attempts to fly.

After a while he moved to Cairo. Again the vultures rose above him circling into the deep sky, and his enthusiasm returned. Here he worked on a book which was to contain the results of his calculations and study, and into which he poured his immense knowledge of bird flight. Once again he tried to fly. With his slowly growing knowledge he built his third and fourth pairs of wings, the latter of over 50 ft span, with an area of 350 sq. ft, and a weight of 100 lb. He became hopeful of success, but before he could get airborne his health finally broke down and in despair he was forced to abandon

14

his attempts. While he was ill he spent much of his time writing, so that others might achieve what was denied to him. His great book, called *L'Empire de l'Air* was published at last in Paris in 1881, and was to become a great inspiration to Lilienthal and the Wright brothers—as yet children. This monument of original work was the result of thirty lonely years during which the author never met a single person who would understand or admit the principle that human flight was possible without power.

When his book was published, Mouillard discovered that he was no longer on his own, for disciples and pupils wrote or came to him, not only from France but from distant America; no longer working alone with only their hopes, they could argue, and be encouraged. During the last ten years of his life Mouillard must have realised that these friends would now carry on where he could not, and that they would succeed. So he started producing writings for their guidance on such subjects as 'a programme for safe experimenting', the employment of barometers as altimeters, and even on the training of pilots, and the use of parachutes.

Although his mind was still far ahead of his contemporaries, his body was failing. At the age of sixty-three, paralysed and exhausted, Mouillard retired to a small lodging house and cut himself off from the world. Many of his friends believed him dead, and ceased to write him letters. He finally died alone and without money in 1897.

The problem of flight had now been studied sufficiently to indicate clearly that a man-carrying aircraft could be built, although it was not understood how height could be maintained. The soaring bird was known to need no engine, since it somehow extracted power from the air itself, but so far no one had studied the air to find how it could contain this mysterious power. This was not surprising since in a non-scientific world there could have been few people to devote their energy to such an abstract theme. However, the gap was filled by another Frenchman, Alphonse Penaud. He was about fifteen years old when le Bris nearly strangled his coachman, and he died at the age of thirty, the year before Mouillard published his *L'Empire de l'Air*.

There is little information on how Penaud carried out his investigations, or what mental and observational processes enabled him to reach the conclusions he did. What is astonishing is that he discovered so much, as can be seen by the diagrams that he left.

Penaud realised that since the wind could not penetrate obstructions, it must either go round or over them, and following from this he deduced that if the obstruction was a ridge, the wind would blow up and over the top. This was confirmed by his observations of birds which soared, without flapping, so long as they stayed in the region of rising air on the windward sides of cliffs and hills.

The understanding of slope lift is not difficult, but Penaud also realised that under some conditions atmospheric waves were set up to the lee of hills, in which birds could soar. He was not able to work out properly what happened, and his diagrams are not accurate by today's knowledge, but it is remarkable that he realised at all that waves could exist in the atmosphere.

His most interesting work was on thermals. He deduced that the vertical up-currents in which birds soared were caused by convection, and he produced diagrammatically his ideas of the structure of thermals, which he believed to circulate in the form of a vortex ring, or 'doughnut'. This theory, which is now generally accepted, was not propounded again until the 1950s. His writings contain clearer observations on thermal activity than are made by many pilots today, even with the knowledge which now exists.

Poor Penaud, he was unable to devise any means of getting himself into the air. He never met, and probably never heard of, le Bris or Mouillard, but like them he followed his lonely ideal beset with difficulties and frustrations from all sides.

The next step forward took place far from the civilised and beautiful land of France. America was a new country, bare and individual, but growing up fast. It was fully extended in

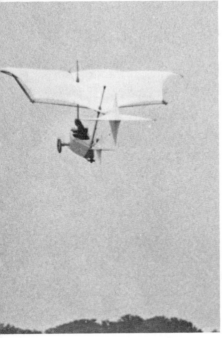

1 (a) Replica of Cayley's 1852 Riding Rudder glider, built by John Sproule; (b) & (c) Replica of Cayley's man-carrying glider of 1853, built by Ken Fripp and flown by Derek Piggott. It was just controllable by what became known as 'the influencer'

2 (a) The magnificent gannet. Span 6 ft, wing area 2.2 sq. ft, aspect ratio 16, weight 7 lb, wing loading 3 lb/sq. ft; (b) Percy Pilcher's Hawk which had a span of 25 ft. More than 50 wires were used to brace the wing and maintain its shape; (c) The general-purpose gull. Span 4 ft 2 in., wing area 2.2 sq. ft, aspect ratio 10; weight 2 lb, wing loading 1.2 lb/sq. ft. It normally flies between 20 and 35 m.p.h., as against the 45–50 m.p.h. of the higher loaded gannet

opening up the West, and making money, but probably far less intolerant of the eccentrics who dreamt of flying. Anything was possible in this new world, even leaping into the air if one wanted to.

John Montgomery was born in 1858, and lived until 1911 when both gliding and powered flight had become accepted. As a result he is known mostly for the flying that he did in his later years, which included launching gliders from balloons, and his early experiments, preceding those of Lilienthal, are often forgotten. Yet he was possibly the first man to make a genuine flight rather than a flying leap.

From 1880, at the age of twenty-two, whilst living in the Californian sun, until 1890, Montgomery devoted almost every moment to his passion for 'the adaptation of man to the flight of soaring birds'. Like most of his contemporaries he modelled his aircraft on birds, but unlike them, did not follow their wing structure with its radiating pinions. Copying this bone and quill construction had resulted in aircraft not un-attractive to behold, but Montgomery knew them to be piti-fully weak. Instead he used straight, parallel spars with curved ribs. His first gliders were quite small, having a span of 21 ft, but they weighed only 50 lb, so could be moved about by one person. The material he used was good American hickory, tough and resilient, covered with shirting.

Montgomery realised that as well as producing an aircraft able to support itself in the air, it was essential to develop some means of control, both directional by rudder, and in an up and down sense to adjust the trim and speed, by an elevator. With a fuselage length of only 8 ft, the tail surfaces of his machine needed to be large, and the rudder was 6 ft high.

Although no one realised it at the time, Montgomery's glider reflected the popular conviction that human flight was possible. Previous experimenters would have been happy to have made wings which merely supported them: Montgomery had mentally overcome this hurdle, and assuming that he would be able to fly, wanted to have control.

Not far from his home he found a gentle grass-covered hill, facing out over the Pacific, where the wind blew smoothly off the sea, and here, at Otay Mesa, he took his first glider. To begin with, Montgomery flew it as a model on its own, first holding it against the wind to try to assess its behaviour, and then launching it from shoulder height over almost level ground. It seemed to go quite well. Encouraged, he gave it bolder launches, until it was making straight glides of 30

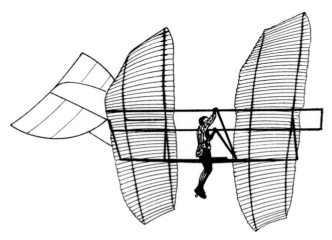

Fig. 3. Montgomery's Santa Clara, which was launched by balloon

and finally 100 yards long. In March 1884 when he was finally satisfied that his ideas were sound, and that the glider possessed adequate stability, Montgomery and his friends carried it to the top of the hill. Montgomery climbed into the fuselage framework, facing a sea wind blowing at 18 m.p.h. It is not clear how he was launched—probably he was just given a pull on a short rope—but the flight was remarkable. For several seconds after becoming airborne the glider lost no height, remaining poised silently above the hill, its forward speed more or less equal to that of the wind. Then it sank out of the influence of the hill wind, and glided steadily to the ground, landing successfully 200 yards out from the hill. It is not difficult to imagine the elation that this brief controlled flight in a glider must have caused. Later the same day Montgomery decided to make another flight. Once again the glider was carried to the top of the hill, a tiring business in spite of its light weight. As they reached the crest, the glider was lowered gently onto the grass; the friends straightened their backs, and probably looked out over the valley to visualise again the wonderful flight. Without warning the wind gusted over the hilltop, plucked up the precious glider, and bowled it over and over in the rough grass. Frantically they tried to grab it, to hold it, but they were too late: the glider was so damaged that it could never fly again.*

Montgomery soon built another, this time adding spring loaded flaps, but for some reason he made the wings flat instead of curved in section. Unfortunately, as a result, the glider would not fly properly.

So he built a third machine. This was given a plan form more nearly representing Mouillard's 'vulture in slow flight' with broad, squarish wings. It had the same tail controls as before, but this time he hoped to obtain lateral control by distorting the rear spar, so altering the incidence and therefore the lift of the wings—a form of wing warping. The glider was slightly larger than the first, with a span of 25 ft, a wing area of 150 sq. ft, and an empty weight of 110 lb. Although in theory this weight was not too great for his launching mechanism, it would not, or could not, fly.

In spite of these failures Montgomery still remained interested in the problem, but in an increasingly theoretical way, doing valuable research into fluid flow both over different surfaces, and surfaces at varying angles. He had flown successfully, but not for many years did he return to flying as a pilot.

* In 1946 a replica of Montgomery's first glider was built and flown successfully.

Chapter Three

LILIENTHAL AND PILCHER

The value of Montgomery's contribution to aviation was simply that he had succeeded in flying. No matter that it was only a single straight glide; it had been successful, and sufficiently under the pilot's control for the glider to be landed, rather than merely hit the ground. What had been done by one could be achieved by another. The hope which had been born when man first saw a bird and for which many people had thrown away their lives was now reality. The dreamers, and the new scientists, had brought together the knowledge, slowly clarified the problem, and proved the possibility. Now the tough continuing process of development was needed to translate experiment into normality. A single successful flight could be argued by some to be a freak of happy chance, but a record of hundreds of flights could only be irrefutable evidence of practical reality.

This was to be the contribution of Otto Lilienthal, an engineer from Potsdam. Even before he left school in 1863 Lilienthal was fascinated by the storks which flew above his town: he observed how they circled up into the sky, and landed so perfectly on their nests on roofs and chimneys. While still a pupil he made himself wings of 6 ft span with which he hoped to fly, much to the opposition of his teachers and the ridicule of the other pupils. This opposition was so great that young Otto was driven to sneaking out after dark to attempt to fly by moonlight.

At sixteen he entered the Potsdam technical high school to study sculpture, and although he changed over during his training to the study of mechanics, he still managed to pass the final examinations with higher marks than any previous

20

student. At nineteen he left college, and with his brother Gustav set up in business to pick up what mechanical work they could. Otto invented all manner of devices such as mining machines, toy bricks, a steam boiler, a reading game, and a reckoning machine, but money was short, and the Lilienthal brothers often worked at their experiments at the expense of eating. Then came the war of 1870, when Otto joined the National Guard, being reported by his fellow soldiers to be always thinking about the problem of flying. One wonders whether, unknowing, le Bris and Lilienthal ever took a pot shot at each other.

Lilienthal's schoolboy leaps with his primitive little wings had made it clear to him that one of the first problems he would have to overcome would be that of taking off. The unwieldiness of his 6 ft wings had been enough of a problem, and they had not even carried him into the air. He realised now that they had been far too small, but knew that running along the ground to gain speed with large wings on his shoulders was going to be both difficult and exhausting. He concluded that some source of power was required to cope with the initial acceleration. Although he realised that the human body had not enough strength to maintain an aircraft in the air, he hoped that it would be possible to use muscular power just to get off the ground. For a short time he toyed with the ever-fascinating idea of the ornithopter, but realised after only one practical experiment the uselessness of man's muscles for this purpose, even when by ingenious ways he used most of those in the body. He decided, therefore, that since there was no source of power available to get him up, he would have to start his flights from a hill, using gravity to provide momentum for the glide down. In this way it would be necessary only to run a couple of steps into the wind to gain enough speed to support the wings. Then he would be able to fly all the way to the bottom of the hill, even if the slope was such that he was only a few feet above the surface.

But all this was so much theory: Lilienthal had no money. His hopes on returning from the war that he would soon succeed in flying were frustrated by the need to go on working to provide for his family. It was not until 1886, when he was forty-three, that some of his inventions started to pay. As quickly as possible he left the business, and moved to Lichterfelde. At last he could devote his time as well as his thoughts to flying. But time was the problem: like others he was going to have to start right at the beginning. Perhaps it was his engineer's approach which stopped him hurling himself into the air with a scaled-up pair of schoolboy wings, but in spite of his longing Lilienthal and his brother first of all got down to some basic research. Between them they did an appreciable amount of measurement on the resistance of the air, and the results of their work were published in a book called *The flight of birds as the basis for the art of flying*. This document became one of the most important aeronautical publications of the 19th century. Still not satisfied, Lilienthal started investigating wing section and camber, centre of pressure movements over the wing, and stability; when, five years later, he finally started seriously to fly, he knew exactly what he was trying to do.

His first trial aircraft was tiny, and tailless. It had a wing area of only 50 sq. ft, for a total weight of 44 lb. In flight the pilot was to hang from the wings, supported from his arms, with his hands gripping an iron cross-bar. Lilienthal intended to control the aircraft by swinging the weight of his legs backwards, forwards or sideways, as the occasion required. To begin with he built a springboard 3 ft high in his garden; from this he jumped several hundred times before he felt that he had observed and learnt enough even to raise the board another 3 ft above the ground. All this practising, which must have been astonishing to the neighbours, was done in calm air, as the turbulence caused by the surrounding suburban complex too easily upset him. He realised, of course, the assistance he would get from flying against a wind, and had a conical hill built at a place called Grosskreuz. It was 50 ft high and so constructed that he could launch himself off regardless of the wind direction.

As in his garden, Lilienthal started his first flights at Grosskreuz almost at ground level. He would run down the gentle slope for just a few paces until he felt the air beginning to support the weight of his swaying wings, then raise his knees to avoid the risk of his feet catching in tussocks of grass, at the same time being careful not to shift his weight and unbalance himself. Then almost at once he would have to start running in the air to prepare for meeting the ground that he could not see beneath him.

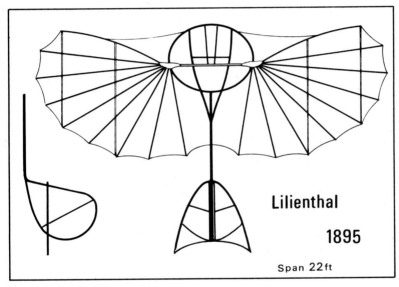

Lilienthal

1895

Span 22 ft

Fig. 4. Lilienthal's gliders were constructed with radial spars, arranged like the pinions of a bird

Otto Lilienthal was a large and colourful man, of heavy upright build, with dark curly hair and a typical 19th-century beard. He dressed deliberately in garments which he felt were appropriate for the moment; these included a white short-sleeved singlet, white knickerbockers, black stockings, and white plimsolls, the whole being topped off with a bowler

23

equivalent. Although this collection of garments may seem funny today, it was by far the most suitable which could be selected from the men's wear of the time. He must in fact have looked most impressive as he stood, ready to fly, in his odd clothes and dark beard, with his flimsy, dangerous little glider. His friends and his family would be there, watching apprehensively, with the inevitable bowler hats, or long skirts.

After a relatively small number of flights with the tailless glider, Lilienthal built a new machine. It is perhaps more true to say that Hugo Eulitz built it to Lilienthal's ideas, because Otto had reached the stage of involvement when he simply had insufficient time to be designer, constructor, test pilot, research worker, and hill builder. The flights of the new glider, which sprouted a neat little tail, were rewardingly successful; stability was improved, and with it an easing of the problems of control. With new confidence Lilienthal was soon running and leaping from the summit of the hill at Grosskreuz, and from a ridge almost 250 ft high in the Rhinow hills. No longer was the glider following a flight path almost parallel to the hill face and just a few feet above it; with the better aircraft Lilienthal was prepared to leap from steeper slopes, and so was often at a considerable height above the ground. Some of these flights were more than a quarter of a mile long, made at a gliding angle of nearly one in seven. Slowly he learnt to control the big wings on his shoulders when standing in gusty winds of up to 20 m.p.h. and to make his leaps into the air without being blown over; on a few occasions he actually gained a few feet of height when his glider flew into gusts of slope lift immediately after getting into the air. On one of these flights Lilienthal was nearly killed, but in spite of the hazardous situation in which he found himself, he was able to observe clearly what was happening. Here is his own account of this frightening moment:

Once, on a soaring flight which started from a greater height, my body and outstretched arms fell into a position in which the centre of gravity was shifted too far back, and I was so exhausted that it was impossible for me to bring my arms forward again. As I sailed along at a height of sixty feet and a speed of about fifty kilometres per hour, the apparatus, which was heavily weighted behind, tipped up more and more, and at last, owing to its motive power, shot up vertically into the air. Desperately I held fast, seeing only the blue sky flecked with white clouds, and expecting from moment to moment that the machine would turn over backwards and end my soaring experiments, perhaps for ever. Suddenly, however, it ceased climbing and began to drop backwards; it was steered into short circling curves by the horizontal tail which was now slanted upwards, until it turned over so far that it stood on its head and plunged down with me perpendicularly earthwards from a height of sixty feet. Fully conscious, with arms and head forward, still holding fast to the machine, I fell towards the green grass. A jolt, a cracking, and I lay with my glider on the ground. The only bad results of this accident were a flesh wound on the left side of my head, which I had knocked against the framework, and a sprained left wrist. The glider, remarkable as it may seem, was quite undamaged. Both the machine and I had been saved by the elastic buffer which, as though guided by a special providence, I had recently attached to the front of the machine. This buffer, which was made of willow, was smashed to bits, single pieces of it being driven a foot deep into the ground, so that they could only be extracted with difficulty.*

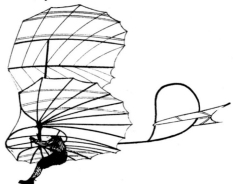

FIG. 5. Lilienthal's biplane glider

* From Kronfeld, R., *Kronfeld on Gliding and Soaring* (London, 1932), p. 29.

By 1896 Lilienthal had logged nearly 2,000 flights, and although virtually all of these were straight glides, he had learnt how to control his direction and was only prevented from attempting to circle by the existence of the hard hill behind him. Despite being nearly fifty years old, his enthusiasm remained great after the crash, and he built yet another glider. This was a biplane, in order that he could obtain a greater wing area for a light structure weight. Lilienthal concluded that he wanted more wing because he felt that he now knew enough to put in a motor. He was not interested in making a powered plane for travel, or carrying passengers, but simply to enable him to take off more easily when there was no wind, and so get more flying. Like many who followed him, he suffered from the frustrations of not being able to have a launch when he wanted one.

One warm evening in August 1896, after the others in the party had gone home, he and his mechanic were left to finish off the day's programme. The fresh wind was smooth as the day declined, and a few late cumulus drifted high overhead. The mechanic helped lift the wings while Lilienthal adjusted them to his body, then he was off, running and leaping from the grass. Shortly after take-off, when the glider was at its highest point above the ground, it hit an unexpected gust. The mechanic watched with alarm as the glider reared up and hung in the air for what seemed an age. Perhaps it was stalled, but there is some evidence for structural failure, or distortion of the weakened wings. Horrified, he watched it suddenly fall from about 50 ft, hit the ground heavily, and roll over twice. The dust settled in silence. The mechanic, trembling with fear and emotion, raced down the hill, and stared at the quiet wreckage. With enormous effort, and full of fear, he managed somehow to get his unconscious master to the village, but Lilienthal's spine was broken and he died a few hours later.

Lilienthal's place in history is assured, but historical fame is often dry and dusty, and it is difficult to know the real person. Here then is an account written by an American

26

journalist who travelled to Berlin and spent a day with
him:

On 2 August 1896, a week before the fatal crash, I met Lilienthal
at Lehrter Station in Berlin. He had with him his fourteen-year-old
son whom he always took along and another man who came to help
him. We set off at sunrise, and after about two hours travelling
got off the train at Neustadt-Dosse where we found a closed
carriage comfortable enough to take us the 20 miles from the
railway to Rhinow. On the way Lilienthal pointed out to me the
flight of some swans.

We had a hurried meal in the little inn at Rhinow, where the
arrival of the pioneer never failed to create interest; the flying
machine was taken out of its shed and put on to the carriage, after
which we went towards the mountains which are two miles from
the village. There a long line of high hills with rounded tops and
abrupt slopes rose above the plain to a height varying from 100
to 300 ft.

The machine was put on the grass and rigged. The 20 ft span
wings were covered with a thin, tough, cotton material which was
tightly stretched. The machine was so well rigged that it was
impossible to find a single slack bracing cord. As well, the fabric
was so tight that the whole machine resonated like a drum when
one tapped it lightly.

We climbed to the top of the hill and Lilienthal took his position
in the framework and lifted the machine off the ground. He was
wearing a flannel shirt, and breeches heavily padded at the knees.

I positioned myself well below Lilienthal with my black hood
[camera] and waited anxiously for the take off, he faced into wind
and took up the position of a runner who is waiting for the starting
pistol. At this moment the wind freshened a little; Lilienthal ran
three paces forward and as well as leaving the ground, went out
from the hill almost horizontally. He passed over my head at
frightening speed at a height of about 50 ft; the wind made strange
noises on the bracing cords of the machine, and it passed me before
I was able to direct my camera towards Lilienthal. Then he glided
above the grass, skimming the stooks of hay. At a foot above the
ground, he shot out his legs forward and landed lightly on the
ground.

I have seen innumerable photographs showing Lilienthal in the
air, but I had no idea of the perfection to which he had brought his
invention. Of everything that I have seen, there is nothing which

could make such an impression on the nerves or excite so much admiration and enthusiasm as the terrible and audacious skill of Lilienthal in mid-air. The sight of a man supported by great white wings, and moving at a great height above you with the speed of a race horse, while the wind produces a peculiar drumming in the bracing cords, makes an unforgettable impression.

While waiting for a few minutes before taking the machine back to the top of the hill we sat on the grass and discussed the first flight. Near us the grass-hoppers clicked on the wing covering. Lilienthal was amused, saying that they loved to jump on the smooth white surface, that they were his only passengers, and that he often heard them jump about on the machine when he was in the air.

The wind freshened a little, and we saw a shower approaching. We lay down under the wings in the company of many small children who had come in a crowd from the neighbouring farms, and stayed perfectly dry during the rain. The sun reappeared at last, and during the time that it took us to reach the hill-top the wings had dried perfectly.

Once again, Lilienthal took his place in the framework and made his flight. The children followed him, running down the face of the hill and shouting. They fell over each other with excitement. Towards evening, after having helped with perhaps a dozen flights, and having carefully observed how Lilienthal maintained his balance, I felt that I had enough courage to try the machine myself. We carried it 40 ft up the slope of the hill, I put myself in position, and lifted the apparatus off the ground. The first impression is of hopelessness. The machine weighs 40 lb and the enormous surface which is exposed to the wind makes the apparatus difficult to hold. It overbalances and touches the ground on one side or the other at the slightest puff of wind, and it is necessary to use all one's strength to keep it level. When one is in the framework, the elbows must be close to the body, the forearms horizontal, the hands holding a cross bar. In the air, when one is supported by the wings, the weight of the body is carried by the upper arms and cushions under the armpits.

I stayed without moving for a few moments, facing the wind, in order to get used to the machine, then Lilienthal told me to go forward. I ran gently against the wind, the weight of the machine lessening with each step; then I felt the force which lifted me. Immediately afterwards, my feet left the ground, and I glided the length of the slope in the air, 2 ft above the ground. The apparatus

28

inclined gently to one side or the other, but I succeeded in landing to my great satisfaction, and immediately determined to obtain a machine of my own and learn to fly. It was a delicious sensation, quite impossible to describe.*

Lilienthal's great contribution to the progress of flying would have been less immediately useful without photography. This art or science had now left its several birthplaces and had become a tool, however limited and cumbersome, in the hands of reporters of the contemporary scene. It was pictures of Lilienthal's flying that enabled experimenters in other lands to bypass many of the original thought processes, and to avoid mistakes in their own flying.

In England, an engineer and university lecturer, Percy Pilcher, incorporated ideas learnt from photographs of one of Lilienthal's aircraft when building his first glider. Called the Bat, it was not very successful, however, as it had too much dihedral angle and no tail surfaces. So Pilcher decided to visit Lilienthal at Lichterfelde. This visit must have been fascinating to the young experimenter because he later went back, and this time Lilienthal got him airborne in one of his own gliders.

On his return home he modified the Bat and from a hill made some flights of 60 yards. He then designed and built four more gliders: the Beetle, Gull, Hawk, and a triplane. The Hawk had a span of nearly 25 ft and an undercarriage, although Pilcher usually carried and launched the machine using his own legs.

Much of the structure of Pilcher's glider was split bamboo, covered with shirt material, and braced with thin piano wire. It could be derigged for stowage and transport. Like Lilienthal's it was controlled by shifting the weight of the pilot's body, a simple matter for a fit man, as the aircraft possessed little inertia.

Pilcher made a large number of flights on the Hawk, some at heights of 150 ft above sloping ground, covering distances

* Originally printed in *Boston Transcript* (U.S.A., date unknown); here trans. from Nessler, E., *Histoire du Vol a Voile* (Paris, 1957), p. 80.

of nearly 300 yards. He got into the air by taking a running leap, by genuine one-horse tows, or by a primitive hand-wound winch, which rolled up 400 yards of cable.

At Eynsford, in Kent, he made flights from the top of the hill, launched by a cable round a pulley which gave him a good fast start, but it was not until 1899, three years after he had built the Hawk, that he actually gained height—a modest 12 ft. To Pilcher it was a triumph, but it was not enough. As it seemed so difficult to find out more, he decided to fit an engine. It was not to be of the carbonic acid type that Lilienthal proposed to use, but a petrol engine driving a propeller. He spent much of 1898 and 1899 working on developing and installing this engine in a family works in Westminster. In September 1899 he went to stay with Lord Braye at Stanford Hall in Northamptonshire to demonstrate his glider. Although the day was wet and gusty, he was persuaded to fly by people who had come long distances to see a man in flight. The first attempt, launched by winch, was successful, because of the great piloting skill which Pilcher had developed. After getting the glider back to the starting point he took off again. This time, however, a bracing wire broke, the tail of the glider collapsed, and, tragically, Pilcher was killed.

The deaths which sooner or later seemed to be the inevitable end of every experimenter never acted as a deterrent to others. Apart from Montgomery, little progress had so far been made outside Europe; this was to be changed by the activities of Octave Chanute, whose family had emigrated in 1832 from Paris to America, when he was a boy of six. He was trained as a civil engineer and only long afterwards, at the age of sixty, began seriously to study the problems of flying. Perhaps because of his age he made a larger contribution than he could have when young and wanting primarily to get into the air himself. Being able to sit back and survey the progress of others dispassionately he soon realised that only one major difficulty lay in the way of progress—the problem of stability and control. It was all very well for athletic young men to behave like acrobats, but this must not for ever remain a pilotage requirement.

Chanute, with his engineering background, carried out a great deal of research, building copies of Lilienthal's glider, and trying out ideas of control and stability on something which he knew would fly. He considered altering the sweep of the entire mainplanes, to give longitudinal control, and attaching control surfaces as on present-day aircraft. He built a number of gliders, even some with several wings superimposed upon each other, and finally evolved a form of construction which became a classic of aeronautical design. This was the biplane with wings of equal size fitted one above the other, the whole structure being braced by vertical struts with diagonal wires. In his work, and particularly in the experimental flying that was required, he was helped by a young American called A. M. Herring, perhaps the first real test pilot.

For their structures, the early pioneers naturally tended to copy the layout used by the only creatures which they could see flying—the birds and the bats. For the wings they used a number of radiating pinions to take the main loads, and a few light members to tie them together. This method was not very satisfactory as it was difficult to make the wing sufficiently stiff, particularly in torsion. A significant advance was to use two or more spanwise spars to take the bending loads, together with a large number of ribs to support the wing skin, and distribute the load into the spars. This method, which was proposed by Henson in 1842, was first tried in flight by Montgomery in 1884 and, being successful, it had become almost universal by the end of the pioneering period. In an effort to make the wing structure as light as possible, many of the early glider wings were braced with wires, Pilcher's Hawk, for example, having more than fifty wires on a wing of less than 25 ft span. Another method of making a light, rigid structure was developed into its classical form by

Chanute; this, the biplane, was used with great success by the Wrights.

Octave Chanute lived to 1910, and saw flying machines doing things he would once hardly have dared to believe.

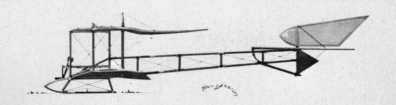

FSV-X

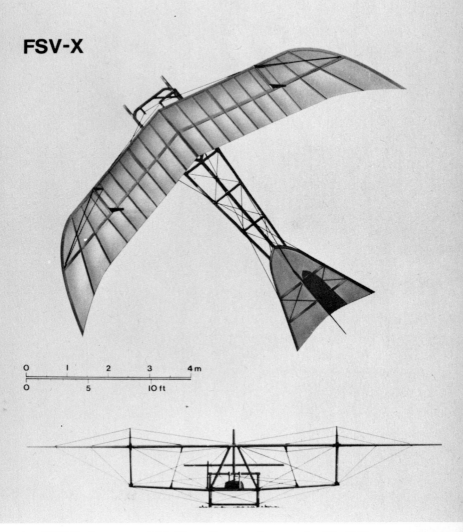

O	I	2	3	4 m
O		5		IO ft

3 The FSV-X of 1912 on which Hans Gutermuth created a World Record of 850 yds distance and 1 min. 52 sec. airborne time on the Rhön

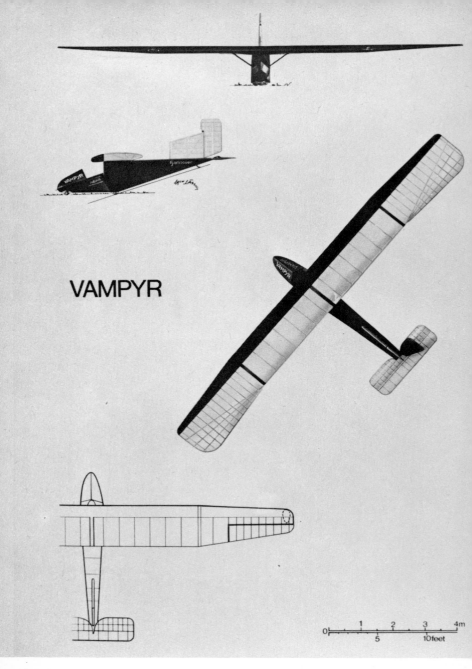

VAMPYR

4 The Vampyr which beat the World Distance Record in 1922 when Hentzen flew 5½ miles. Span 41 ft 5 in., empty weight 265 lb

Chapter Four

THE BROTHERS WRIGHT

For the third time in the history of flying two brothers were together; the Montgolfier brothers had invented the hot air balloon, Gustav Lilienthal had helped his brother Otto with gliding, and now there appeared Wilbur and Orville Wright. In 1895 they were working together in their own small bicycle business, where they were mechanics, inventors, and designers, always on the look-out for new ideas. Any technical literature that they could lay their hands on they read, and it was in this way that they first heard of Lilienthal. Up to that moment they had not seriously thought about aeronautics, although they could still remember a toy helicopter, like a flying screw, which they had been given as children seventeen years before.

They were fascinated by the accounts of Lilienthal's flights, and when within the year they read of his death, they felt that they must themselves attempt to fly and solve the problems which had beaten him. The difficulty was to find out how much knowledge already existed. As the Dayton public library, not unnaturally, could produce little, they wrote to the Smithsonian Institute in Washington, which sent them lists of books, and extracts and pamphlets written by or about most of the pioneers up to that time.

The brothers got down to their books much to the fury of their younger sister who had brought home a girl friend from college and expected entertainment. Their reading turned out to be somewhat depressing, as it was often contradictory and strangely incomplete.

They worked out that although Lilienthal had made nearly 2,000 flights, his total time in the air had been only some five hours. They realised that from this small experience Lilienthal had achieved more than could reasonably be expected, and that the only way to make faster progress was to find a means of staying in the air longer on each flight. Unlike Pilcher who put his hope in up-currents, the Wrights came to a more pedestrian conclusion. They decided to try to make an aircraft with a flying speed equivalent to the strength of wind that could normally be expected near an exposed coast. Such an aircraft would remain virtually over the same spot in flight, and be readily observed. If longer observation times were required in the early experiments, the glider could be held by lines about 20 ft long and flown as a kite. It was hoped that this ability to study the reactions of the glider in the air would enable more progress to be made in a short time.

In spite of all their reading, or perhaps because of it, the brothers decided to test every existing theory or pronouncement, and prove or disprove it for themselves. They knew that flying was practical, but realised quickly that essential to the development of the aeroplane, their final goal, was a full understanding of stability and control. This had not been mastered by anyone. Experiments with a biplane whose flying surfaces could be distorted led them to a modification in which both ends of the top and bottom wings could be warped, so that when one went down the other was raised, like embryo ailerons.

It was planned to use an elevator, but this was to be placed in front of the mainplanes instead of at the rear as on most modern aircraft. Initially there were no vertical tail surfaces, and although a fin was added later, this was not made movable. They decided that if they were to learn how to control an aircraft, the experiments should not be confused by its possessing any inherent stability. The wings were, therefore given neither dihedral angle nor any other self-righting tendency, and the aircraft made wholly dependent on the pilot's operation of the controls, for remaining in the proper attitude, correcting gusts, or manoeuvring.

The brothers completed the construction of the components of their first man-carrying glider in 1900. It was designed to fly at only 21 m.p.h., and consequently was given a greater wing area than most previous aircraft. Their choice of a flying ground, although sensibly based on the idea of using a site with strong steady winds was nevertheless a surprising one. Correspondence with the U.S. Weather Bureau led them to select Kitty Hawk, a small hamlet on a spit on the Atlantic seaboard off North Carolina. Neither of the brothers had ever been there, nor met anyone else who had, but on the evidence of a single report about the winds, they decided to carry out all their experiments there, despite the fact that it was over 500 miles from home.

It was agreed that Orville would stay and look after the bicycle shop, until Wilbur had settled in at Kitty Hawk. On 9 September 1900 Wilbur set off by train, carrying with him all the materials, equipment and parts needed to build the glider, as well as food, clothes, and camping equipment. On arriving at Elizabeth City, the nearest railway station, he enquired the way to Kitty Hawk, only to find that no one seemed to have heard of it. He discovered in due course that it was near Roanoke Island, to which a boat went once a week. This had left the previous day, so Wilbur went to the waterfront with his strange collection of bits to see what other boats there were. Finally he persuaded one Israel Perry, who lived on a small flat-bottomed schooner, to take him. Wilbur was horrified at the filthy boat, which looked as though it would sink at any moment, but was so determined to get to Kitty Hawk that he took his precious cargo aboard and prepared to suffer 40 miles of misery.

After arriving, Wilbur went to the home of William Tate, where he was hoping that he might be able to stay. He had eaten almost nothing for forty-eight hours, but Mrs Tate soon dealt with the situation by filling him up with ham and eggs.

The next day Wilbur set up the 12 ft by 22 ft tent about half a mile away from the house in an exposed place where there were few trees, and where the wind could blow uninterrupted from the sea. Then in the heat of the day he dragged the crates, boxes, and his water supply to the tent. Without delay he unpacked the sheets of fine white French sateen, already shaped and stitched at home, and the 16 ft long spars for the wings (he had been unable to get them 18 ft long, so was going to make the machine a bit smaller), and started to assemble the glider. But he had been much slower than he expected, and by the time Orville arrived three weeks later there was still a great deal of work to be done. The brothers stayed at the Tates for a couple of days, and then moved into the tent, which they lighted with a bicycle acetylene lamp. However, once organised, the final assembly of the glider did not take long. It was a biplane, with no tail, but with a front elevator, a wing area of 165 sq. ft, and a place for the operator to lie on the centre of the bottom wing. The whole aircraft weighed only 52 lb.

The first unexpected difficulty was that the winds were by no means as steady as they had been led to expect; one day they blew at great strength, the next not at all. Then they discovered that the data accumulated by others was not correct, in that a glider of 165 sq. ft wing area needed more than the estimated 17–21 m.p.h. wind to support it like a kite with the pilot on board. As this meant that the chance of flying the machine for protracted periods was not going to materialise as often as hoped, they put on board a lighter weight than either of them, and flew the glider at a height of about 20 ft, holding and controlling it with cords while observing its behaviour.

They realised, of course, that observation from the ground could not teach them much, and that they could only learn about flying by doing it themselves. So they dragged and carried their precious glider to Kill Devil Hill, a huge sand dune about 4 miles away, helped by Mr Tate; and after a day's pause for the almost gale force wind to drop, they took turns making straight flights off the top of the ridge. The slope of the hill was $9\frac{1}{2}°$; using the front elevator to fly parallel to it at a height of a few feet, they found that they were gaining speed. This showed that the glide angle was flatter than the slope, which was encouraging. Having learnt to fly on the elevator alone, they reckoned that they could cope with the complications of a second control and unlocked the wing warping mechanism; to their satisfaction this too was successful.

The flying from Kill Devil Hill, which gave them a total airborne time with a piloted glider of a mere two minutes, instead of the hours that they had intended, ended their experiments for the year. Before they returned home they weighted their discarded glider with sand, intending to leave it behind complete. The locals were both sad and horrified to see such beautiful fabric apparently being thrown away, so the brothers gave the glider to Mrs Tate, and from it she made sateen dresses for her daughters, who became the envy of the neighbourhood.

During the winter the brothers built another glider, basically similar, but larger, with 290 sq. ft of wing area instead of 165, and weighing 98 lb. This was the largest glider that had ever been built, and the Wrights hoped to realise their intention of flying it as a kite for long periods with the operator/ observer on board.

Returning to Kitty Hawk the following year (1901), the first job was to build a wooden hanger just big enough to house the glider. They continued to live in the tent, and solved their water problem by a crash programme of well-digging, finding water 12 ft beneath the sand. The brothers must have worked incredibly hard to achieve as much flying as they did, since their aeronautical sessions were always confused with basic domesticity.

This year Octave Chanute came to see how they were getting on; he asked them to add to their camp a young medico, George Spratt, who was interested in their experiments, and a man called Huffaker who was building a glider financed by Chanute. It was hoped that the extra crew would help speed progress, and that the exchange of ideas would be useful.

The first flights of the new glider were made on 27 July, one of them being just over 100 yards in length and lasting

19 seconds, their longest yet. Despite this, they decided that the performance of the aircraft was not as good as that of the earlier glider due, they thought, to the excessive camber of the wings. Accordingly they resolved to modify it. This sounds simple, but it involved taking both top and bottom wings virtually to pieces. They rebuilt them in the primitive hangar, beset by sandflies and mosquitoes, whose virulence more than once nearly caused a major postponement in the history of aviation.

By August they had learnt all they could from flying the new glider, but although they had made flights better than anyone hitherto, they were depressed. They had not yet flown at any height, and with each step forward the problems, particularly those hardy ones of stability and control, went on growing. On the journey home Wilbur even went so far as to declare his belief that man would not fly within a thousand years! They were fully prepared to give it all up, and to return to the sensible and more lucrative life of making better bicycles.

It was Chanute who finally persuaded them to continue. He even managed to persuade Wilbur to address the Western Body of Engineers on 'Some Aeronautical Experiments'. Taking the preparation of this paper as seriously as they did all experiments, the brothers made a wind tunnel to check the published data of the effect of air pressures on plates. They found this method of testing to be so valuable that they went on to check hundreds of models of wing sections, and even complete aircraft, finding that many of the previous results were wrong or incomplete. The ingenious feature of the wind tunnel was their method of measuring forces, both lift and drag, or 'drift' as they called it. Instead of measuring absolute values, which would have demanded not only an accurate balance but also precise control of the airflow, they made their measurements in relation to the drag of a small flat square plate placed in the same airstream. The results which they obtained encouraged them to believe that they now had enough reliable data to make it worth while attempting to build and fly another glider. So the bicycles were put aside once more while they constructed the new aircraft.

The 1902 machine was taken to Kill Devil Hill on 25 August, but because of the work involved in repairing the gale-battered shed and then adding living quarters to it, they did not start flying until 9 September. This new glider was

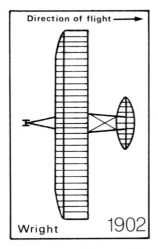

Fig. 6. The Wright 32-ft-span biplane glider which immediately preceded the aeroplane of 1903

even bigger than the last. It had a span of 32 ft, a wing loading of 1·2 lb/sq. ft, and an aspect ratio of 6 : 1 instead of the earlier aircraft's 3 : 1 ratio. Previously the wing warping had been operated by the pilot's feet, but on this machine the mechanism was connected to a cradle moved by the pilot's hips. For the first time, vertical surfaces were incorporated; these took the form of two fixed fins mounted on outriggers behind the wings.

The first trials were tremendously encouraging and it seemed that the winter's wind-tunnel work was going to pay off more than they had dared hope. At last they found that they could achieve concentrated flying. During September and

October they made over 1,000 flights; some were more than 200 yards long and as much as one minute in duration. On a few occasions the glider maintained height for a few seconds in the rising slope wind. A remarkable feature was that with their more effective controls they were able to operate in winds as high as 36 m.p.h.

It was not until many trips had been made that the Wrights realised their aircraft would be easier to fly if it were fitted with some form of directional control. They removed the two fixed fins and replaced them with a single movable rudder; rather surprisingly, instead of having separate controls for the elevator, the wing warping and the rudder, they inter-connected the rudder to the wing warping, using the same cradle worked by the pilot's hips.

The 1902 glider showed that human flight was now practical and controllable. In the minds of most people at the time, however, there was still little understanding of the nature of the problem—even Mr Tate's brother, Bill, watching one of the Wrights' more rewarding flights, remarked, 'All she needs is a coat of feathers to make her light, and she'll stay in the air indefinitely.'

As the warm late summer weather slowly gave way to the sharper winds of approaching winter, the little group packed up, Chanute and his friends returning to their homes, and the Wrights to the bicycle shop, no longer depressed and feeling that flight was a thousand years away. They now knew that nothing except the lack of an engine prevented them climbing into the air, to travel as they wanted, as they needed.

Chapter Five

BACK TO THE BIRDS

It was not long before the engine was found, and the aeroplane invented. The world quickly became fascinated with the new shuddering flying machines, with their noisy stuttering motors, and the excitement of being able to fly in the sky at will. There was no longer use for gliders, and they were almost forgotten. Only in a few places experiments continued, as a cheap way of working on the eternal problem of stability, or merely as a means of getting into the air somehow. Gliding was not considered as a sport—it was practically not considered at all—nevertheless, it did have some attractions for the young and the athletic. In spite of the lure of the power plane, it was delightful to have wings attached to one's own shoulders, to leap from a hilltop and sail down into the valley below. So, although gliding was almost forgotten, it did not die. In the backwaters of the new aviation there were a few individuals who were interested only in the 'adaptation of man to the flight of birds'.

One of them was a Frenchman, José Weiss, who at the age of thirty-five became a naturalised Englishman; in fact he was better known as a landscape painter in America than as an aviation pioneer in England. He was an intellectual of courage, never afraid to differ from current thought, but although he had since youth experimented with models, it was Lilienthal's death which turned him to really serious work, just as it had with the Wrights.

Weiss made hundreds of beautifully constructed model gliders, all of birdlike shape, with which he had great success. By 1909 he felt that he knew enough to build one that would carry a man. Vastly different from the Wrights' austere

41

biplane, his was a monoplane of 26 ft span. It had strut-braced wings of crescent shape, with pronounced sweepback at the tips, like a swallow. The tips could be bent to alter their incidence, and were the only control surfaces, being worked by two pedals which were moved together to change speed, and differentially to roll the aircraft. There was no tailplane or fin. The pilot sat in a streamlined fuselage.

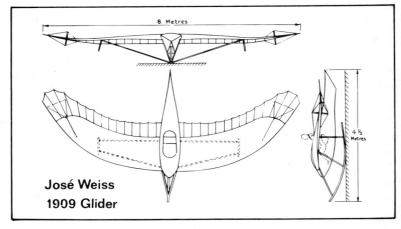

FIG. 7. The 1909 glider of José Weiss

Unlike the Wrights, Weiss was convinced that if the aircraft possessed inherent stability, flying could be made easy and safe. This was why he used the swept-back wing, with considerable wash out towards the tips, and some dihedral.

The full-size glider was flown from the Sussex downs at Amberley, near Arundel. Weiss launched it by running it along rails pointing into the wind, getting acceleration by a drop weight. He soon found that this was not necessary, as the glider in running down the sloping rails quickly gained speed to fly and took itself off.

Among those who flew the Weiss glider was a young man called Gordon England, who soon became expert with it.* It

* Much later he was to be Chairman of the British Gliding Association.

was with the machine in England's hands that Weiss was able to show evidence for the presence of usable up-currents in the air. He knew that these must exist from watching soaring birds, and quickly realised that not only was a suitable glider needed to utilise them, but a pilot who could sense the existence of the up-currents and manoeuvre quickly but delicately within their confines. Gordon England learnt quickly from his master. He found that although the glider was too stable to enable him to turn rapidly, he could fly for short spells without losing height. If he was launched into strong gusts of wind sometimes he actually gained a few feet; on 27 June 1909 he rose nearly 40 ft in lift—presumably hill lift but possibly augmented by thermal—and travelled a distance of nearly one mile. This was the first ever appreciable gain of height. Many flights were carried out in the Weiss glider, but no one else was able to gain height. It was probably as well that neither Gordon England, nor anyone else, flew in the rough air of strong lift, as the Weiss glider, although designed carefully, was in fact, weak, and might not have withstood much turbulence. Despite the shortcomings of this aircraft, due to its stability it was flown safely by people without previous flying experience. A group of these new pilots banded together, and in 1912 formed probably the first gliding club in the world. It was called the Amberley Aviation Society, and had about a dozen members. One of the followers of Weiss, although not one of the club members, was Frederick Handley Page, who also believed in safe, stable aircraft. He built his first aircraft on the lines of the Weiss glider, but his real interest was in aeroplanes.

With others flying his glider without difficulty, Weiss became increasingly interested in methods of launching. One idea was a turntable platform on which the glider was lifted, which possessed a chute down which it could be launched into wind. Later he, and a club member, Dr Alexander Keith, built a glider designed to beat its wings just enough to get off the ground, the power being provided by a furiously pedalling pilot. Once in the air, the wings were to remain fixed. The glider was built and flown both with and without a pilot, and proved quite stable. It was a strange-looking bird with a tall single undercarriage stalk on which there were pedals and a landing wheel, and projecting forward a fearsome-looking scythe blade. This appeared to be ideally placed to impale the pilot should he be unfortunate enough to be catapulted out after a heavy landing, but was presumably intended as an anti nose-over device. Although it was unfortunate that the war started before the bicycling and flapping experiments could begin, it probably saved the designer some disappointments, since others had already discovered that man's own muscles were inadequate. Weiss's health was greatly affected by the war, and at its end he wrote to a friend, George Howard, that he had not long to live; in this letter he declared his conviction that gliding and soaring would be one of the finest sports when gliders were built which could travel 'thirty times the height of the launch in distance.' He hoped that others would carry on the work that he could no longer do himself, but he could not know that within twenty years his belief would become reality.

During the years between the end of the 19th century and the Great War there were others whom the birds continued to inspire. In Austria, the Etrich brothers, and in Switzerland, Carl Stieger, were building gliders. There was also an engineer called Wolf Muller who created a 36 ft span imitation stork, the wings of which were intended to flap, but did not. Although it never flew it was of interest in that it possessed a fully enclosed fuselage complete with mica windows.

Some of the creations built at this time had real hopes of success, some were first steps up the ladder of finding out about flying the hard way, and some were magnificent flights of fancy translated into useless hardware; far from the mainstream of development, they were weird of shape and remarkable in conception. But from all of them slowly the glider grew.

There was a Monsieur Liurette, an administrator in the Colonies, whose main inspiration was vultures. He did not appreciate that they were supported by warm air up-currents (or thermals) and thought it impossible to fly only on still wings. So despite the evidence of his own eyes he concerned himself with trying to overcome the problem of dynamic flight. In this field he might have achieved great things had it not been for his job, for although he built three aircraft, just as he completed each, he was posted to administrate in another part of the world. He was probably the world's first really frustrated pilot.

There was Dr Magnan. He concluded that when a bird faced the wind, an increase in wind strength would result in a gain of height for the bird. After some further research into dynamic soaring, he built two quite modern-looking gliders, one with the wingplan of a vulture, the other with that of an albatross. He fixed up a rig from which these aircraft were suspended, in order to measure the effect of gusts on them— a sort of open-air wind tunnel. The 1914 War was upon him before Dr Magnan got his birds airborne, and although the albatross glider, flown by a M. Canivet, showed considerable promise in its first trials, time ran out. The sad bird mouldered away in a hangar at St Inglevert, while further east the new military aeroplanes took off in anger.

But as well as the exotic and the unpractical, away beyond the firing in the depths of Germany work was being done which lay in the direct line towards the gliding of today. The modern glider was born in an architect's office, on the drawing board of Frederic Harth, who started to try to fly in 1910. Although he had seen the designs of others, his architect's training enabled him to combine line and structure in a way which produced a more refined aircraft shape. This ability was more valuable than Harth could have realised, since the performance of a glider is largely dependent on the economy of its lines. His 1914 glider was not so very different superficially from the improved training gliders still being used in the 1940s. Harth, like the Wrights, discarded the imitation bird and set out to design a purely practical aircraft. As with the Wrights, the whole aircraft was built with flying as the

45

first objective, the only concession to the pilot being to give him adequate controls; if there was no seat, or a hard one, or if the pilot was cold, this was unimportant. Harth's other concern was how best to use any gust, or rising air, which his glider might meet. It was this determination to utilise only the energy in the air as his source of power which finally separated the designer of the glider from that of the aeroplane. No longer was an aircraft something which might or might not contain an engine. From now on the basic aims of designers would diverge.

Harth concluded that gusts could best be utilised by altering the incidence of the wings as the faster-moving air hit the glider. In the cockpit he installed large levers connected to each wing; if moved forward the incidence would be reduced, and if backwards it would be increased. If both levers were moved together in the same sense, the pilot would be able to utilise the speed of the gust, or modify his flying speed, but if he moved them in opposed directions this would make the glider turn. The machine possessed neither normal elevator nor rudder. Harth found that there was no problem in locating the arrival of a gust, because as it met the wings the effect was transmitted directly to the two levers, rather as the pull of a fish attracts the notice of a fisherman. Harth would then pull on his levers, increasing the incidence; as the gust passed, he would allow the incidence to return to normal. Before 1914 Harth made several flights near his home at Hildenstein with this glider, managing to maintain height for short periods. In August 1916, during the war, he managed to stay above his gently sloping hill for three and a half minutes.

Harth's interest in gliding was, like most men's in his time, a largely technical one; his enjoyment came primarily from the success of his brain-child, not from the sheer pleasure of flying. Gliding in this sense, as a sport, began one day in 1909, when a group of boys from Darmstadt high school went to an aeronautical exhibition at Frankfurt-am-Main. They were so fascinated by the aeroplanes and strange flying machines, that immediately on returning home they began to make

46

models. These were of gliders, simply because the idea of flying with wings on their own shoulders was attractive to them. The first real aircraft they built were copies of Lilienthal's gliders, both monoplanes and biplanes, which they flew from a mound in the school playground. They must have had a surprisingly liberal headmaster, for they were allowed to continue.

The next year two of them, Hans Gutermuth and Berthold Fischer, set out to find a proper flying hill of their own. Throughout the summer holidays the two boys wandered among the forest-covered hills of Germany, finally coming to the Rhön mountains. Here they found exactly what they wanted, on the huge rounded slopes of the Wasserkuppe. They managed to borrow a cowshed, to use both as camp and workshop, and during the summer holidays of 1911 and 1912 Gutermuth and his friends built nearly thirty simple gliders there. Without proper drawings, the machines were made from almost any materials which could be obtained cheaply; the spars of local timber, and the wing coverings of bed-linen— probably the sheets that their fond parents had sent them to sleep in. As can be imagined, the gliders were crude beyond belief, yet they flew, and none of the boys met with any accident. The first glider that they finished made flights of 400 yards and in 1911 Hans Gutermuth flew nearly 1,000 yards down into the valley, and without soaring was airborne for 1 min. 52 sec.—which is quite a long time hanging from one's arms. Some of the gliders the boys built were enterprising if unconventional in shape, but the majority were hang-gliders similar to those of Lilienthal, controlled by shifting the pilot's weight. They loved the excitement of running headlong down a slope, until they felt the wings lifting their feet from the ground; it was pure delight to fly far out over the valley on their own wings, with the cool wind tearing at their clothes. They competed with each other to see who could land furthest from the starting place. It is easy to imagine the end of a good flight, when after sailing along quite high, the earth seemed suddenly to rush up towards them, the trees and grass blurred, their feet running in anticipation, perhaps stumbling as they touched. Then, back on the ground, with the unwieldy wings suddenly heavy on their shoulders, they would look back up at the high hill, at the little ants of their friends on the skyline, and not really believe what they had done.

As they learnt more, the boys built gliders in which they sat on seats in a fuselage, and installed more conventional controls. They had all the excitement of test-flying a completely new creation. But these days were soon to disappear. The war started, and Hans Gutermuth was killed, with many of his friends.

It was the physical exhilaration and skill the boys found, combined with the intellectual exploration needed to extract from the air the knowledge that birds so perfectly understood, which gave gliding its own special direction.

5 (a) F. P. Raynham flies his hurriedly constructed glider at Itford; (b) E. C. Gordon England flying the glider he designed himself; (c) Peyret's tandem monoplane which beat the World Duration Record flown by Alexis Maneyrol of France

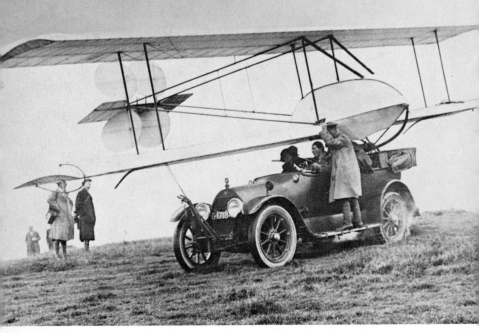

6 (a) G. W. Cain's flying bicycle at Itford. It only bounced; (b) Anthony Fokker's biplane which made several good soaring flights, including a World Record with a passenger of 49 min.

Part II

EARLY DAYS

Chapter Six

RETURN TO THE WASSERKUPPE

When the war was finally ended, and it was possible to think about living instead of dying, creating instead of destroying, aviation had changed. The aeroplane was now a weapon or a tool, no longer the dream of an individual. It was built in factories and many of those who built it were neither interested in how it flew, nor in who would be its pilot. Quite soon the wartime bombers were to be given cane chairs and carry passengers, and as 'airliners' open up routes across the world. The aeroplane had become organised.

Once more gliding was almost forgotten. It was remembered and brought to life largely by the efforts of one small man, Oscar Ursinus, editor of the German magazine *Flugsport*. He used his paper to call for enthusiasts to come again to the Wasserkuppe and together fly for fun, build new gliders, start again. He persuaded and browbeat individuals and organisations into giving money; he published maps for reaching the Wasserkuppe; he organised prizes for the best flights and the best gliders; he arranged for wooden barracks and workshops to be erected on the mountain. Everyone had to bring their own bedding, their knives and plates, and above all their tools; they could wash in the good spring water of the Fulda river. The first camp was to be held from 15 July to 15 September 1920. No gliders could be provided, and there was no means of launching any that arrived other than by the energy of those who might come.

Twenty-four people turned up. Among them were Wolfgang Klemperer, Eugene Von Loessl, a Swiss constructor named Spalinger, and of course Ursinus himself. Some were engineers, some ex-military pilots, and some, like young Peter

Riedel and Wolf Hirth, had never flown at all. Fortunately their enthusiasm matched the efforts of Ursinus, and resolved itself into hard work instead of being defeated by the enormous difficulties of trying to start from virtually nothing. This was just as well, for it was quickly found that the old know-how had been lost, and discovering the best way of designing, building and launching a glider had to be done all over again. Inevitably, progress was slow: not until three weeks after the camp had started was a flight made that even approached in

FIG. 8. Willi Pelzner's hang-glider of 1921 which weighed only 20 lb

length any of the pre-war glides straight down into the valley.

Three days later young Von Loessl was launched to try to beat his own previous longest flight of 40 seconds. The wind was strong, with large cumulus drifting overhead. He had flown half a mile out from the hill, and been airborne for just over a minute when he flew suddenly into severe turbulence. The tail of his glider was not strong enough, and with a sudden crack, heard by the watchers on the ground, the elevator broke. At first the glider seemed to come down slowly, but when it hit the ground the impact was enough to kill Von Loessl.

The high hopes with which everyone had arrived on the mountain were being dissipated fast. But although depressed the little group were determined to go on; agreeing that the best way to remember their friend would be to return to the Wasserkuppe each year and succeed in making finer flights. In the meantime, with the camp coming to an end, there was little to show for all the effort. The old type hang-gliders, particularly those flown by W. Pelzner, who had developed superb muscular control of his flying, still seemed to offer the

52

most fun; because of the physical effort and co-ordination required, even a straight glide was satisfying. In the final days of the meeting, however, the young engineer from Aachen, Klemperer, brought a new glider to the launch point. It was an unusually chunky looking monoplane with trousered skids, painted white and called the Black Devil; the cantilever wing

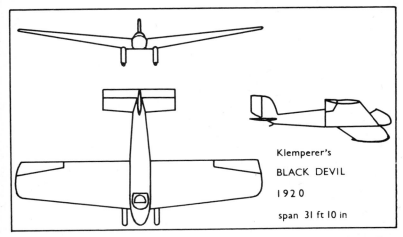

Klemperer's
BLACK DEVIL
1920
span 31 ft 10 in

FIG. 9. The Black Devil, Wasserkuppe, 1920, which weighed 134 lb

was thick, but the whole aircraft weighed little. Instead of running down the hill to launch himself, or being pulled by a rope to gain speed, Klemperer had himself catapulted into the air with a rubber shock cord, or bungey, so that he was off in a few yards. To everyone's delight he flew for 2 min. 32 sec. gliding a distance of over a mile. Three days later he flew in a stronger wind and rose in the slope lift 30 ft above his launch height before making the inevitable glide into the valley. Depression vanished with this sign of genuine progress, and the first Rhön meeting ended in unexpected optimism.

During this time Harth was continuing his experiments at Hildenstein, and in the Black Forest Frederic Wenk was secretly building a tailless machine. This had a big swept-back wing, mounted above a short boat-shaped fuselage; it was

53

hoped that its performance would be better than any other glider of the time. In it Peschke flew the first figure-of-eight ever to be made in a glider, during a flight lasting 2 min. 30 sec. Although the first part of this flight was made in slope lift, this was not exploited because it was not understood, even though as long ago as 1911 Orville Wright had soared for 9 min. 45 sec.

On the opening day of the second Rhön meeting, in 1921, fifty people arrived on the mountain top, bringing with them no less than forty-five aircraft. There were still a few hang-gliders, to be flown with enjoyment by enthusiasts like Pelzner, but most machines were new in design and construction. These were gliders intended for soaring in the elusive rising air above the hills, and not merely for gliding down into the valley. One of the prizes offered this year was for the best soaring flight of at least five minutes duration, ending not more than 160 ft below the launching point.

Wenk's tailless soarer, piloted by Wilhelm Leusch, was one of the favourites for the prize. This large glider with its swept wings was launched by being hoisted from the shoulders of its crew, who ran down the slope until the glider gained enough speed and lifted from their hands. As soon as the wind seemed right, Leusch decided to make an attempt. The glider was thrown into the air, but continued to rise steadily, even when it was beyond the region where slope lift could be expected. The sky was full of snowy white cumulus, darkening to the deepest indigo near the horizon. One of these clouds was near; boiling upwards as the fierceness of its up-current thrust ever higher. Soon it would become a thunderhead, sucking air or gliders from below up into the growing storm. Into this turmoil Leusch was inevitably drawn. To the watchers it was unbelievable. Used to seeing their friends float out over the valley, small and frail against a background of corn and trees, they were now looking at an equally frail glider against a background of dazzling cloud, higher than they had ever seen one before.

Silently the glider continued to rise, standing out straight towards the storm. On nearing the surging cloud it began at last to turn away. With relief the watchers assumed that the pilot rightly intended to avoid getting too close. The turn continued, becoming steeper. Then it grew steeper still. The excitement on the ground at this first real soaring flight changed to apprehension. As they watched the long wings silently changed their shape—then collapsed. After a second of silence came the sound of destruction, the dull rending crack that told them that Leusch would soon be dead.

No one fully understood why the glider had gained height after the launch. To begin with lift could have been obtained from the wind blowing up the slope, but out from the hill it must somehow have come from the cloud. Such up-currents were even less understood; but it was clear that the air near big cumulus possessed the power to destroy.

It was Klemperer who once again helped to rescue the meeting from depression. This year he had brought the successor to his Black Devil—the Blue Mouse, with similar short broad wings, and cockpit which perched the pilot up in the breeze. With it he flew for 13 min. 30 sec., but did not win the prize because he did not soar, using the performance of his glider to float far down the valley. This time Klemperer had a rival, Arthur Martens. His glider, the Vampyr, had been designed and built by students at Hanover, and its shape was to lead directly to the sailplane of the future. It was a high-wing monoplane with a higher aspect ratio than the Blue Mouse, and a cockpit which was fully enclosed except for the pilot's head. Martens managed to make two complete circles, and finally landed even further away in the valley, having flown his Vampyr for two minutes longer than Klemperer. Then Klemperer beat Martens. But no one properly soared, and in spite of the high hopes there was no award.

The need to achieve more than glides into the valley was becoming desperate. It was all very well for Lilienthal to have done this, his gliders weighed only 50 lb, and the problem of carrying them a hundred yards back up the slope was not onerous. But flights in gliders weighing up to 200 lb could now end several miles away, and 1,000 feet below: soon it would be possible only to have two trips in a day on one glider. However much the flights achieved, the retrieves involved were becoming extremely tedious, even to the industrious Germans; it is not surprising that they got into the habit of starting to fly at dawn.

Fortunately, before the year was out Frederic Harth succeeded in hill-soaring properly. For 21 min. 30 sec. he floated in the slope wind at Hildenstein, flying to and fro along a stretch of ridge, making circles, and finally landing 170 yards from where he was launched, and only 40 ft below. This was a world record, and the first time in which up-currents of any sort had been deliberately and effectively exploited. It is difficult now to realise the extent of this achievement, and the quantity of skills and knowledge which had to be acquired without teachers before Harth could carry out his flight. He made it easier for others; as with the four-minute mile, once someone had succeeded, success was available to many.

For the third meeting on the Wasserkuppe in 1922 several prizes were offered for flights, some of which seemed impossible of achievement. Although only one genuine soaring flight had ever taken place, there was to be a prize for the greatest duration, one for the pilot who could make the longest distance using any form of soaring, and one for landing nearest to a specified point several miles away across the mountains.

Credit must be given to Ursinus for providing a challenge to meet the mood of the moment, a mood which possessed something of a Wagnerian quality with its fierce driving force and fascination for the unknown, interwoven with the atmosphere of the remote mountain. It is almost possible to feel the sultry air and see the great clouds massing and threatening throughout each hazy afternoon. In such a place high drama was inevitable.

During the first two weeks of the 1922 camp no worthwhile flying was done; a number of gliders were smashed, and three pilots, including Wolf Hirth, injured. Then, quite suddenly it seemed, the technique of hill-soaring which had looked so difficult was understood and came within reach. On 18 August Martens was launched from the west slope in his Vampyr, and as Harth had done, flew back and forth along the ridge in the rising air and stayed up. Quite quickly the Vampyr climbed to 300 ft and for 25 minutes soared above the heads of the many spectators who had come to see this strange engineless flying. Then the wind dropped. Gradually Martens sank lower and lower until it seemed that he must land and miss the duration prize, for which he had to fly for 40 minutes; but at the last moment the breeze strengthened again, and once more the Vampyr gained height, cheered on by everybody. It stayed airborne for the record time of 1 hr 6 min.

Delighted by his success, Martens had himself launched again, and this time flew off to try to win the distance prize. After leaving the slope lift, in which he had climbed as high as possible, the distance he could expect to fly was whatever he could obtain from a straight glide. It seemed, however, more like a miracle to the spectators when he landed 6 miles away, although 1,700 ft below. Not enough credit is given to the courage of these early glider pilots when it came to landing in strange places. Although the glide angle of their aircraft was not particularly flat—only about one in fifteen—they had no aids such as dive brakes for controlling the glide path; their controls were not very effective, and their total flying experience was negligible—a pilot with five hours would be quite an expert. Because every second and every yard was an achievement they would go on and on, flying straight until almost on the ground, leaving only the barest margin for avoiding trees or turning into wind.

The next day, on 19 August, after Marten's retrieve from the hot valley, Heinrich Hentzen, flying the Vampyr again, stayed up for the longer time of 2 hr 10 sec., and to consolidate this, gained a further world record with a flight of 3 hr 6 min. a week later, during which he climbed 1,000 ft above the top of the hill. These flights were not only records;

soaring flights of this length at last enabled pilots to stay long enough in the air to improve their flying skill, and with this new and greater ability to experiment seriously with soaring. The pace could now accelerate.

The last days of the meeting showed how much progress was being made. No less than six or seven gliders were to be seen soaring together. Usually the two Hanover machines were highest, seemingly poised in the same place 1,000 ft

FIG. 10. A hang-glider at the Combegrasse meeting, 1922

above the hill, heading into the strong wind. They remained soaring at the top of the slope lift until it was almost dark, remote from the excited chatter below.

In this year there were also gliding meetings in other parts of Europe; perhaps the biggest of these was at Combegrasse in Central France, to which fifteen French pilots came with their gliders, and at which a pilot called Bossoutrot made three circles gaining height in a blue, or cloudless, thermal over the landing field, without the aid of any hill lift. Although incidental it was probably the first use in the world of a genuine thermal. Undoubtedly many theories were produced as to the cause of this lift, but it would seem that no thoughts were clear enough to link it in any practical way with the soaring of birds; otherwise more attempts would have been made to repeat the flight, to learn about this form of up-current. The work of Penaud, which could have provided the basis for experiment, was long forgotten.

Chapter Seven

ITFORD 1922

Another notable meeting took place in England, at Itford in 1922. Itford was a peculiar event in the history of gliding. It started as a publicity stunt organised by the *Daily Mail*, who offered a prize of £1,000 for the longest glide exceeding thirty minutes in duration. The inspiration came from the rather garbled accounts reaching this country of what had been going on in France and Germany; the *Daily Mail* wished to demonstrate that we could do as well and also to 'increase airmindedness'.

In eight weeks the organisers, largely under the drive of Harold Perrin of the Royal Aero Club, succeeded not only in publishing the rules of the event, but in finding a suitable site, interviewing landowners, obtaining large marquees as temporary hangers, and setting up an Operations Organisation. Even more surprising than this was the fact that no less than thirty-five gliders were entered; most of them specially designed and constructed in the short period of eight weeks which separated the announcement of the prize from the start of the competition. The entries ranged from those produced by established aircraft manufacturers such as de Havilland and Fokker, through those made by people with flying experience but lacking manufacturing facilities, to the inevitable lunatic fringe who lacked everything except misguided enthusiasm. With the exception of the latter, many of the entries followed on the lines of the development on the Continent towards machines of large span, high aspect ratio, and light weight. Because there were no airworthiness requirements and because also the question of durability was hardly considered, the standard of design and construction was, by present day standards, distinctly crude. For example the Handasyde glider, flown by the well-known F. P. Raynham, was assembled in such a hurry that there was no time to connect the aileron control to the stick, and the glider was flown by the pilot using one hand on the aileron balance cable and the other on the stick.

The site chosen was on Itford Hill near Lewes, a westerly-facing slope on the left bank of the river Ouse. The site was presumably selected because of its steep slope facing into the direction of the prevailing wind. Needless to say, during the period of the contest, 16 to 21 October, the wind instead of coming from the west blew constantly from the N.E. Fortunately Firle Beacon, later the site of the South Down Club, could be used instead. As few of the entrants and virtually none of the spectators had ever seen a glider before, there was a lack of practical knowledge of operational procedure. However, this was more than made up during this unique event by the remarkable drive and energy which was displayed by both entrants and organisers.

Gordon England, who had flown with Weiss at Amberley thirteen years before, brought a glider of his own design, built by his brother at Walton-on-Thames. There were two de Havilland gliders, both wire-braced machines of 50 ft span. From Germany came an Aachen monoplane, similar to the Black Devil of Klemperer, which was flown by J. Jeyes of Northampton. Anthony Fokker brought from Holland two biplane gliders, a single- and a two-seater. A practical but distinctly crude aircraft had been assembled by Squadron Leader A. Gray by fixing the top wing of a Fokker D7 biplane on to the fuselage of a Bristol Fighter; this was reputed to have cost 18s. 6d. (5s. for the fuselage, 5s. for the wing and 8s. 6d. for fittings, dope, etc.). From France came a peculiar-shaped glider designed by Peyret, and flown by Alexis Maneyrol. It had two identical strut-braced wings, one mounted at the front of the fuselage and the other at the rear, with the pilot sitting between them. Along the trailing edge of each wing were full span flaps, which by means of a bevel type differential mechanism could be used either as ailerons or as elevators. There were also a few other fairly conventional gliders and a number of devices which can only be described as remarkable. The rules of the contest prohibited the incorporation of balloons to assist flying, but they did allow machines with motive power, provided that this was produced entirely by the occupants. Machines powered in this way ranged from flying bicycles, and an ornithopter of no less than 54 ft span, to a two-seater helicopter in which it was intended that the front man should drive an airscrew for propulsion while the rear man drove the lifting rotor. Even more exotic was an entry which although it actually arrived at Itford, did not fly. This Kingwell aircraft consisted of a biplane incorporating a perpetual energy engine, comprising a fan, some inlet pipes off a radial engine and an airscrew. The theory was that the wind would blow into the fan, make it spin around, and thus turn the airscrew which would drive the machine along. *The Aeroplane* commented, 'viewed as a mechanical proposition it seems to be several 100% better than standing in a clothes basket and lifting oneself by the handles'. None of the fringe element took the air.

On the first two days of the meeting a few flights were made at Itford itself, bungey-launching off the top of the hill, a method which was used throughout the meeting. Then the wind changed to N.E. and all the rest of the flying was done at Firle. Fokker flew his two-seater for 7 minutes with a *Daily Mail* journalist on board, and Raynham succeeded in staying up for 11 min. 30 sec. before the wind dropped. Later in the day the wind returned and Fokker, flying his two-seater solo, stayed up for 37 minutes. The minimum duration for the £1,000 prize had been achieved, and there were still several days to go.

On Tuesday, Raynham stayed up in his Handasyde for two hours, despite the peculiar method of working the ailerons. On the next day flying was stopped after a spectacular accident in which Jeyes hit the hill with his wing tip, cartwheeling and writing off his glider. Then came disaster of a different sort—to quote Terence Boughton in *The Story of the British Light Aeroplane*:

The wild night which followed put an end to the hopes of Mr E. T. Prosser, a pre-war pilot who had laboriously erected his large biplane glider inside one of the tent hangars, only to find that it was impossible to get it out. The problem of whether to dismantle the tent or the glider was solved for him by the wind, which blew down the tent in the night, and completely wrecked his machine.*

This was not the only remarkable occurrence. E. D. Herne who had brought a D.H. glider decided after a few flights to try to improve his lateral control by converting his ailerons to wing warping. The modification completed, he was bungey-launched, fortunately over fairly level ground, for at about 20 ft the warping wings started warping on their own and went on doing so until they finally twisted themselves off, and the fuselage fell to the ground leaving a whole, but distinctly surprised pilot.

Friday was a calm day after the storm, but Saturday was soarable again with a N.E. wind. Gordon Olley, flying the Fokker with a passenger, set up a world two-seater record with a flight of 49 minutes. Then Maneyrol took off at half-past two and surprised everybody by the manoeuvrability of his odd-looking glider, managing to keep continually in the hill lift. Raynham, thinking that his previous flight of nearly two hours might be beaten, tried to soar but failed, landing at the bottom of the Downs. Squadron Leader Gray then had a shot with his £1 glider, failed, and was launched again. When dusk came he and Maneyrol were still soaring strongly, much to everyone's surprise. Maneyrol succeeded in beating Raynham's previous time and it suddenly seemed possible that he might break the world record. The two aircraft went on soaring into the darkness while a landing strip was hastily prepared with motorcar headlights. Finally Maneyrol was informed that he had broken the German record for endurance

* From Boughton, T. A. B., *The Story of the British Light Aeroplane* (London, 1963), p. 28.

by the cheering and hooting of motor horns; twenty minutes later both he and Squadron Leader Gray made perfect landings on the top of the hill within 100 yards of their take-off points. Maneyrol had stayed up for 3 hr 21 min.; a remarkable achievement as it was only his second flight in the aircraft and his first on the hill.

Looking back at Itford, the most surprising feature is that nothing came of it. Some ten pilots had tasted the joys of soaring first-hand and a lot of people had had a great deal of fun designing and building simple gliders. Apart from Walter Merriam who tried to get a glider club going in the Isle of Wight, and Gordon England who, in spite of breaking his glider and suffering a double fracture of an ankle at Itford, was involved in a revival of gliding in this country in 1930, none of the people concerned appears to have got further involved in the sport. As for manufacturers like de Havilland and Fokker, it is easy to understand why, since they were already engaged in developing light aircraft. Of the other pilots and spectators, one would have thought that at least a few would have decided to continue, but this was not the case. It is possible that they considered the problems of designing, building and operating gliders on their own too difficult, but it seems more likely that impetus was killed by the competition's very success. After the prize of £1,000 had been won, other achievements might well seem tame.

7 (a) Itford 1922. The warping wings went on doing so. Herne in the de Havilland;
   (b) A lack of knowledge of operational procedures; Barbot in the Dewoitine

8 (a) Kronfeld's recording-breaking Wien of 1929. Span 63 ft; (b) *l.* to *r.*: Max Kegel, Wolf Hirth, Ferdinand Schultz, Fritz Stamer, Robert Kronfeld and Edgar Dittmar outside the Wasserkuppe school buildings

Chapter Eight

WIND ON THE HILL

Although the art of slope-soaring was now understood, and it had become possible to fly for hours high above the hills with almost the freedom of a bird, a paradoxical situation arose. The sport of gliding had been started in more and more countries, yet enthusiasm soon declined, and in some places the infant sport died away altogether. In Germany, even the tremendous pioneering spirit of the Rhön lost some of its drive.

To begin with, the great challenge had been in finding out how to fly at all. Then the subtle division between the protagonists of the engined plane and those who believed that enough power to fly existed in the air itself, showed itself among the pioneers. In Germany immediately after the war this separation was concealed by the Versailles Treaty: for a while there was no choice—if anyone wanted to fly, they had to think only in terms of the glider. This enforced specialisation helped to speed up early progress, but by 1923 the aeroplane addicts were once more thinking about power.

The gliding fanatics were on their own again, but there seemed little to look forward to. The true direction of glider design had now shown above the morass of theories, some strange and others ingenious, and the basic shape of the working glider was established. From now on, new aircraft would be refinements of an existing theme, their development no longer the inspiration of artists or the brain-child of inventors, but routine work by technicians and engineers: the fascination of designing some exotic personal bird had gone for ever. In flying, the hang-gliders with the physical fun they gave were out—outclassed and outdated. The excitement of sailing out from the mountain top and landing far down in the valley was soon over, too, killed by the inevitable tedium of getting the thing back up the hill again. Even the exhilaration of the first slope-soaring flights had gone. As long as world records could be beaten by flight times counted in minutes, the challenge and the success was great, but when, as soon happened, hours and yet more hours of just sitting in the air above a hill were needed to show progress, enthusiasm faded. Aeroplanes could travel to other places; and birds migrate over the countryside or the sea; but even though it was now clear that the energy in the air was enough to support man and his glider, it was not known how, or even if, it could be used to enable him to fly from one place to another. Gliding was too limited, and seemed to have little future.

Investigation into the possibilities of soaring across country was given direction by Ursinus who tried to encourage flying to a goal—usually some point further along the mountains which could not be reached without careful planning as well as some skill in slope soaring. Since the goal was often in sight from the top of the Wasserkuppe it was fun for those on the ground as well. Prizes were offered for distances much greater than any so far achieved, but no one found out how to do it—even when soaring birds circled up from the valley, and then flew away overhead.

The only people for whom there now seemed to be real opportunity were young pilots with a scientific approach to their flying; those who were prepared to study in detail the behaviour of the air and the performance of their glider. These people linked closely with the designers, for their minds were mostly similar, and so gliding became a sport with a highly technical flavour, just as it is today.

The only other people who found any real interest were the meteorologists, and those who liked teaching, for gliding had reached the stage where newcomers were no longer pioneers anxious to experiment with their own creations. There were others, mostly students, who simply wanted to learn to fly; and so some people, because they liked it or because there was a job to be done, became instructors.

As the appeal of gliding narrowed, so many of its older devotees fell away, and the years 1923–28 were lean. Only the dedicated pioneers remained, and a few newcomers who fitted into this special enthusiasm.

At this time there were two centres of gliding in Germany. As well as at the Wasserkuppe gliders were flown at Rossitten on the Baltic sea, where the wind blew over the sand dunes along the coast. The site had been chosen because the possibilities for slope soaring were considerable, although quite different from those of the mountainous, sometimes gloomy Rhön. The heaps of sand which made up the long coastal ridge were sometimes only 30 ft high, washed by heavy surf. To soar along them the pilot had not only to keep extremely close to the ground, but also to fly very slowly while doing so, to achieve the minimum sinking speed for his aircraft. Flying in the spray-filled air must have been stimulating in light, slow gliders: from an open cockpit the roar of surf could be heard above the whistle of the airflow, and the lips always tasted of salt.

Some remarkable flying was done at Rossitten by a local schoolteacher, Ferdinand Schultz, who built himself a glider similar to, but even more primitive than, the early 'broomstick' single-seater trainers. This machine was controlled by two levers above the pilot's head, and had neither seat belt nor proper foot rests. It is astonishing that Schultz never fell off in flight: he was unable to use this glider at the Rhön meetings as it was not sound enough technically. Nevertheless, when he heard that Germany had lost the world duration record to France with Maneyrol's flight of 3 hr 21 min. at Itford, he had himself launched and remained airborne over the dunes in his dreadful glider for 8 hr 42 min. to win the record back for his country. Several national meetings were held at Rossitten. During one of them Schultz flew for 9 hr 30 min. with a passenger. Later he flew on his own for 14 hr 7 min. in a better glider, again winning a world record.

Several attempts to beat distance records were made from Rossitten entirely in the lift provided by the sea wind as it blew over the dunes. Even if thermal soaring had been understood at this time, there would have been little chance of these up-currents so close to the coast. To some extent the specialised technique required to soar efficiently so close to the ground probably delayed the practical development of thermal soaring.

On one remarkable flight Schultz soared along the sand nearly to Memel, over 36 miles away. There is no record of the maximum height he attained, although it is unlikely ever to have exceeded 800 ft. Much of the flight was done lower than this, probably only at 200 ft or so. Since the dunes were not a regular ridge Schultz had gaps to cross, which he managed by conserving every foot of height, and utilising every gust by careful and sensitive flying. Sometimes he would find that he was almost brushing a wing through the waving sea grass, or even the sand itself. When he came to a gap in the dunes which was too wide to cross using only the slope wind, Schultz discovered that by flying with immense care out over the surf itself just above the swell, the glider would stay airborne, supported presumably by the air pushed up by the waves; then he would drift back on to the next dune, and work his way up once more.

This exhilarating technique which Schultz developed was copied by a young student, Johannes Nehring, a brilliant pilot who usually flew from the Wasserkuppe. Despite having done very little flying in the sort of conditions which existed at Rossitten, he set off to fly as far as he could along the dunes. He explored even further the lift which existed above heavy surf, and used it to soar just above the waves a hundred yards out to sea. He also discovered that even houses or trees in the path of the steady sea wind could deflect the air sufficiently to keep him just airborne. It was probably as well that his glider could fly and land slowly.

In 1923 and 1924 the annual Wasserkuppe meetings were held, but the weather was poor, and so little opportunity for new flying existed. The old flights down into the valley and in the slope lift above the mountains had been done many times, and there was not much interest in doing them again. When the monument to the pioneer pilots who had been killed flying was unveiled, it is even possible that the price of progress may have seemed too high. At the time of the ceremony there was the usual Wotan-type thunderstorm brewing, in spite of which pilots selected for the honour of flying at this memorial hour decided that they must do so. The result was inevitable. The glider of Thomson was not strong enough to cope with the turbulence, and the wings distorted more and more as he tried desperately to bring it safely down. At 20 ft one of them broke off, and the pilot was lucky to get away with his life. Another glider, inappropriately named the Gallows-bird, crashed into the face of the hill injuring the pilot. And finally, as though this was not enough, the wing of Max Standfuss' glider broke in the violent turbulence about 100 ft up, and he was killed. It was just as well that there were some who were not easily put off.

One of these was a young joiner called Gottlob Espenlaub. He had first come to the Wasserkuppe in 1920, where, without money or equipment, he had settled down to make flying his life. In the autumn he bought a sack of oatmeal and some dripping as food for the winter, and started to build himself a glider. By 1923 he had made two and took them to a meeting in Vienna. Not being a pilot himself, he lent one to someone who could fly.

This pilot promptly broke it. Espenlaub was so furious at the wanton destruction of his work, that he declared that if his precious aircraft were going to be wrecked he would do it himself. Getting into the second glider, he had himself launched off a 1,000-ft hill, glided 2 miles, landed safely, and found himself the recipient of a prize for the longest flight; not only did Espenlaub not know how to fly, but his glider was built without any technical or design knowledge, and had not even been test-flown.

But even with such enterprising people as Espenlaub, Nehring and Schultz, by 1925 gliding was slowing to a stand-still. There seemed to be little future for the sport, and the weather continued to be awful. To encourage others to go on flying, Schultz would get airborne regardless of rain or hail. Nehring carefully worked at developing the technique of hill-soaring to an extent which has never since been surpassed. If there was slope lift anywhere he could make use of it. He was prepared to fly very close to the rocks in huge span gliders or make figures-of-eight with immense patience almost in the tops of trees if this meant that he could stay up.

Fig. 11. The glider in which Schultz flew for 8 hours

He would work his way steadily along the ridges, assessing the behaviour of the wind on every spur, or in each gully. Nehring was almost certainly the most skilled pilot in the world at slope-soaring; but this flying, however superbly executed, still chained the glider to the hills, and most pilots had neither Nehring's patience nor his skill. For them there would probably be yet another valley landing, with its tedious retrieve.

The widespread cry 'Where do we go from here?' was urgently needing an answer. Looking back now, it seems extraordinary that despite all the observations of soaring birds, the knowledge of physics possessed by many pilots, and the papers that had been written, the way ahead could not have been both seen and implemented sooner. It may be that the very preoccupation with hill-soaring had kept everyone's heads to the ground, and their minds on the mountains, instead of studying and recognising what they could see happening in the air above them. Perhaps what was needed was just someone to stand back and look.

The preoccupation with hill-soaring had of course affected the shape and performance of the glider. Just as the albatross had evolved to soar the big waves of the southern oceans, and the vulture to float effortlessly over one spot waiting for carrion, so the man-made bird could now rise on the merest breath of wind over the hill; it was becoming just as specialised. Then, in 1926, something took place which was to help lift gliding out of its rut. Professor Walter Georgii became Director of the Rhön–Rossitten Gesellschaft research institute, and at the same time took over the Department of Flight Meteorology at Darmstadt. A new rallying point was shortly to appear.

Chapter Nine

EXPLORE THE SKY

Professor Georgii had long understood that there must be thermal up-currents in the air, and he now knew them to be strong enough to support a glider. He realised that cumulus clouds were produced by convection and must therefore be formed by up-currents. The problem was how to find the best way of using this energy that would free the glider from the hill and allow it to roam the sky with a freedom hitherto thought impossible.

One pilot who was interested was Max Kegel, but his first experience was somewhat inadvertent. On one August afternoon during the 1926 meeting he was slope-soaring over the Wasserkuppe when a thunderstorm brewed up with surprising suddenness; within minutes Kegel had been sucked into it. He had, of course, no blind-flying instruments, no parachute, and no idea of the power or size of the storm. Fortunately the newer gliders were stronger, and Kegel's held together in the turbulence while he endeavoured to keep control. After what seemed an age he was thrown out of the side of the storm higher than he had ever been before. Kegel quickly realised the opportunity which now existed and flew off straight to land safely more than 30 miles away. Although this was the first cross-country flight in the world which had not used slope lift throughout, Kegel's success in escaping from the hills did not encourage others to follow him. His lurid account of the flight only succeeded in frightening his friends to such an extent that storm-flying was officially declared inadvisable by the organisers of the meeting.

Although the doldrums of the last few years had resulted in few young pilots coming up to challenge the sadly small number of pundits, Kegel's flight sparked off fresh interest, and Georgii's scientific work quickly brought life to the movement. It now looked as if, after all, gliding could have much to offer. When in the spring of 1928 Georgii encouraged a programme of experiments for investigating the lift under cumulus clouds, Nehring found that when flying a light aeroplane with the engine throttled back immediately underneath them he could maintain height.

During the 1928 Wasserkuppe meeting the utilisation of lift under cumulus clouds, as distinct from trying to find and use thermals, was made one of the events. One of the pilots who had thought about the possibilities of using this cloud lift was Robert Kronfeld, an early pioneer of the Rhön who had so far not achieved any big flights. He had come to the conclusion that there were two ways in which contact might be made with it. The first was to get as high as possible in the slope lift directly above the hill, and then, as the cumulus drifted overhead, transfer straight from it to the cloud up-current. The other way was to fly out upwind from the hill at as great a height as possible to meet the cloud as it approached.

After slope-soaring for some time Kronfeld saw a large well-developed cumulus approaching the Wasserkuppe and determined to try to connect with it. He was surprised to find this easier than he had expected, and using the new idea of circling, was soon drifting along under the cloud 1,400 ft above the ground. It occurred to him that this lift might provide a means of reaching the Himmeldank mountain a few miles away and returning home again. Using slope lift alone it would have been possible to get there, but not to return. As his cloud drifted past the Himmeldank, Kronfeld left the sky and dropped down to slope-soar on its ridge. Watchers on the distant Wasserkuppe were not clear how Kronfeld proposed to get back and, after he had spent some time flying to and fro slope-soaring, neither was he. At this moment Max Kegel, who had decided to make an attempt on the same out-and-return flight, arrived at the Himmeldank high above Kronfeld's head and turned immediately to go back. It was a moment of great indecision for Kronfeld, who much wanted to follow Kegel home although he knew in his heart that it was impossible. So he watched, as he flew back and forth, seeing the other glider getting lower and lower until it sank down to land in the valley in the lee of the Wasserkuppe. Kronfeld was still in the air. After a time he realised that another good looking cloud was approaching, so positioning himself on its line of drift he waited until he could feel its up-current and then started to circle. To his delight he found that once again he had managed to connect, and although while circling he was drifting still further from home he gained height quite fast. He was soon up near the base of the cloud, and setting course for home directly upwind found no more difficulty as there was now a continuous street of cumulus under which to fly. He even had enough height to spare for some exploratory wanderings on the way.

Surprisingly, few pilots had observed closely what was going on, and even fewer put any conclusions they might have reached into effect. One of the few to do so was a pilot called Bachem, who climbed sufficiently high under a cloud to enable him to fly round the Himmeldankberg and return without using any other lift.

Although gliding could now free itself from the hills, developing new techniques, and learning skills such as navigation took time. There were some pilots who were reluctant to change their ideas or leave familiar territory: when suddenly the doors of the world open it is difficult to decide where to go. Some time later when a prize was offered for a flight over a new district, obviously with the intention of encouraging thermal-soaring and opening up new ground, the protagonists of slope-soaring declared their conviction that the best distance flights would continue to be achieved in the hills; it was just a matter of finding somewhere in the world a hill that was long enough. But in spite of their voices, no new pilot would again attempt to reach anything approaching Nehring's skill in slope-soaring. For them the new cloud-sailing was the object.

Nevertheless, when a German newspaper offered a prize of £250 for the first pilot to fly 100 km. (about 62 miles), this was felt to be rather overdoing things. Attempts were made, but again initially on the hills. Ferdinand Schultz was the first to try, along his beloved sand dunes at Rossitten, but they did not continue far enough without gaps which he was unable to cross. He tried again in the depths of winter, but had to give up owing to the difficulty of distinguishing what was snow still in the air and snow blowing along the surface of the sand, from the frozen spume of the waves. This almost impossible situation was aggravated by the salt which encrusted his goggles in the sub-zero temperature.

Throughout the winter, while the redoubtable Ferdinand was pressing on in the vile North Sea weather, Kronfeld was having a new glider built. He realised that to make a serious attempt on the prize, not only was a high-performance glider needed but particularly it would have to have good manoeuvring qualities to circle round and round under the clouds.

Unlike most vehicles, where the performance is measured in terms of how fast it can go or what load it can carry, the effectiveness of a glider depends on how slowly it can descend vertically through the air, and how flat is the angle at which it glides. To achieve a low rate of descent, or sinking speed, it is necessary to have large wings, low weight and a good shape, whilst to obtain a flat angle of glide the shape is all-important.

Test flights in the early spring showed that the new glider, the Wien, might fulfil Kronfeld's hopes, and on one trip he managed to circle all the way up to 6,000 ft. In the meantime Nehring had discovered a range of hills near the Odenwald where he reckoned that, regardless of sun or clouds, in a good hill wind he would be able to gain the prize. Early on 3 April 1929 he was launched, and without great difficulty soared along the ridge until he reached Heidelberg. Here the Odenwald hills ended, and between them and the Schwarzwald there was a valley. Nehring tried every trick he knew to get high enough to bridge the gap, and if it had been possible to get across on slope lift Nehring would have done it, but it was not possible, and he had to land after flying 42 miles.

Some time later he tried again along the same hill, and reached the gap. As he approached he flew as slowly as he could, conserving not feet of height but inches, and re-flying any short beat from which he thought he might be able to extract just a little more height. When the moment came that he had to try to cross, he set out with little hope. At last,

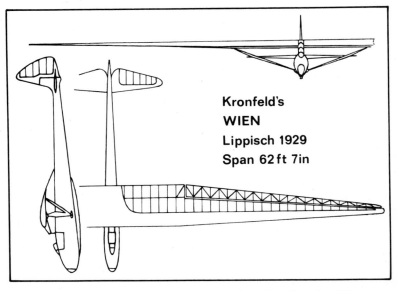

Kronfeld's
WIEN
Lippisch 1929
Span 62 ft 7 in

FIG. 12. The first glider to soar more than 60 miles, the Wien

despairingly, he tried to connect with the lift of a passing cloud, but was much too low. He had failed again, although this time his total distance was 43 miles.

When Kronfeld made his first attempt, it seemed that he too had not yet the faith to fly out entirely over flat country. He chose the hills of the Teutoburgerwald as suitable to fall back on, if the erratic and still suspect lift under cumulus let him down. Before starting, he explored the many low hills in the area on his motorcycle, noting down good ridges and gulleys for different wind directions, the slope of the fields for emergency landings, and the height of some of the more insignificant slopes. He did not, however, have enough time to carry out the thorough survey that he would have wished. Kronfeld's first attempt was made in stable weather, purely in hill lift, and it ended only 21 miles out.

On 15 May he started again, on a superb day in early summer, with cumulus sprouting all over the sky. The lift above the launching slope was good and he worked his way steadily along it, but whenever he came to a gap he waited for a passing cloud. As it drifted overhead, rippling its shadow across the fresh green fields, Kronfeld turned to meet it, sometimes circling, sometimes just heading out towards it and feeling it urge his glider upwards. He never stayed with the clouds, but took just enough lift to enable him to float across the gaps in the hills and then went on his way, low over the wooded slopes near the sounds and scents of the earth. In this way he flew the 60 miles and won the prize. It was a fine flight, but if he had soared downwind using only cumulus, instead of across wind along the hills, the flight could have been done more easily and more quickly—but who is to say with what greater fun?

However much they really enjoyed scraping along the hills, both Kronfeld and Hirth hoped to be able to become independent of them, and of the influences of the ground. They wished to link themselves with the clouds, to fly across country high in the summer sky, with the landing place distant and unknown. Kronfeld's chance came at the annual Rhön meeting of 1929. From the Wasserkuppe, hills did not continue far enough for any long flights to be made using only slope lift. Already the limits of the high land had been explored by many pilots, all of whom had had to land on reaching the plain. On the third day of the summer camp the weather was hot, and quite obviously this heat, trapped in the valley, was going to erupt in a thunderstorm during the afternoon. Kronfeld had already enough experience of these to realise that if he became seriously involved with the cloud, even in his new tough Wien, there was an appreciable risk of structural failure. It would be only prudent, therefore, to wear a parachute. As the day became more stuffy, and the hot wind fitful and erratic, Kronfeld talked with Georgii about how best to use the massive explosion of power which they could see slowly climbing up the sky, and which would soon be upon them. Georgii counselled the need to keep before the cloud edge, if possible in the clear air, as the storm front would probably have some roller action as it advanced, the cold air undercutting over the hot land. Hirth had already been launched and was in the air 3,000 ft above them, studying the storm, and awaiting his chance to integrate himself with it.

Just before it broke, in the few moments of calm spattered by single big drops of rain, Kronfeld was launched. Immediately he started to rise, and turned downwind to stay ahead of the dark cloud which was reaching out over the top of him. As Georgii expected, he gained height fast, and was able to soar alongside the cloud wall without being enveloped by it, although he flew into enough rain to choke his airspeed indicator. He was almost surprised when he realised that not even one beat along the familiar slope had been needed. Soon the Wasserkuppe was invisible behind and below the cloud and rain, and he was riding high enough to see not only the unknown land far ahead, but the extent of the storm itself stretching towards the horizon on each side. Not content to stay in the same area of lift, and despite the freezing air Kronfeld started systematically to explore ahead of the storm front, and found that even a couple of miles in advance of the cloud there was still lift. His height varied between 6,000 and 10,000 ft above the plain—7,500 ft above the Wasserkuppe. To him this was a fantastic and lonely height, so far above the misty ground drifting imperceptably below. Kronfeld had been launched in the late afternoon and his cross-country speed was of course only that of the thunderstorm which carried him. After $4\frac{1}{2}$ hours he was forced by approaching night to land near Hermsdorf, cold and wet. At one time he had been sucked into the cloud itself, where without instruments he had lost control of his Wien, but he had created a new world distance record of 85½ miles. This flight was not only an exhilarating and great achievement, but was the finest possible stimulus at this time.

It was not long before results began to show: newly taught pilots attempted to reach the clouds and fly in them almost as soon as they had obtained their 'C' Certificates, and in a summer of fine weather were quickly catching up the pioneers in the development of a new skill. It was at this moment that the whole purpose of gliding—the exploration of the limitless sky—came into focus and within reach.

FIG. 13. The white birds on blue ground of the 'B' and Silver 'C', originally designed in Germany and later adopted by the Fédération Aéronautique Internationale

Chapter Ten

FIRST THERMALS

The cloud and thunderstorm flights of Kronfeld, Hirth and others put new life into gliding, but thermals, away from clouds, were still not properly understood or used. Heat thunderstorms are only the ultimate expression, so to speak, of thermals and develop from them only when the air is extremely unstable. As has been seen, a great deal about thermals was in fact known; even in 1901 Wilbur Wright wrote 'when gliding operators have attained greater skill, they can, with comparative safety, maintain themselves in the air for hours at a time in this way, and thus by constant practice so increase their knowledge and skill that they can rise into the higher air and search out the currents which enable the soaring birds to transport themselves to any desired point, by first rising in a circle, and then sailing off at a descending angle'.

Looking back on any of man's advances it is often surprising how ignorant people are of the work of others in their own field. We now know that had previous knowledge and ideas of thermals been neatly listed and available on the Wasserkuppe, Klemperer could have soared in thermals in 1922, as in fact did Bossoutrot and Coupet in France that year. But when in the late '20s Georgii tried to encourage pilots from the Wasserkuppe to fly out over the valley on days when there was little or no wind to find the elusive bubbles, the response was discouraging. Only Nehring made an attempt, and to everyone's surprise gained 300 ft.

It was difficult to have faith in something that was totally invisible. The thunderstorms and the big cumulus were so obviously sources of power, the energy of which could be felt

9 (a) Klemperer's Black Devil of 1922; (b) The Peyean Boot 1924; (c) The Kassel
in which Eric Collins beat the British 2-seater record in 1933; (d) Wolf Hirth's
Minimoa of 1936; (e) The world's biggest glider—Kronfeld's Austria of 1931;
(f) The Rhönadler, designed by Hans Jacobs 1932. Glide ratio 1:20

10 Concentration on the Wing:
(a) The Professor of Alexander Lippisch, 1928
(b) The highly developed wing of the gannet
(c) The gull-winged Minimoa of Wolf Hirth

as the clouds passed over. The preoccupation was still with the cloud itself, and not with the thermal which produced it. Even when pilots started circling beneath clouds there was for some time no real attempt to explore the area of lift. Almost certainly some of the doubt and reluctance was due to the character of the Rhön itself. Apart from the deeply ingrained tradition of the place, only bungey- or shoulder-launching was needed to soar in the hill wind. When there was no wind the glider inevitably went down into the valley and was lost for the rest of the day. If the Rhön had not been such a good slope-soaring site, more effort would have been devoted earlier to developing ways of launching gliders higher above the ground. If such means had been available, so that it would be possible to land back at the launch point without soaring the reluctance to search for thermals would not have existed; since the thermals were obviously there they would have been found and used.

It is interesting that the preoccupation with storm-flying manifested itself mainly on the Wasserkuppe; in Poland and France at this time the search was far more for ordinary thermals, as used by soaring birds. However, understanding was coming. Kronfeld, who was one of the first to use a variometer, a device suggested by Alexander Lippisch, wrote in the spring of 1930:

When flying in the upwind of a cloud, it seems to me that the only way to remain successfully within areas of lift, the cross-section of which corresponds approximately to the outline of the cloudbase, is to circle continuously. The principle is none other than that used by a bird wheeling in a small, local column of warm rising air. The relation between the size of the object in flight, and the area of lift must, in most cases, be about the same.*

However, the first real thermal soaring, without either hills or thunderstorms, took place in the United States. An American pilot, A. Haller, and a German far from home, Wolf Hirth, were the first to realise their opportunity.

* From Hirth, W., *The Art of Soaring Flight*, trans. Naomi Heron-Maxwell (Stuttgart, 1938), p. 37.

Hirth, who had only one leg, went to America in 1930 to visit the first soaring meeting at Elmira, taking with him his Musterle glider. He found the American site, as well as the weather, quite different from Germany. At a more southerly latitude the days were warmer though shorter. The air was drier, and so there was often little or no cumulus in the blue sky. Hirth knew that this was not for lack of thermals, but it was nevertheless strange to fly in clear air and expect to find lift. He had installed a variometer in his Musterle, and although he had flown with this instrument in his Klemm monoplane he had little experience of it in a glider. However, he had thought about using thermals more often than others and knew what he was trying to do.

Here is his account:

On the last day of the Competitions [in Elmira, N.Y., October 1930], I myself succeeded in making the following flight, which, far from being a haphazard cross-country flight was a planned long-distance goal-flight to Norwich, N.Y. The Soaring Society of Norwich had offered a prize for which I was anxious to compete. Long before the Competitions had begun I had thought out two possible ways of making this flight, both of which necessitated clouds for locating thermal up-currents.

Six machines were already in the air when I was launched off the South slope of the soaring site near Elmira in my sailplane. In a few minutes I had risen above the school-machines, and after 20 minutes had caught up with Haller who was flying at a height of about 1,000 ft. For a time my 'Musterle' flew together with Haller's 'Schloss Mainberg' in long-drawn-out figures of eight far above the other sailplanes; then in the middle of a turn I suddenly noticed that my companion was going up like a lift at the other end of the slope. I at once steered my plane in that direction and to my joy found a vast area of thermal upcurrents, in which, after 10 minutes of uninterrupted tight circling, I climbed to 3,000 ft above starting level. This was the greatest height that had ever been reached in America, either during the Competitions or at any other time. However, on this beautiful sunny day, there was not a cloud in the sky, and for a moment the absence of this up-current indicator made me wonder whether there was any point in setting off along the prescribed course with a cross-wind. Then the temptation to make the flight became too great and I soon found myself flying down the broad Chemung Valley. During the next 15 minutes I lost a great deal of my previous height, when suddenly, not far from Waverley, I caught sight of two soaring birds wheeling and gaining height rapidly. What were they doing at such a height? These vagrants usually only fly in search of prey, but sometimes they undoubtedly consider it great fun to soar higher and higher for sheer pleasure. This time I could share in their joy, for they showed me where I could find further lift. A small detour brought me above them and for a short while I too rose steadily. The birds did not pay the slightest attention to me; possibly they did not even see me, as they much prefer to look down rather than to strain their necks by looking up.

Far below lay Waverley. From now on the way lay up the Susquehanna Valley. Haller had flown Southwards down the valley with the wind behind him in order to make as long a flight as possible and was already out of sight. Once again I was losing height foot by foot. Were there no more up-currents to be found? The ground was approaching rapidly and the only slope which appeared to hold out any hope of lift lay far ahead of me. Fortunately, down below there were not, as is often the case in this part of the country, many miles of woodland, but several suitable-looking landing-grounds; and I had already chosen a lovely long field ahead of me in which to land when, in surroundings which according to the rules of slope-winds should have produced down-currents, I suddenly felt myself being lifted up. Once more I gained height, though not for very long. Then I lost it again, only soon afterwards to find another and still stronger up-current. My altimeter showed me that I was climbing steadily and in a short while I was once more 3,000 ft above starting-level.

I can well remember, as though it only happened five minutes ago, how at this height I tried to take a deep breath because I felt so elated. I say 'tried' because I was so tightly wedged in the cockpit of my machine that there was only room to take very small breaths at a time! However, to make up for that, I felt myself completely identified with my sailplane and at that moment would not have exchanged it for the fastest and most expensive power-plane in the world.*

Although towards the end of this flight Hirth showed his

* From Hirth W., op. cit., p. 55.

reluctance to rely entirely on thermals, it was clear that gliders would no longer be tied to geographical features on the ground, or even to the clouds. By 1930, too, aerotowing was beginning to prove a safe and practical means of launching, and this meant that gliding could take place from fields far from any hill.

Before leaving America, Hirth made a rather surprising flight. He was launched by winch in his Musterle from one of the less cluttered quays on the Hudson river, beside New York city. He found thermals everywhere, and ambled round over the city itself, able to maintain an almost constant height of 1,000 ft. As can be imagined, crowds gathered to watch this strange silent aircraft floating above them in the blue sky, apparently supported by nothing. Eventually, signalled at by the police, Hirth landed back on the quay, having brought all traffic to a halt at the north end of Broadway.

Although thermal soaring had now been proved a practical proposition, with what seemed a limitless future, the development of any effective technique for using this new-found form of lift took time. Some of the older pilots made no attempt to search out thermals and still remained happily soaring on their familiar slopes. Others produced theories and ideas in remarkable variety. One difficulty which at the time seemed a constant source of confusion, is to us incomprehensible. It was the problem of how to turn in a thermal. Many believed that the glider would rise faster if only flat turns were done, and the glider circled on rudder alone. Hirth, on the other hand, became famous for his steep turns when circling, which was of course why he was successful. After years of hill-soaring, where the object was to fly constantly at the slow speed which gave their glider the minimum sinking rate, pilots were appalled at the idea of worsening its performance by turning steeply or flying faster. Hirth knew that the sinking speed of his glider would be increased if he circled steeply, but knew equally well that if he was to go up in the thermal it was essential to stay within its boundaries; he preferred to do this with some margin rather than risk losing it altogether. The protagonists of the rudder-only turn worked out remarkable reasons why, although soaring birds circled with banked turns, gliders should not: they were a sort of flat-earth society.

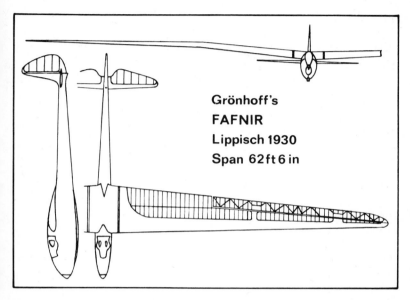

Grönhoff's
FAFNIR
Lippisch 1930
Span 62ft 6 in

FIG. 14. The world's first really beautiful glider, the Fafnir, which weighed only 440 lb and had a wing loading of 3.2 lb/sq. ft

Often when some new and important development comes along which cuts across established practice it is not readily accepted because people try to fit the new ideas into their existing convictions, instead of trying to work out a new conception with a fresh mind.

Returning to Germany from the experience of America, Hirth, with Kronfeld and the young Gunther Grönhoff, led the way at a startling pace. In May 1931 Grönhoff, flying his Fafnir, broke the world distance record by flying 169 miles on a storm front from Munich to Kaaden in Czechoslovakia.

During the Rhön competitions Kronfeld soared 103 miles to Westfalen on a day without either cloud or wind: on another day Hirth and Grönhoff both exceeded 100 miles on pure thermals. Hirth wrote of this flight:

On 2 August the weather conditions were unusual for the Rhön competitions, for there was a sharp east wind blowing. Circumstances prevented me from appearing at the start until noon, after others, headed by Marcho-Silese Pfeiffer, had already reached nearly 3,000 ft above starting-level from the east slope of the Eube. Grönhoff was already out of sight, and by the time I took off the wind had abated considerably, and I was only just able to maintain height.

For a time the three of us flew backwards and forwards skimming the tree-tops by inches, and only occasionally were we lifted up over the Obenhausen valley by spasmodic thermals. At last after about forty minutes I found a thermal bubble which, without containing very much lift, was sufficiently expansive to enable me to remain within its limits.

I had first exploited the idea of 'tight-circling' in thermals in America the previous year, and having further practised this method in the course of five flights in Grunau, I was now once again able to gain height steadily without clouds and independent of the slope-wind. At a height of approximately 650 ft I left the slopes of the Wasserkuppe and circled steadily up to 2,000 ft. Five or six miles away from the Kuppe it became apparent that there was no more lift in my original bubble, and I was unable to find any new up-currents in my immediate vicinity. However, I suddenly caught sight of some butterflies which had obviously reached that height under thermal influences, and I hastened to make use of the same locality. This did not get me much higher, but at least enabled me to cover a few more miles without much loss of height.

Not far away, somewhat south of the Fulda, a soaring bird wheeling 300 ft below me then called my attention to further air-masses that were apparently pressing upwards. When I had made a few circles and was taking a look round, I saw a plane flying straight towards me from the north. For the second time I had met Grönhoff in mid-air, without having made any previous arrangements to do so. The first time was in a thunderstorm, when it was natural that we should see each other again on the 'front' of the storm. But this time it was pure chance that brought us together after many hours flying, and in spite of having taken off at different times.

We now stayed together, which was, of course, to our mutual advantage, for first one then the other found a bubble which both of us were able to use. In this way, we circled around each other often for as many as ten consecutive turns. From below, it must almost have looked like a dogfight, whereas in reality we were helping each other.

The country over which we were now flying was unknown to me; but I supposed that Grönhoff was familiar with it and that we were flying approximately in the direction of Frankfurt. We maintained an average height of 3,000–3,500 ft above the Wasserkuppe, and in the search for lift often found ourselves far apart, and one of us at times even flying 4–500 ft above the other. When we had been soaring together for about 1¼ hours a large river appeared on the landscape. At first I thought it was the Main, but soon realised I must have been mistaken. At this point I lost sight of Grönhoff and in spite of looking for him everywhere was unable to find him again. So there was nothing for it but to continue the flight by myself. Hitherto the thermals had occasionally been capped by fine white puffs of cloud; but as evening drew near, these gradually dissolved.

Shortly after losing Grönhoff, I was forced down to 650 ft above starting-level, and as I later discovered, this loss of height must have occurred near Limburg-on-the-Lahn. Here, there were some large, half-reaped cornfields from which I hoped to find further lift, and as it turned out I did quite right in changing my course and heading straight for them. With the help of a sustained thermal, I covered several more miles, and climbed so high that I had no difficulty in crossing some mountains which had appeared below. I had now been flying for 3½ hours and on looking about me I caught sight of a broad, silver ribbon, winding its way through the countryside far away in the distance. A suspicion soon became a certainty. Joyfully I whispered to myself, 'The Rhine, the Rhine —if only I can reach it!'

But I did not like the look of the terrain over which I now found myself. Slowly I lost height! The mountains before me grew larger and at Bad Ems I was only 1,000 ft above the ground. Anxiously I looked about me. How to continue flying? The solution seemed difficult; but once again luck came to my aid. After soaring for a short while behind one of the bowl-shaped Lahn Mountains, I once more found a perfectly good bubble of warm air and with it spiralled away up and on.

At the height of at least 3,000 ft I crossed over the Rhine between Oberlahnstein and Koblenz. Steamers were working their way up the river, and thousands of people were sunbathing near Koblenz. It was the first time many of them had ever seen a sailplane in the air, and one of the bathers whom I met on my return journey next morning asked me a typical question: 'Is it possible to fly straight in a glider?' For he and all the others had seen me appear over the mountains on the edge of the river circling steadily and in the same way disappear again in the direction of the river Moselle.

As I crossed over the Moselle there was no more lift evident so I proceeded to steer my plane in a more northerly direction. In the old days I had often toured this part of the country on my motorcycle and I knew that owing to the thermals subsiding towards evening my only hope lay in the slope-wind of the Eifel. But the Eifel was too far away. I lost height more rapidly than was comfortable, and therefore turned back south towards the Moselle.

There remained one more difficulty to be overcome: that of landing in a place full of small orchard trees, high-tension cables and fields surrounded by hedges. But my luck held and my 23rd cross-country flight in a sailplane ended, as had previously always been the case, without damage to my plane.*

Hirth's distance was 120 miles; he was not retrieved until the next morning because it turned out that there were three places called Brohl in the district, and his crew visited and searched the other two before they finally arrived at the correct one. He probably had little time to think about what was happening in the States since his visit, but Americans cannot be accused of idleness. The Soaring Society of America was formed in 1932 and in the same year Jack O'Meara beat the American distance record with a flight of 66 miles. But tradition dies hard, even in the New World, particularly when there is a superb slope-soaring ridge not far from home. The following year Richard du Pont soared along the Blue Ridge in his Bowlus Albatross I for 122 miles, although he beat this record using clouds to go 158 miles in 1934. Nevertheless, only months later Lewin Barringer in an Albatross II made the world's longest ridge-soaring flight of 155 miles.

* From Hirth, W., op. cit., p. 68.

The next few years were not spectacular, used as they also were in Britain for steady growth of the sport as a whole, but by 1938 the Americans had learnt not only how to use thermals but found where the really good ones grew. In April that year Barringer flew 212 miles from Wichita Falls, Texas, northwards to Tulsa, Oklahoma. This was the first U.S. goal flight record and in a land famous for its aeroplane flying he was launched by winch. His success was shortlived, for in June 1939 P. Brown set off, also from Wichita Falls, with a declared goal of Wichita, Kansas—263 miles. He reached it, but it was not enough to gain the still unofficial category of world goal record because one month earlier, in Germany, Kurt Schmidt had flown 299.8 miles from Trebbin to Holz Kirchen.

Chapter Eleven

THE GOLDEN AGE

One always hopes for a golden age, but it is easy not to realise when it is there. One can look back and see it slip away into history, or as a glimmer in the remote past, but is it possible ever to recognise that one is actually living in it? Probably not —time sweeps by too fast, and life is so much fun. Certainly for German glider pilots the golden age of the 1930s must have vanished too quickly. There were only seven short years of wonderful sunlit flying high above the plains and woods of Central Europe: seven years of exhilarating progress, new gliders, new techniques, new records. Then the world became too serious, and there were other pulls and other affiliations. The golden age had gone for ever.

The excitement of flying in thunderstorms, and soaring across country, as well as the sport-for-youth propaganda, had brought to the new clubs being started all over Germany large numbers of students and other young people. By 1932 many of these beginners had become enterprising soaring pilots in their own right. This infusion of talent and physical enjoyment inevitably resulted in a rush and tumble of progress out of which came the best soaring pilots that the world had so far produced. One of these was Heini Dittmar, younger brother of Edgar, who had held the world height record of 2,530 ft in 1928. He went to the Wasserkuppe on leaving school to work as a model aircraft constructor for the youth section, and while he was there helped to build Grönhoff's Fafnir, perhaps the first really beautiful glider in the world. He desperately wanted to fly it himself, but a pupil's progress learning by hops in a single-seater open Primary was frustratingly slow. To speed things up he decided to design and build his own soaring plane, which gives an idea of how much progress he reckoned he was making in the school. A few weeks in hospital gave him the time to produce the plans, and 2,000 hours of hard slogging work, the glider. He called it the Condor and in it won the junior class of the 1931 Rhön competitions. During the late winter of 1933 he took his Condor to Darmstadt to learn blind-flying, and then became the ninth pilot in the world to win the new Silver 'C'. Such energy and talent were soon spotted by Professor Georgii, who was in a position to give him a job as a meteorological research pilot. In 1934 he went to South America with an exploratory soaring expedition, beat the world's height record by climbing to 14,100 ft, and started a gliding club in São Paulo. On returning to Germany, he set out to fly further than anyone else had done, and soon became famous for his long-distance flights.

Hanna Reitsch, who started gliding at Grunau in Silesia in 1932, was another of the famous, and not only because she was one of the rare women pilots. At one time she held the world women's record for height, duration and distance, and was the first woman to hold the Silver 'C'. A tiny person of great courage, she became involved in research and test-flying, expeditions to other countries, and top-class soaring, finally winning the senior class team-flying prize in 1935 with Heini Dittmar and Peter Riedel. She is perhaps one of the few pilots in the world who has ever had a glider tailored to fit, Hans Jacobs building for her the Sperber junior, a scaled down version of his fast and handsome Rhönsperber.

By 1934 a great deal had been learnt about how to fly long distances across country using both clear-air thermals and cloud lift. During the summer, Grönhoff's three-year-old flight of 169 miles was beaten by Wolf Hirth, who flew 220 miles. But this record stood only for one day. On 27 July Heini Dittmar went 234 miles to Liban in Czechoslovakia in Grönhoff's old Fafnir, which he had flown since its owner was killed in 1931. No longer were there prizes for duration flights, which were regarded as mere pole-squatting. The only aim now was distance: to soar as far as possible, and next time to go further.

91

The first to fly more than 250 miles was a young pilot, Ludwig Hoffman. His passion since childhood had been flying, but he was given up as hopeless by his instructor; then quite suddenly he became good, then very good. The new record was well earned, for he had already flown in two weeks a total distance of 625 miles, ranging as far as France. From one of these flights he travelled back overnight, and without going to bed, set off again. Several times he fell asleep in the air, and after flying 140 miles decided that he would have to land, although he still had 2,000 ft in hand. In the 1934 Jubilee contests, he had won the prize for the greatest aggregate distance, having achieved 727 miles.

In the spring of 1935, while testing the new Rhönsperber, he again totalled 625 miles, including one flight from the Hornberg to Zürich, so becoming the first pilot to soar into Switzerland. With this flying behind him he was not only well equipped to do great things in the 1935 competitions, but he must have possessed an almost unique experience of being retrieved. On the first day he reached Olesnice in Czechoslovakia, 296 miles in seven hours, and no sooner had he got back to the Wasserkuppe than he was off again at 0930 hrs towards Belgium, landing 200 miles away near Arlon after nine exhausting hours. The weather was not particularly good and often he had to wait or go back on his tracks in order to stay airborne while waiting for new thermals to come up and fresh cumulus to develop; anything was worth while that would make sure of just a few more miles of distance.

Just distance. In competitions there were no set tasks, and no starting times. Pilots took off as early in the day as it seemed possible to stay in the air and drifted away on the weak lift of the morning to gain distance regardless of all else. Distance, just as far as it was possible to go: the escape from the hills had run riot.

But now there came a new problem. Distance flying was magnificent fun, but there was a limit to this too. Thermals were produced by the sun, but even on a fine day in midsummer the hours of warmth were limited, and could not be

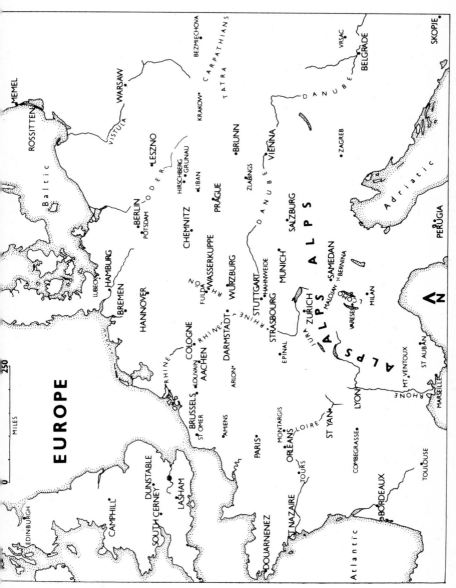

Fig. 15. Gliding map of Europe

93

increased. It might be possible to find a hill as thermals died
away in the evening, slope-soar all night, and fly on again
when the thermals started next day—if they started—but
weather was not that reliable, and the human frame tired. It
was necessary to learn to fly faster, and thus fly further in the

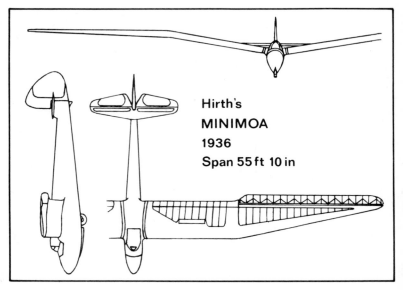

Hirth's
MINIMOA
1936
Span 55 ft 10 in

FIG. 16. Hirth's Minimoa, built for circling in thermals; 110 were built

hours of sunshine. This could be achieved by climbing up in
thermals more quickly, flying on between them at a faster
speed; and designing gliders to suit this technique.

One of the first to realise this was Wolf Hirth, who in his
new Minimoa succeeded in flying 262 miles to Zlabings in
Czechoslovakia, a flight which on that day was nearly 60 miles
longer than that of any other pilot. Hirth's glider had been
designed more for manoeuvrability than for speed, but the
very ability to centre and circle easily in the strongest part of
a thermal, and therefore to climb rapidly, led directly to speed
flying as we know it. Hirth started to be selective about the

lift he used. On a good day, instead of circling in all that was available around him, he would leave weak lift and fly on to find something better. It was obvious that such tactics would increase the risk of losing the thermal altogether and having to land, but Hirth was sufficiently confident of his ability to assess the sky, know when it would pay to discard poor lift and when it was necessary to hang on to every scrap he could find.

It is difficult now to realise how essential it seemed simply to stay up in the early days of cross-country soaring, and how much less important to try to fly in a straight line. Many pilots tended to drift vaguely downwind from cloud to cloud, with no goal to aim for and no line drawn on a map. If the distance flown was great, this was terrific but to some extent fortunate. By 1935 ideas were changing rapidly. The newer pilots had started flying in the certain knowledge that thermals could be relied upon to support them. They accepted thermals, and took only what they wanted from them in order to fly faster.

The competitions of that year highlighted the fast approaching limits of idyllic wandering in the sky. On one day no less than four pilots exceeded 300 miles, landing at Brünn in Czechoslovakia. There was a strong wind in which the gliders travelled 314 miles in only 5½ hours; an average speed of 57 m.p.h. These flights not only created a new world record, but put up the highest cross-country speed so far achieved. One of the pilots, Oelzschner, was killed during the aerotow retrieve, and the other three pilots asked that the record should stand in his name alone.

With such distances, whether achieved through learning to fly fast, or being helped by a strong wind, a further problem was created; the nights were not long enough for the return journey, and the next day's thermals might be missed. Distance flying was magnificent, but the top pilots were beginning to realise that attempting to fly to a goal, perhaps across wind, or out to some point and back without landing, might be more practical. The retrieve could be speeded up, if needed at all, since the crew could start off along the route at the same time as the glider, or if the pilot flew to an airfield there would be facilities for him to eat, and care for his glider; even to get an aerotow home again.

It was only that it seemed like tempting providence to announce beforehand where one was going to fly to in a glider. But after Wolfgang Späte had planned to fly to his home in Chemnitz, 135 miles away, and had got there, and Wolf Hirth had flown from Hamburg to Hanover, and back again the next day, it was realised that goal-flying was not so difficult. In this same year (1935) Peter Riedel reached Hamburg from Berlin, 164 miles, and on 21 August Erwin Kraft created a world goal-flight record of 206 miles to Cologne from the Hornberg:

The choice of Cologne for my goal-flight was determined by the fact that long cross-country flights of over 180 miles are only possible from the Hornberg in three directions, if one does not want to land in a foreign country: i.e. the courses indicated by a S.E., S. and S.W. wind.

As the thermal conditions had greatly improved in the third week in August, it was only a question of taking advantage of a day with a relatively favourable wind.

On the morning of 29 August 1935, the sky was clear with a steady East wind of 18 m.p.h., and at 1000 hrs it was already obvious that excellent thermal conditions would obtain. Between 1030 and 1100 hrs the first typical lift clouds could be seen forming, and I went to report my intention of making a goal-flight to Cologne with a Rhönsperber. My proposal met with a great deal of scepticism, as the wind conditions could certainly have been better. For the greater part of the way I would be flying with a cross-wind, which would undoubtedly impede the success of my goal-flight, if not frustrate it altogether. But I had carefully planned the flight and was determined to attempt it. In the meantime the clouds had become well-developed, and the sky was covered with the most promising looking cumuli.

At 1145 hrs I was towed up to 650 ft, where I released and rose with a very slight lift to 1,000 ft. However, losing this, I soon found myself forced to search for up-currents, which I found after losing a little height in very turbulent air conditions on the lee-side of the Hornberg. Circling steadily, the Sperber now rose to 3,000 ft above the Hornberg, and the moment came to set off across-

(a) Eric Collins with his Grunau Baby; (b) Heini Dittmar, Ludwig Hoffman, Otto Brautigam, and Wolfgang Spate; (c) Robert Kronfeld in the Wien; (d) Philip Wills in Hjordis; (e) Geoffrey Stephenson, first across the English Channel; (f) Kit Nicholson, killed in the 1948 World Championships

12 (a) Dunstable, 1937: Philip Wills in Hjordis going off the top
(b) Dunstable, 1937: Author learning on a Dagling

country. Flying in a north-westerly direction, I pushed the stick slightly forward till the A.S.I. registered 60 m.p.h. and the vario-meter indicated a fall of 7–8 ft/sec. After flying straight for about 6 miles, the variometer again moved towards 'rise'. I at once began circling while the needle of my variometer rose to +10 ft/sec. and I soon found myself at cloudbase, which lay at 7,000 ft above sea-level. In order to gain as much height as possible, I allowed myself to be drawn into the cloud at the rate of 8–9 ft/sec. After eight minutes blind-flying, the light filtered through above and soon the cloud lay in gleaming white below. Through the cockpit cover could be seen the blue of the heavens; but I had no time to enjoy the splendour of the scene. My altimeter registered 8,000 ft above sea-level and it was now a matter of converting this height into distance. So once more on a north-westerly course, I pushed the stick slightly forward and speedily covered ground, for as I had only six hours in hand and a cross-wind with which to contend, it was necessary for me to maintain a high ground speed.

After three-quarters of an hour, I found myself over Heilbronn, where a strong lift again brought me to cloud-base. As before, I rose rapidly by flying blind inside the cloud, and reached my greatest height of 8,600 ft above sea-level, i.e. 5,200 ft above releasing point. Once again I flew along at high speed, while below me the River Neckar wound its way through the country-side, and Heidelburg came into view. In order not to waste time, I flew straight through small belts of up-currents. At 1300 hrs I caught my first glimpse of the Rhine and at 1320 hrs flew over Mannheim. Up till now my average speed had been highly satis-factory, for in 1½ hours I had covered 80 miles.

While flying high over the Rhine in the direction of Worms, I saw ahead of me a towering cumulus, which appeared a likely source of lift. But I was to be disappointed, for when the Sperber arrived beneath it, it was in process of dissolution and I found myself in a belt of strong down-currents.

So once again I slowly lost the height which I had struggled so hard to gain; but in the meantime I had crossed the Rhine and the country over which I was now flying was unknown to me. My altimeter registered 3,000 ft above sea-level, and for the first time I began to doubt whether I should make Cologne. It was certainly a blow to see the last cloud dissolve before my eyes. I seemed to be in a wide belt of down-currents, and the chances of finding further thermals were growing very thin. I kept glancing hopefully at the variometer, but it remained maliciously below zero, until the

97

altimeter registered only 2,300 ft. Suddenly the air became turbulent; the needle of the variometer quivered a few times, then slowly crept up to zero. I drew a deep breath for I knew that for the moment I was safe. Very cautiously I began circling, while the needle of the variometer slowly moved to + 3 ft/sec. The strain of the last quarter of an hour was over, and once again I felt that everything might turn out well after all. In spite of the cloudless blue sky, my altimeter soon registered as much as 6,500 ft, and as soon as the lift ceased I stopped circling and set off across-country again. I had now become more cautious than before, and endeavoured to draw lift from every possible source.

At 1515 hrs I once more looked down upon the deeply incised valley of the Rhine, and neither to the right nor to the left was there a landing-ground to be seen! In view of the high landing-speed of my plane, conditions were somewhat dangerous, and I knew that if I should be forced to land, no amount of skill would prevent me from crashing. In order to reach Cologne, a certain amount of risk would have to be taken, even though the prospects of finding lift continued to grow more remote. Latterly, my cruising speed had deteriorated, for in the last two hours I had covered only 45 miles and a good 80 miles still lay ahead of me. Without heeding the country below, I flew on, losing height steadily, but right over the Rhine a fresh belt of up-currents came to my rescue and drew me upwards at the rate of 6 ft/sec. However, the terrors of a forced-landing on the declivitous slopes of the Rhine Valley were again impressed upon me, as I once more lost the height, which I had only recently gained after a fierce struggle. The variometer recorded a fall of 10 ft/sec. Boppard, a small town on the Rhine, drew closer, and in despair I realised that I was only 1,500 ft above the Rhine and still falling at the rate of 13 ft/sec. A landing at this juncture would mean either coming down on the waters of the Rhine or landing in the vineyards on its banks.

Behind Boppard the Rhine curves sharply to the right. With the wind blowing as it was, it should be possible to find slope up-current at the corner. It looked like my last chance, and I was only 650 ft up when I made towards it in a desperate attempt not to be forced down. Suddenly it became extraordinarily turbulent, and I was thrown about violently, the wings shuddering under the vicious bumps. At last, the variometer again moved up to zero, hesitated, and—Great Scott!—fell back to −3! In my despair, I could do nothing but gaze at the dial hopefully. Another bump! The needle flickered, then travelled surely and steadily to +3!

I at once began circling to the left, my Sperber dancing about madly; but after gaining 1,300 ft my variometer registered a lift of 6 ft/sec, and I could once more breathe freely. The last quarter of an hour had been a terrible nervous strain. In the meantime I had again reached 6,500 ft and once more set off across-country. It was already 1615 hrs, and it was debatable, to say the least of it, whether I should have time to reach Cologne. I had passed Koblenz and could see Bonn in the distance. The up-currents now became more frequent and several times I was able to climb to 6,000 ft above sea-level, eventually leaving Bonn behind me at a height of 4,000 ft.

Only 20 miles to go! But I was gradually losing all my height. On the dusky horizon I could already see the rooftops of Cologne; but I was lower than ever! Should I be forced down so near to my goal? But luck was with me, and there was still a slight ascent of warm air.

In despair I made use of even the weakest lift, and by dint of struggling for every inch of height once more rose to 3,000 ft. But then it was all over!

In a long glide, my Sperber carried me to Cologne, and I soon fell to 1,300 ft. In wide circles, I searched for the aerodrome, but could not find it anywhere. The situation was becoming critical and I was only 700 ft above the rooftops, when literally at the last moment a power-plane came to my rescue. As it was climbing towards me still at a very low altitude, it could not have taken off so very long ago. So, pushing the stick forward, I flew rapidly in the direction from which it had come. At last the aerodrome appeared in sight, and clearing the last obstacles with 6 ft to spare I landed right in front of the hangars at 1735 hrs completely exhausted after a 6-hr flight. I was almost too tired to climb out of the cockpit; but I was in high spirits, for I had flown 206 miles: the longest goal-flight ever made in a glider.*

* From Kraft's account, given in Hirth, W., op. cit., p. 172.

Chapter Twelve

END OF AN ERA

Preoccupation with exploring the cumulus of summer skies left little time for thinking about other possible forms of lift, but there was still one way of soaring to be explored— wave; in the vast surges of air which may be created in the lee of mountains under certain meteorological conditions. Although a great deal of soaring had been carried out over hills and mountains, this was done above the windward face in the rising air. Pilots kept clear of the lee slope because they knew, often from hard experience, that the down-currents could treat them roughly and deposit their glider on the ground too rapidly for comfort. What had not been realised was that the air could rebound up again, and in the upflow it was possible to soar. In some parts of the world the topographical shape of the land stimulated such big wave systems that indications of the unusual disturbance affected the appearance of the sky; but in hills and mountains, such as the Wasserkuppe, even if wave lift developed it might be almost impossible to recognise without prior knowledge of its existence. This is because it would be weak, transient and confused with other more common forms of atmospheric disturbance.

In 1931, during the spring following Hirth's American visit, he was in Silesia talking to the director of the Krieten observatory, who told him of a strange stationary cloud that appeared in southerly winds above Hirschberg at night as well as day; its cause was not known and sometime it might be worth investigating with a glider. The locals had always called the odd smooth-edged cloud the Moazagotl.

On 3 March 1933 Hirth was instructing on Hirschberg

airfield, when in the late afternoon he noticed that one of the gliders from the Grunau Soaring school a few miles away was much higher than it could possibly be from a normal launch. As he watched it started to fly straight upwind towards Hirschberg town continuing to gain height. In the sky a strange elliptical cloud was forming—it was the Moazagotl.

Hurriedly, Hirth stopped instructing and jumped into the nearest glider, shouting for the Klemm towing aeroplane as he did so. The air during the tow was violently rough and it was a struggle to reach even 300 ft; several times Hirth nearly had to release the steel towing cable. Then they flew into smooth rising air and soon reached the other glider at 2,600 ft. Hirth released and flying close saw that it was his friend Hans Deutchmann. Flying almost side-by-side and heading into the strong south wind, both gliders rose steadily in strong lift. In the excitement of soaring into the sky so unexpectedly and so easily, it was difficult to work out the cause of this strange lift. For a while Hirth flew around the area; he found that the strength of the up-current was 13 ft/ sec. with down-currents of the same value if he ventured too far to the north, although it was never difficult to find the lift again and climb back up to 4,600 ft. When it began to get dark Hirth and Deutchmann flew back to their respective airfields, having soared for $1\frac{1}{2}$ hours. Although it was obviously associated with the mountains upwind, Hirth realised that unlike ordinary slope lift, where the possible height gain was limited, this new-found lift might go very high indeed; the Moazagotl cloud must have been formed in it, and this had remained thousands of feet above them.

The flight of Hirth and Deutchmann attracted a great deal of curiosity, and it was soon realised that the lift had been caused by the Hirschberg mountain setting up a wave system in the air, not dissimilar to that created in water downstream of an obstruction. It was thought probable that elsewhere in the world there might be even bigger waves to the lee of the great mountain ranges. Now that this first flight had been made, other pilots endeavoured to fly in the wave whenever its presence was heralded by the strange cloud. As it was explored, and associated waves found, pilots managed to climb higher; within two years 13,000 ft had been reached, and by 1937 18,750 ft. In this flight both the first and second waves of the system were used, found at 10 and 19 miles respectively to the lee of the mountain. Hirth was also flying and climbed so high that at about 19,000 ft the needle came off the top of his barograph chart. A two-seater flown by Erwin Ziller reached 16,000 ft, a world record height with a passenger. Later in the same year Dr Kuettner reached 22,000 ft, and soared on the face of the Moazagotl cloud itself.

In the late '30s all sorts of new ideas for soaring flights were tried out. One of these was a grand tour of Germany; a course of 482 miles was set out starting and ending at Darmstadt, with goals (stopping places) at Wurzburg, Munich, Augsburg, Stuttgart, Mannheim and back to Darmstadt. The total distance had to be covered in 8 days, and it was achieved by four of the eight pilots who entered.

In 1937 there was a contest to soar across the Alps from Salzburg to Italy. Six gliders, including a two-seater, were successful. During the Rhön competitions of this year, twenty pilots declared Wurzburg, nearly 100 miles away, and nineteen got there. By 1938 out-and-return flights were added to the list of records, Bernard Flinch establishing the first with a flight of 191 miles, Bremen-Lubeck-Bremen. Only 7 years after the first thermal cross-country flight, nothing seemed to be impossible. It is, however, unlikely that anyone remembered the last words of José Weiss which had now come true: that as soon as gliders had achieved a performance which gave them a gliding angle of 1 in 30, gliding would be the most wonderful sport in the world.

A remarkable feature of this period was the high standard of talent of those engaged in the development of new gliders. This was apparent in several European countries, but it was particularly marked in Germany, where many new designs were produced by Academic Flying Groups associated with universities or technical colleges. Several of those engaged in this work either as students or teachers afterwards achieved fame, particularly von Kármán, Lippisch, Messerschmitt, Kupper, Klemperer, and Dornier.

But time was running out. Gliding for a German could no longer be wholly his life, or his love: comfortable clothes on the Wasserkuppe had given way to uniforms. Technical students on holiday no longer launched the gliders; this was done by regimented boys with smart shorts and armbands.

By 1938, unknown and unknowing, the great days of the Rhön were coming to an end. The famous spirit of the Wasserkuppe, the Rhöngeist, was about to die, and for ever after the mountain would be just an ordinary place where gliders flew. It would still be unique, even magnificent, but it could never again possess the almost mystical atmosphere of the dedicated days.

In this last year of German peace, as well as the usual competition, there was to be an investigation into the structure of thunderstorms, to find out more so that they could be

FIG. 17. The Monument on the Wasserkuppe

avoided, or their use organised. Where better than on the Wasserkuppe? When better than during the competitions, where there would be plenty of pilots to help with the investigation, to take readings, to report what they found? Thunderstorms on the Wasserkuppe in August were likely, and in new strong gliders, with instruments and parachutes, there would be a good chance of a record too. All was prepared, and after a few days the weather came just right; the air was hot and sultry, and during the afternoon pink thunderheads emerged imperceptibly from the haze.

As the storm brewed, so the pilots waited, looking past the Monument to the Fallen Fliers out to the dark windward distance. Already the first rumbles of thunder could be heard. As the storm overwhelmed the sky, gliders were pulled out and made ready, crews rushed about in the sticky heat while the pilots watched the ominous darkness closing in. Then the wind dropped. A little lightning flickered out in the valley; there was some shouting, then, one by one, quickly into this moment of time the gliders were launched; one after the other they flew out to contact the storm. Drops of rain, sudden and chilling hit the watchers. Some of the gliders disappeared, rising up towards the dark cloud without turning, like dust to a vacuum cleaner.

The storm was of unexpected ferocity, the courage of the German pilots unquestioned. In gusts of wind, gliders which had failed to connect with the storm landed back and were hurried into shelter before the rain or the hail spoiled their polished skins. But those who knew the interior of such a storm were afraid. What had been done? Slowly the oppressive darkness passed overhead, and the cloud became grey and weepy with the remnants of the freezing rain; the wind dropped light in the flat air. Glimmerings of pale clearance appeared on the horizon. But that was all. No gliders could be seen either in the air or on the ground, and none returned to land on the Wasserkuppe. It was some time before the reckoning could be made.

On the plus side there was a world height record. Captain Drechsel, of the new Luftwaffe, had gained 6,687 metres (21,400 ft). The up-current had reached 100 ft/sec. with down-currents of similar strength, and he had found the turbulence extreme, particularly in the narrow junction between the two. Several pilots had exceeded 5,500 metres, battling with the beginnings of anoxia in the wild air, with ice on their wings. Some of them landed in fields safely, thankful to be alive. Others were not so lucky.

Several gliders broke up inside the storm. Fantastically, all the pilots were able to get out by parachute, in spite of the enormous possibility of injury caused by the violent behaviour of the splintering aircraft. All but three of these landed safely. These three, Lemm, Schultz and, in a Horten, Bleh, unknown to each other, but possibly quite close together, must have hit extreme turbulence high in the cloud, in sub-zero temperatures, and fierce lift. Freeing themselves from the wreckage, they had leapt into the darkness and the piercing hail, static lines pulling open their parachute canopies. The relief of knowing that they would soon be out of the biting cold, the terrifying thunder, and the fierce stabs of the lightning must have been great. It will never be known how soon they realised that they were not coming down because the lift in the storm was too strong; enough to bear their parachutes higher and higher. Perhaps they never knew even this; when their bodies were ultimately found, one had been charred by lightning, the other two frozen to death.

The meeting went on, the thunderstorm research was continued, and within a year those left were at war. The Rhöngeist was dead.

This moment in time passed almost without notice, for the sport which had sprung from the Wasserkuppe mountain was now thriving all over the world. The Americans were developing their own brand of gliding; in Poland a centre had been set up at Bezmiechowe in the Carpathians. The Poles brought a technical approach to their sport, and thought it right that money should be spent on research: their first soaring flight was in 1928, and in the '30s were making many long thermal flights with gliders of Polish design. In France, Italy, and even as far away as Australia and South America there were active gliding clubs. In 1939 there were 816 German pilots with Silver 'C' badges; the Poles had gained 159, the British 50, the French 29, the Swiss 19, and the Americans 17. About half of these pilots for one reason or another were never to fly a glider again.

But it was the Russians who held the major records when the war stopped play.

As far back as 1927 the Russians had encouraged and sub-

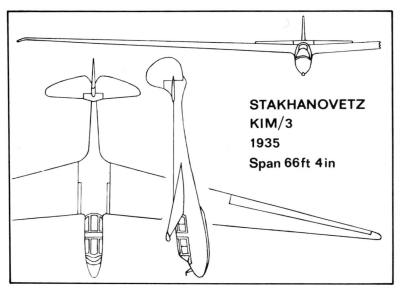

**STAKHANOVETZ
KIM/3
1935
Span 66ft 4in**

FIG. 18. The record-breaking Stakhanovetz used by the Russians in 1939

sidised gliding. Involvement in sport was necessary if their thousands of people were to be brought into the 20th century: to achieve results quickly, young people were encouraged to interest themselves in learning new things, particularly those needing a modern and technical approach. By 1937 Russia had taught thousands of pilots. Not a large proportion of these had done any soaring, but those who did went at it with the same sense of purpose which was becoming characteristic of anything that they took on. They soon realised that hill-soaring tended to breed an unenterprising sort of pilot, and so they moved their centre out to the plains, the vast flat expanse of eastern Europe, with its hot dry summers, miles of waving corn, and great slow wandering rivers. Far from the crowds they taught themselves how to fly on thermals, and in such an arena it was impossible to think small.

In May 1937 Victor Rastorgueff flew 335 miles, starting from Moscow. On his return he took off again, flying 374 miles to the east and a few days after that, on 27 May, 405 miles. On this day V. M. Ilchenko flew a two-seater with a passenger, V. Emerits, 253 miles, a world record which was beaten the next year by two more Russians, I. Kartsheff and P. Savtzov, in July. But the most surprising of all to the world was the new distance record on 6 July 1939 of 465 miles. This was nearly double the longest distance ever made, and it was flown by O. Klepikova—Miss. But speculation and congratulation was lost in the noise of war, and almost six years were to go by before the summer skies would be free once more.

Part III

BRITISH BEGINNINGS

Chapter Thirteen

THE THIRTIES

Apart from the meeting at Itford, the sport of gliding was virtually unknown in Britain until late 1929, when newspaper reports gave stories about pilots who had ridden on thunderstorms, and of the distances Kronfeld had flown on the rising air of storm fronts.

It is always a little surprising that the successful 1922 meeting at Itford led to nothing. Or is it? At that time the prospect of the little aeroplane, in which one would be able to fly all over the place, seemed a more attractive proposition. It was difficult for people to see what use, even what fun, there was in gliding: it was just a sort of aerial tobogganing. Even the soaring backwards and forwards along a hill, which had seemed exciting at Itford, did not in retrospect seem to be a very interesting way of flying. Detractors wrote letters to the papers: 'Gliding! It is a case of collective folly.'

Certainly to most people the crude aircraft of which they had seen photographs did not seem to have much to offer. So many people were required to launch them into the air, and when they had glided down, time and energy had to be spent carrying them up the hill again. Why do all this, when with an engine it was possible to fly where one wanted? Within a year of the Itford meeting any interest in gliding was diverted by the light aeroplane trials at Lympne. This was real flying. Within another two years the firm of de Havilland had produced the famous Moth, which sparked off a flourishing flying club movement and made private ownership practical.

So few people thought about gliding in England in the '20s; and kindly ridicule greeted the individual who had ideas. But the new storm flights were different. Interest was stimulated by the dramatic quality of the thunderstorm flights, particularly among those who would have liked to fly, but for various reasons had not yet been able to. *The Aeroplane* wrote at length on this new development in gliding, and one of the results of this was that Mr D. C. Culver wrote suggesting a meeting of anyone who might be interested. He arranged a 'gliding lunch' at the Comedy Restaurant in London on 4 December 1929 for the thirty people who indicated that they would come. To the consternation of everyone, fifty-six people arrived.

Suddenly, with an odd spontaneity, enthusiasm was huge; a committee was formed which eventually led to the formation of the British Gliding Association, and plans to start gliding clubs were made. Doug Culver's lunch had been a success.

There was, however, little except enthusiasm, since nobody knew anything at all either about how to fly, or to operate a glider. It was sensibly agreed to invite some German experts to advise; Professor Georgii came to talk on soaring and meteorology, and the Chief Instructor of the Wasserkuppe, Herr Stamer, about teaching *ab initio* pupils to fly. Their visit was followed a few months later by another. This time Robert Kronfeld and Carli Magesuppe came to demonstrate slope-soaring on the South Downs, at almost the same place as the little remembered Itford meetings of eight years before. During one of these flights Kronfeld decided to see how far he could fly along the hills, and set off towards the west. The low chalk slopes covered with short turf, with the sea not far behind them, were very different from the Wasserkuppe, but soaring on them gave Kronfeld no difficulty and he was soon out of sight: the demonstration was over as far as the audience were concerned. Only some hours later did the news come through that he had landed at Portsdown Hill, near Portsmouth, 50 miles away. To the uninitiated it seemed unbelievable; gliding was not just aerial tobogganing after all. It was possible to fly far away and land in some unknown place. This was attractive to the imagination.

All over the British Isles gliding clubs were started. Small groups of enthusiasts got together, and found some hill with a landing place at the bottom, however improbable. A primitive glider was bought from an enterprising firm like R.F.D. of Guildford, or designed, or even just made from photographs, by any club members who felt able to wield a saw. The curious, the enthusiastic, even the bored joined together, and the clubs were in business—more than a hundred of them within two years.

But all the enthusiasm in the world could not make success out of such a situation. There simply was not enough knowledge, or equipment, to go round. Most of the clubs were doomed to failure before they had finished the inaugural meeting.

Few of the people who started were pilots, or were in any way involved in aviation. They had little idea of what constituted an airworthy glider, how many people were needed to launch it with a rubber rope, let alone anything about the theory of flight. To them gliding was to be a sport like sailing; they had little intention of getting involved in the hard school of serious aviation. But they found that they had to begin completely at the beginning. On the continent flights of 100 miles long were being done, and gliders towed into the air by aeroplanes. Similar aircraft were in use in British flying clubs, which could have been used to tow gliders, but there was no link with these clubs; instead, almost a determination to show that gliding was different, even superior. The aeroplane people, on the other hand, could not see it as other than inferior. It seems extraordinary that no one, at the beginning, went to Germany to learn properly how to fly and soar, and to start their club with both experience and good aircraft.

Within two years many of the clubs which had started with such enthusiasm had disappeared. Of those which still struggled on, most were left in a deep rut of misplaced ingenuity. Even the aeroplane pilots in gliding had somehow got off on the wrong foot, and were regarded as poor risks, though in almost all cases it was the result of incompetent and inexperienced instruction. This was not surprising since many instructors had done practically no flying themselves. They were

113

trying to run clubs in which they as well as their pupils would learn basic pilotage, but this took a long time since no glider remained unbroken for long. Ideas of soaring were forgotten, and gliding was right back in the era of aerial tobogganing, which in the beginning had been rightly spurned.

Editorials and letters in the magazine *Sailplane* declared the importance of soaring as the purpose of gliding, and told of the technical and flying achievements of other countries: in America they were already thermal soaring and aero-towing; France had abandoned the hand-pulled rubber launching rope in favour of the winch; Spain had aerotowing, Egypt auto-towing. But it was no good. In England the ability and the experience simply did not exist, and unlike some subsidised countries, there was little money either.

Only in the London club, settling in on the chalk downs near Dunstable, was there enough talent and ability coalescing into experience to show progress.

It was not only that the London Club had a large population to draw from, it made fewer mistakes than many other clubs. In the first place, it started with more than one glider, so that a bad landing did not completely stop club flying. It managed to attract, rather than discourage, aeroplane pilots such as Mungo Buxton: some London Club members went off to Germany for their holidays to see how it ought to be done. Slowly, not particularly efficiently, it started to teach its beginners. But when beginners feel that they are going some-where, or can achieve something, efficient organisation is not so important: the pupils teach themselves. On 21 February 1931 two members who had first started flying with the club soared on the hill in the cold winter air for just over five minutes. Their names were Graham Humby and D. C. Smith and they were the first British *ab initio* glider pilots to obtain the 'C' certificate.

At last, after countless hours, weeks, and months of national effort, there was some return.

A few other clubs had also overcome the worst of their problems and were flying regularly. In the South of England,

13 (a) The Dagling Primary; used for the 30 second 'A' flight
    (b) One horsepower retrieve of a Falcon III
    (c) King Kite after the first competition launch on the Wasserkuppe

14 (a) Hanna Reitsch talking to Philip Wills, British Team Manager, Professor David Brunt, and John Fox on the Wasserkuppe, 1937; (b) The British team haul Hjordis back up the hill; (c) Bill Murray and John Fox, pilots of the 2-seater Falcon III, at the 1937 Internationals

there were the Southdown and Dorset Clubs, and in the North, Newcastle, Barrow-in-Furness, Derbyshire and Lancashire, and a group which later amalgamated to become the Yorkshire Club. Only one university, Imperial College, had started gliding. In Northern Ireland the Ulster Club, developing more as a group of private owners than a conventional club, was starting its successful history.

One of the people who helped to rescue British gliding from the despair into which it had so soon fallen was C. H. Lowe-Wylde. Not attached to any club, he was an aeroplane pilot who designed and built a whole series of effective and work-manlike gliders. They were not as advanced as most of the German machines, but they were sound and cheap. He also introduced auto-towing as a practical means of launching pupils on training flights. To this he found opposition, on the grounds that the catapult launching of pupils in single-seater gliders was safe because the flight could not last long, but auto-towing was dangerous because the 'flight' could be continued after the pupil had lost control. Anyone who has ever been catapulted in a glider which he did not understand how to fly will know the paralysing effect of the acceleration, and the fallacy of this argument. The almost furious opposition to auto-towing shows the extent of the ignorance, and the non-engineering approach of the time to gliding. While the argument raged, Lowe-Wylde steadily piled up irrefutable evidence of the value of auto-towing, which is today one of the ordinary methods of launching. It was a calamity when he was killed in 1933; it is believed he was taken ill in the air, probably as a result of overwork.

On 24 May 1931, at Dunstable, the British soaring record of 3 hr 21 min. made by Maneyrol at the Itford meeting nine years before was at last broken. Henry Petre, an aeroplane pilot, stayed up for 3 hr 28 min. in a London Club glider. At last the stalemate was nearly over.

Chapter Fourteen

DOWNWIND FROM DUNSTABLE

Sometimes when a group of people get together, and they are the right people at the right time, they create an organisation which develops a momentum of its own: they are still part of it, but it is more than all of them. So it was with the London Club. By 1933, Dunstable was beginning to mean gliding. Probably more flying was done at Dunstable than at the rest of the clubs added together. Its private owners went on expeditions all over the country, cheerfully towing their trailers with motorcars which boiled on every hill. With their Wrens and Scuds, they launched off mountains, landed on rough moorland, and returned to Dunstable with ludicrously funny stories of what had happened. By April that year forty-three Club pilots had obtained their 'C' certificate.

Among the growing number of pilots who had started their flying at Dunstable was a smiling young man, small in stature. He became so fascinated by gliding that he bought himself a cottage nearby. His name was Eric Collins. There are not many born pilots, but Collins was one of them, and even though he had not the advantage of aeroplane-flying experience, he soon knew more about soaring than any other pilot in England. In the spring of 1933 he was flying passengers in the two-seater, and with them regularly connecting with the lift under cumulus clouds. To help him he fitted, and learnt to interpret, a primitive variometer. Then he taught himself to fly blind in clouds.

During June the British Gliding Association held its second National meeting on Huish Hill, a south-facing slope near Pewsey in Wiltshire. In order that as much use as possible should be made of the facilities, it was decided not only to attempt soaring, but to give training flights in a two-seater with Collins as Instructor. A few days after the camp started Collins several times found himself in thermal lift while doing circuits in the Lowe-Wylde B.A.C. VII two-seater. Then on 2 July good cumulus developed in the light breeze; Collins was able to get only 600 ft from the launch, but whenever the variometer gave indications of lift he circled. So near the ground, the thermals were not strong, nevertheless he managed to extend the usual two-minute flight of the training glider to five and then six minutes, while trying to learn as much as he could about the form of this lift in the short time available. The next day, with his wife as passenger, he managed to circle in a thermal up to 950 ft under a clear blue sky, and from this exalted situation decided to set off for the first cross-country flight on thermals in Britain. He found one further up-current in which he regained some lost height, before landing in a field 6 miles away.

Back at Dunstable, Collins soared 22 miles on 3 August to South Mimms, reaching 2,300 ft on the way. This was the second, but not the last time, that he would hold the British distance record. The pilot with whom he was going to share the honours had obtained his 'A' certificate at Dunstable in April that year. He was a young aeroplane pilot called Philip Wills. Not a natural pilot like Collins, Wills possessed an ambitious determination which drove him on until he reached the top. Such a force was just what was needed at the time, for Wills's flights, and particularly his written accounts of them, did a great deal to remove the outdated image of gliding and show it as a new and marvellous sport.

At Dunstable, 18 March 1934 dawned with a freshness in the air and a clear sky. As the wind began to strengthen in the early morning, its direction was studied with great care by several London Club members, and when the first wisps of cloud grew out of the blue, showing it to be just north of west, there was jubilation. The wind was on the hill. It was cold, but the spring sun would warm the day and the air was

Fig. 19. Gliding map of Britain

118

wonderfully unstable. Soon the little wisps formed into cumulus, and the cumulus grew into great streets of cloud marching across the sky.

Collins reached Dunstable early, and got out the Kassel two-seater. He took it to the top of the hill and, with his wife as passenger, was bungied off into the lively air. Along the ridge he found the slope lift excellent, but even better were the thermals bubbling off the sunny slope. Having climbed quickly to 1,700 ft he left the lift to land and give another passenger a taste of such delightful flying. On the next flight the thermals were strong, and there seemed to be lift everywhere. It was obviously a day to attempt to fly away across country. Collins landed again, and with a German visitor, Herr Exner, in the back seat, took off.

While all this was going on, another London Club pilot, Sebert Humphries, had got airborne in the Crested Wren and joined Collins in the hill lift. This Wren was one of a family of light-weight gliders, with a remarkably sensitive all-moving elevator which made obvious to people on the ground any twitchiness on the part of the pilot. During the early afternoon a particularly fine cloud street could be seen developing upwind over the flat Aylesbury plain, drifting slowly towards the hill. As it approached, 'Humph' flew out towards it, gaining height steadily as he flew into wind underneath it, with Collins in pursuit.

When several miles upwind, probably higher and further from Dunstable than he had ever been in his life, Humph had to decide what to do. He was at cloudbase, and if he continued he would soon be in cloud; if he turned downwind his ground speed would be nearly 60 m.p.h., and he would be quickly swept past the familiar home field—unless he burnt his boats, and went off across country. But even though he had never done this, it did look possible, and an opportunity not to be lost. So Humph turned tail and fled downwind. He lost no height sailing back under the cloud street, since the cloud above was still lifting.

To the watchers on the ground the tiny Wren flew above

them at what seemed an incredible height. They wondered if it would turn again to keep above the Downs, but it did not, and soon vanished from sight over the new country which lay beyond. They turned to look for the Kassel, but it too had disappeared.

While all this was going on, Philip Wills arrived at Dunstable in a fever of excitement; quickly he rigged the club Professor and took it to the hilltop. At 1315 hrs he was launched, just as the other two disappeared. The club members who had been rushing down the hill catapulting everyone into the air, went off to get some lunch and to await events.

The cumulus were now growing into huge masses, some of them becoming dark and violent, trailing a fringe of hail. At 1,600 ft Wills left the hill, circling in lift ahead of a hail-storm without a variometer. In this he reached 3,800 ft and, maintaining his height, continued circling. He travelled some 15 miles before the hailstorm caught him up and enveloped him. Fighting his way out of its chilly wetness he found that he was near a town, but having no map only discovered afterwards that it was Welwyn. Having now lost the up-current he selected a good landing field and circled round it while descending gradually to 1,800 ft.

Considered with today's knowledge of cross-country techniques, this continuous circling was a waste of both time and height, but not only was it Wills's first cross-country flight in a glider, but one of the first in England. Flying over strange country without an engine was an adventure in itself; the important thing was to do it, and not necessarily to go anywhere.

Another cloud street was now approaching, and under its leading edge Wills found more lift; abandoning thoughts of landing, he climbed rapidly to over 4,000 ft. After circling under the cloud, he reached North Weald airfield at about 1430 hrs and decided to land. After twenty minutes of circling down and around the airfield, there was still no sign of life, which was disappointing. Then the Professor flew into lift again. Once more Wills used it, drifting away while climbing to 3,200 ft. Quite lost again, there was some companionship in meeting other aircraft in the air; he was immensely cheered when he saw two Moths, one with the registration **G-EBVK** which came close. Flying along just underneath the Professor which was almost twice their size without noticing it, they went on their way leaving him alone and still lost. Further

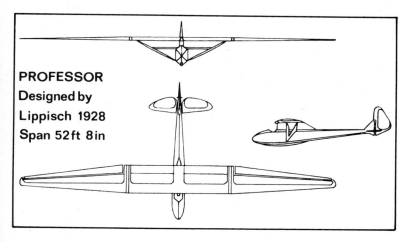

PROFESSOR
Designed by
Lippisch 1928
Span 52ft 8in

FIG. 20. The German Professor, in which Philip Wills broke the British Distance Record in 1934. It was not an easy glider to fly, and spun easily

efforts to recognise something on the ground brought the realisation that there was water not only ahead but on both sides. He was obviously reaching what must be the end of the flight. He circled down, landing in a field of blackberry bushes at 1545 hrs near the river Blackwater.

Back at Dunstable, the telephone over at Turvey's Farm started to ring. It was 'Humph', who seemed much more concerned with reassuring Eric Collins's father that he had not beaten his son's 22-mile record, than with giving his landing position. Barely able to say where he was, he finished his call with the cry 'Hurry, hurry, they're tearing the poor Wren to shreds!' and rang off. Mrs Collins rushed up to the

Club with the message, and then tore back to the telephone. The next call came quite soon from Collins himself. He had flown 46 miles with his passenger, and gained the British two-seater distance record; but he had to wait in his field while the trailer, which had recently been blown over, was repaired. This was done by the willing hands of whatever members were at the club. It soon almost needed repairing again since, by an extraordinary coincidence, it nearly collided at a remote crossroads with the trailer returning to Dunstable with Humphries and the Wren.

Then Wills rang, and to everyone's relief avoided stretching the almost non-existent retrieve organisation beyond the limit by having stored the Professor in a safe barn. He had flown 56 miles, breaking the British distance record.

It is difficult now to realise the jubilation of this day. Three cross-country flights had been made at one time, including two new records. Two of the pilots were pupils of Dunstable itself—and the year 1934 was only just beginning.

During April, Eric Collins ceased to spend most of his days in the Kassel two-seater, diverting part of his time to his new Rhönadler. This was a fine new glider from Germany, with a much higher performance than any over here. It was resplendent in clear varnish with pale translucent wings. The acquisition of this aircraft, a present from his father, not only gave Collins something approaching an equal chance to the German pilots, but it stimulated the whole British movement by showing at first hand the progress that was being made elsewhere.

On the 22nd of this month, cumulus sailed majestically once more over Dunstable in unstable westerly air. Eric Collins was launched at noon in his Rhönadler into a wind which was still light, but after a couple of beats along the ridge, he could feel the boost of thermal lift at only 100 feet up. He circled carefully and managed to climb in it to 1,000 ft, when he flew upwind from the hill to find lift under a nice fat cumulus. Under this he worked his way up to 3,500 ft, from where he could see the pattern of the cumulus, dappling the fields with purple-blue shadows. Entering cloud base near Whipsnade, he found himself rocketing upwards, experiencing for the first time the energy contained in a fast-developing cumulus. With his self-taught instrument-flying he was able to keep control.

In spite of having no variometer, he managed to connect properly with the lift under five more clouds, circling under them and zig-zagging his way over the countryside in order to try out every one that looked suitable. It was on this flight that, for the first time, London appeared as an obstacle to soaring. It had been quickly realised that there was much more to cross-country flying than just drifting vaguely downwind and getting lost, but even on his first flight Wills had reached the sea on the Essex coast. From Dunstable the best direction to fly for long distances was towards Kent, using first the hill lift, and then the cumulus of a N.W. wind. In this direction there was nearly 100 miles of land, and one day it might be possible even to reach France, and distance unlimited. But, long before this could happen it was necessary to find a way into Kent between London and the Thames estuary; not even the most intrepid pilot viewed with enthusiasm the idea of drifting, engineless, over the top of the city.

On this flight in the Rhönadler, Collins endeavoured to fly across the wind whenever possible in order to find a south-east passage, but he was forced to land in Essex, at Rayleigh, 52 miles away. It was not a record flight, but it completed for him the requirements of the new international Silver 'C' award —the highest which could be obtained. On the continent there were twenty-four pilots who had flown the 50 kms distance, the 5 hours duration, and had climbed 1,000 m. in a glider; there was now an Englishman.

No more cross-country flights were made until 15 July, when Collins flew 30 miles in an attempt to get round London to the west. This required more cross-wind soaring for a longer time, but the route was not affected by the downwind drift of the city's smoke, which often cut off the thermals. When Wills arrived at the Club, he heard that Collins had disappeared to the south, at right angles to the W.S.W. wind, at a height of 5,000 ft. Within twenty minutes he had rigged, and pushed, shoved, and towed the Scud to the top of the hill. Willing pupils awaiting their own turn for a hop bungied him off and he was quickly away under a passing cloud. He decided that he would try the south-east passage, using the following wind to help him to travel faster, and risking the London haze.

He had neither parachute nor barograph. At a time when the glider was so likely to be back on the ground at the bottom of the hill within minutes of taking off, when so much soaring was done only a few hundred feet up, and when the total cross-country flights in England could be counted on the fingers of one hand, it seemed pomposity itself to dress up in flying-suit with goggles, gloves, parachute and barograph on a hot summer day, just in order to do a quick hop down into the gulley. It was only when a pilot had found himself frozen stiff in his shirt sleeves at 5,000 ft a dozen times, or screeching round out of control in a dirty wet cloud, that he was able to have the courage of his convictions and drape himself in all his paraphernalia with a clear conscience in front of a crowd of spectators.

Towards Harpenden, Wills ran into further lift at 3,000 ft. The thermal was not large, but surprisingly it seemed to go on and on, until at 5,000 ft without any warning at all the world disappeared. The Scud had shot up into cloud; the wing centre-section, which was immediately above the pilot's head, having hidden its approach. On this occasion his glider was fitted with a variometer, and its indicator jumped violently to 10 ft/sec. 'up'. From always longing to get into cloud, Wills now wanted to get out, as this one seemed more powerful than was desirable for an experimental attempt. He started diving out at 50 m.p.h., but the variometer still firmly indicated 5 ft/sec. up. Realising that results were needed quickly he pushed the nose down until the poor little Scud, with its open cockpit, was pointing earthwards at 70 m.p.h., way beyond its per-mitted speed—and still going up at 2 ft/sec. His spectacles started to disengage from his ears. Then quite suddenly the glider shot out of the black maw into serene sunshine. Re-organising his glasses, Wills set off to the S.E. until, beyond Epping, the air quietened and he landed at Abridge Airfield.

In the meantime Collins was plugging along the westabout route, in clear air. At Watford the Rhönadler was at only 2,500 ft but he used lift below another cloud over Northolt. Over the houses he went to Heston, over the fields and gravel pits of what is now London Airport to Hanworth. Slowly he crept on over the Thames, but felt defeated by the sea of houses ahead, and prudently returned to a safe landing at Hanworth. London was still the obstacle to progress.

On this same day another cross-country flight took place. Not from Dunstable and not by a club pilot, not even by a man. Joan Meakin, a young English girl, had learnt to fly in Germany. She had bought a new German high-performance glider, and in it was towed by a light aeroplane all the way from Germany to England. Her knowledge of soaring and ability to handle the more advanced gliders of the time were probably more than anyone else's in England, but she did not do much flying in the clubs, having been engaged by Alan Cobham's circus. In her Rhönbuzzard she would be towed up to 1,500 ft by an Avro 504, and do aerobatics, with loops, all the way down again, to land neatly in the minute fields from which the circus operated. On this day, something that glider pilots everywhere had secretly hoped for took place. Joan Meakin went up, not down. After soaring happily around for a while instead of doing her aerobatics, she saw two display pilots coming up in aeroplanes to fly alongside. They signalled her down at once. She found, however, that far from receiving a ticking-off for messing up the programme, she was asked if she would like to have a go at the distance record. Taking off immediately, she was towed to 2,500 ft above the display field, just outside Bristol, and eventually landed near Salisbury, a distance of 40 miles.

Although the best distances from Dunstable were to be extracted from the polar air of a N.W. wind, Dunstable hill was also soarable in a wind south of west. Weather from this direction did not often seem to have the same cumulus-giving properties as the N.W. wind, but it was hoped that it might be possible to fly long distances up into Norfolk.

On 5 August 1934 Collins reached Holkham Bay (98 miles) and regained the British distance record. The wind was southerly, blowing almost parallel to the slope at Dunstable. At its north end the hill curves round enclosing a steep smooth gully known as the Bowl, and when the wind is in the south, this is the only place where lift can be found. After his launch Collins flew straight there, but in this restricted place he had to turn continuously, flying close to the ground, to utilise every scratchy bit of lift, however near the earth. Patiently he worked his way above the top of the hill into the freer air where he could explore better, gaining a little more height with every minute that passed. At a few hundred feet, instead of looking at the couples in the grass who had come from the town to be alone, he could study the sky and find a cloud to start him on his way.

Several times he was able to reach 4,800 ft as he wandered on towards the great flat lands of the Bedford River, Ely, Raynham, and so to the Norfolk coast, which he reached at Wells. It must have been a tremendous moment for him when after hours of intense concentration on locating the elusive energy of the clouds, and navigating, he found that he had reached the North Sea with still a precious 3,000 ft in hand.

On looking at a map, the obvious direction in which to fly long distances from Dunstable would seem to be towards Cornwall, using the N.E. wind of an anticyclone. Until much later, when aero-towing became available, it was very difficult to get away from Dunstable in easterly winds. Instead of being able to soar on the west-facing slope, with an east wind pouring down the hill it was often impractical to fly at all; even a winch launch could not get the glider clear of the down-current. In any case anticyclonic skies did not look particularly good for soaring. It was therefore going to be difficult to improve much on the record, starting from Dunstable. There were other sites from which a start could be made, but in a sport so dependent on just the right weather for success it was impossible to get off work, organise a launch, and tow the glider perhaps hundreds of miles by road, in time to take advantage of a day's thermals. The problem could have been overcome by keeping the glider at an aero club near home, having persuaded the management to fit a towing hook on one of their aeroplanes, since most of these clubs were open every day: there would have been much less restriction on the direction in which flights could be attempted, and this would have resulted in more soaring days being available. Four more years were to pass, however, before Philip Wills was able to obtain aerotows from Heston. At the time there were even some who felt that he was gaining an advantage, instead of widening opportunity for everyone.

It is easy to get an impression of gliding as a sort of aerial pot-hunting, with this apparent concentration on records, but this was not true. The challenge in distance flying was not to gain a man-made trophy, but to pit skill and intellect against the strength and weakness of the unknown sky—a sort of 20th-century voyage of discovery in which the difficulties, even dangers, which might beset the traveller were unknown. Each flight was different, with moments of deep despair when no lift could be located, and the glider would be in imminent risk of being back on the ground, followed by relief and elation when some tiny scrap of lift was found and worked with care and skill until, once again, the pilot was almost literally on top of the world. The challenge was not that of going further than the other man, but of flying as long as the glider could possibly be kept in the air.

In 1934 Dunstable was still the only practical place from which to attempt to beat the distance record. Even so, it was to be another two years before this happened again, and then it was quite unexpected. The forecast for 5 July 1936 gave little indication that the weather would be unstable, and the moment might easily have passed by.

The sky was overcast at Dunstable and few pilots were

bothering to rig. But at 1215 hrs Philip Wills did so and had a winch launch into the flock of school gliders chasing each other's tails in the Bowl. Thankful for the good performance of his new glider, Hjordis, he quickly managed to gain just that few feet over the others which made life a little less hectic. After about three-quarters of an hour of this sort of flying lunch called, but was dismissed from his thoughts by the arrival of a feeble thermal. This was followed by a break in the clouds, and sunshine; the thermals burst out and he was away. The lift, though steady, never became strong nor did cloud base rise above 3,000 ft. Although enough had now been learned to avoid the endless circling that had gone on before at almost all stages of a flight, the small operating depth involved nibbling at every thermal in order to keep as high as possible. Soon the new enclosed and small cockpit gave Wills a headache, cramp and thirst, and then for a while he could find no more lift. At 800 ft matters seemed desperate when, in his own words, there was 'suddenly a miracle: lift, slight but sufficient. Headache or no headache, though paper bags should beckon, circle we must. A quarter of an hour later, feeling biliously triumphant, we had achieved 2,000 ft and the situation was saved.'

Gradually he worked his way onwards in the weak lift, and after a while recognised Duxford. Then on again to reach the sea on a compass course. Without a map he could only try to remember how to get the maximum distance from Dunstable, and after flying a few miles along the coast he landed at 1625 hrs—104 miles out, with once more, the record.

But now what? To beat the record again from Dunstable would someone try to soar north up the spine of England into Yorkshire, with a difficult start hill-soaring in the Bowl, or would they go over the sea to France?

Chapter Fifteen

CLUBS, COMPS, AND CAMPS

Although distance-flying was the ultimate challenge in soaring, it was a faraway dream to most pilots. For them was the long process of learning, followed by the achievement of staying up successfully in hill lift for the first time, and perhaps after two or three years the chance of flying across country. But life was carefree and gliding fun, as part of an account by Hugh Bergel in 1935 will show:

We got to Dunstable at about 10 a.m. on Saturday, July 6th. The wind was blowing up the hill from somewhere north of west, at about 15 m.p.h., and long streets of cumulus at an apparent height of 3,000 ft or so promised a lot of lift—unless, indeed, they grew so quickly as to cover the whole sky, which looked possible.

Rigging and inspection of the London Club's Grunau Baby I and transporting it to the hilltop took about an hour, by which time Wills in the Scud had been launched. To our surprise and regret he seemed unable to get more than 200 ft of height along the ridge, and he appeared to be soaring in absolutely smooth and stable air.

A three-a-side launch put me in the air ten minutes later, and then I could feel for myself that the air was unexpectedly stable. About that time Wills caught a thermal to 1,400 ft. As he came down I stumbled into one and went up to about 1,200 ft, where the variometer needle went back to 3 ft per second fall. Another ten minutes' slope-soaring, and Wills caught another thermal—the one which started him off to Heston.

To my fury I was then deposited (with the Grunau Baby) at the foot of the hill. All lift had vanished completely, though there still seemed to be as much wind blowing up the hill as ever.

Using up all my stock of bad language I waited for the towing car. Very luckily (for me) no one else turned up to fly the G. B., and at 12.45 p.m. I was launched again, with no hope of doing more than another 20 minutes slope soaring, for by this time the clouds were thinning and becoming flatter and less promising altogether.

About three minutes after the launch, when I was about 150 ft above the hill-top, I ran into a thermal. I was so angry with having apparently lost my opportunity that I threw my customary caution aside and circled. It worked, so I circled again. It went on working, so I went on circling interminably, till I found the base of the clouds at 3,200 ft, after what felt like 3½ hours of hard work. Taking a deep breath, I waved good-bye to Dunstable and tried to spot my position. It turned out that I was over Hemel Hempstead, due south of Dunstable—which was impossible.

It then dawned on me that the wind at 1,000 ft and over was due north, or even east of north (against all the rules), and I got in a panic about being carried over London. So I set off east, where Wills in his greater wisdom had gone west.

Soon I was down to 800 ft over Radlett, having conspicuously failed to find lift under the clouds, and having been reduced to just setting off into the blue in hope.

As a last resort before landing ignominiously at Radlett (a bare ten miles from Dunstable) I made for some red-roofed villas grouped together. Thank Heaven, it worked, and again I settled down to interminable circling, at last reaching cloud-base level at 3,400 ft (the clouds were steadily going higher).

Once again I set off east. Once again I lost height very rapidly, till I reached Southgate (or thereabouts) at 1,200 ft. Once again, in desperation I went for houses and in particular a burning rubbish dump. And again it worked (I smelt the rubbish dump half-way up) and I went on round and round and round till I got to 3,800 ft (cloud level again).

After that it was a bit of a nightmare. With a howl of terror I found I was in sight of—London Bridge! I raced off east, circled a bit over the Mile End Road, got to Barking and circled a bit more. I now had my eyes on what looked like a usefully flat and open field running down from a main road to the Barking Power Station. As I was then losing height I kept my eye well on it as a hopeful landing ground. When I was down to about 1,800 ft I looked a bit closer, and found that the whole field was one gigantic spider's web of 133,000 volt cables!

Shivering with fright and cold (but mostly fright) I pushed off east to the Ford Works at Dagenham and got another few hundred feet of lift, and was at last preparing to land in the first reasonable

5 The Wasserkuppe: (a) Falke waiting to take off; (b) Launch point 1937: the Swiss Spyr III of Sandmeier; (c) Ceremony 1937; the British Team behind David Brunt, on the left

16 (a) The Reiher of 1938 designed by Hans Jacobs
   (b) The Atalante, later the Mü 13, designed by Kurt Schmidt, 1936
   (c) Philip Will's Minimoa and his Talbot retrieve car
   (d) Kit Nicholson's Rhönsperber at Dunstable, 1937

looking space when I spotted Hornchurch R.A.F. aerodrome about 1½ miles upwind. I got there with about 800 ft to spare, and landed just half an hour before two squadrons were due to land there in formation after the Duxford Review.

Whereupon I was made very welcome by the R.A.F., who with limitless generosity gave me beer and tea and beer and supper and beer till I was rescued 6½ hours later by a trailer designed, apparently, to hold the *Mauretania*—with more room to spare for the *Queen Mary*.

With the best will in the world, I simply cannot ascribe the flight to anything but luck. I did not know where I was (till afterwards), or where I ought to go, or what I ought to do, and blundered about, and Heaven sent me a thermal every time when things looked their blackest.

My chief impression was one of terror and helplessness most of the time. I was working frightfully hard going up, and praying frightfully hard coming down. My spare hand gripped the edge of the cockpit with such agony and emotion that it was still numb three days later.

The Royal Air Force were charming. They couldn't understand —being used to seeing 'Bulldogs' approach at 3,000 ft and just land over the hedge—why it took me some 5 minutes of 'S' turning to get rid of 800 ft. And they expected me to take off again after a beer or two and just go back to Dunstable—like that! It took much sternness to refuse the offer of a tow behind a 'Bulldog' and/or a Hawker 'Demon'. Their beer and food were glorious.*

The London Club was by now not just a going concern, it possessed the same inevitable force as an avalanche, except that it was going up, not down. It lost count of the 'C' certificates that its members gained, and record flights were objects of celebration, not of awe.

The Derbyshire and Lancashire Club members were clearing rocks from their new landing ground at Camphill, from which L. R. Robertson had already soared 52 miles. Espin Hardwick was fighting battles on behalf of the Midland Club, because of the fear that gliders would frighten away grouse on the Long Mynd. Sutton Bank was becoming the centre of the North, and Ulster was going strong.

* From *The Sailplane and Glider* (London), August 1935.

The big gliding event of each summer was the National Competitions. There were prizes for duration flights, for the longest distance and the greatest height; not until much later was there any task flying or formula for scoring. Before 1937 there were just winners, and others. But the prizes were not important. The 'Comps' were the occasion to meet friends

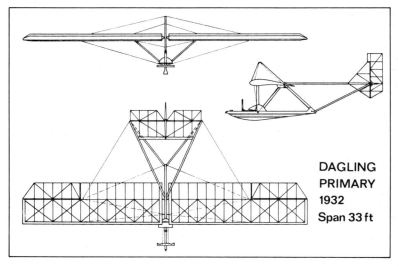

DAGLING
PRIMARY
1932
Span 33 ft

Fig. 21. The R.F.D. Dagling, produced by Slingsby. The solid unsprung skid quickly taught pilots the importance of gentle landings

not seen for a year, to swop tales, and to have fun. Everyone who could flew in the Comps, and those who could not came just the same.

A blow to this companionship was the death of Eric Collins. Early in 1935 Collins, who, as well as being a superb and sensitive soaring pilot was also good at aerobatics, was engaged by Cobham's circus to give displays in a Grunau Baby. There seemed little that he could not do—loops, bunts and tailslides. But the little Grunau was never designed for this treatment and luck could not last. On 30 July, the day

132

before he was to return to the London Gliding Club as their
Chief Instructor, the left wing of his glider broke in the middle
of an outside loop, shortly after releasing from tow at 3,000 ft.
He did not, or could not, use his parachute and he died. The
loss to British gliding was immense, even though he had
already made the greatest contribution possible—the start of
thermal soaring in England.

At this moment the London Gliding Club was about to hold
their first large-scale instructional camp. There were many
offers of help to take Collins's place as it was felt that the best
tribute which could be paid to him was to have a successful
camp for new pilots. In the hands of Sebert Humphries
enthusiasm rose to fever heat, and stayed that way. He had
many willing assistants, including Basil Meads and Dewsbury.
Jack flew so much that some were convinced that he would one
day come down covered with feathers, sitting on a clutch of
eggs.

The camp was a quite remarkable success. In the eighteen
days 65 pupils did 3,000 launches, ate 3,000 meals, and
obtained 34 'A', 30 'B' and 1 'C' certificates. Six single-seater
primary gliders were used, as well as two Pruflings and two
Grunau Babies.

Training everywhere at this time was carried out solo, on
'broomstick' gliders with insensitive controls and little performance. They were bungey-launched by a rubber rope,
stretched out by as many people as the instructor reckoned
the circumstances required. For early launches there would be
two on each side of the V-shaped rope, because the glider was
only intended to slide along the ground while the pupil tried
to keep the wings level. Sometimes it slid along the ground,
but sometimes it did not. Instead, it would shoot into the air,
so that the pupil shut his eyes and hung on waiting for the
crash. When this came and the noise and dust had died down,
the pupil would be surprised to find himself unhurt, but
horrified to discover the wings collapsed and on the ground.

From slides, the pupil progressed to hops, in which he was
expected to learn to control the elevator in 12 seconds

flat. After a few hops to 20 or 30 ft, and in the hope that the pupil had got the idea, the glider would be hauled a little way up the hill, and flung off from there for a higher flight. If the pupil's nerves were still in good order he would be bungied off the very top of the hill, feeling as though he had never been higher in his life, as he peered between his knees straight at the earth 200 ft below. Trying to avoid doing anything wrong usually meant trying to avoid moving the controls at all, while the air shrieked through the wires. Then the ground rushed up until the rudder bar, and the pilot's own feet, were scything off showers of buttercup heads; and with a bump the flight was suddenly over.

After a straight flight or two from the hilltop, the pupil was expected to try a few gentle turns, which he was apt to do largely on rudder, because this felt more natural and because he was still terrified of tipping the glider up. Ultimately all his 'learning' was added together in an attempt to hill soar for five minutes in a primary glider of 'better' performance. Whatever sort of pilot this sort of training turned out, there was one thing which could be guaranteed: he was fit and with no fat to spare.

England is not all hills, and in some parts of the country there were clubs which had to do without them. One such place was Cambridge. Even in its early days, the University Club had not been quite like others: living in the flat lands of East Anglia, it had had to devise means of getting airborne without launching and soaring from a slope. To the Cambridge Club, but at the time not to many others, the answer was quite surprisingly simple. Why not just winch up the glider directly into the thermals? The idea was right and the mechanical aptitude and human energy there in plenty, and so, in spite of the weather, they were successful.

By late 1936 the Club achieved, for the first time in England, a height of 1,000 ft from a winch launch. Thermal-catching from the winch quickly became a highly entertaining pastime, and gave rise to a large amount of serious research on thermal distribution, periodicity, size and shape, at much cost to the exam results of several undergraduates.

Not being tied to a hill, the Cambridge Club tended to go off on expeditions at the least excuse to explore new places with their gliders. One of the first of these was to Kimmeridge on the Dorset hills, where a strange caravan of cars and motor-cycles arrived in the middle of the night with two gliders and a winch. The meeting was of great exploratory value in more ways than one, since most of the ridges were soared on, and many of the bushes and walls rammed. Further entertainments included the Dagling primary being blown over in its trailer by a spring snow-storm, and one 'C' certificate.

From the beginning there was always a quality of the unexpected about the Cambridge Club operations, as on the day when an instructor was repairing a break in the cable; to stop other unthinking members from pulling the ends away from him and back to the launch point he tied it round his waist. But engineering enterprise was one step ahead—one undergraduate decided that a car would be better than man-power for pulling the cable. It was some time before anyone realised why the instructor was running quite so frantically across the field.

British gliding might still have been behind the Germans in terms of absolute performance but at least it knew how to enjoy itself.

By 1937 the movement was, in fact, rushing breathlessly forward, so breathlessly in fact that it was decided to enter the International Competitions on the Rhön, and take on those expert nations, Germany, Poland, Yugoslavia, Austria and Switzerland. Five gliders could be entered by each country, and Fred Slingsby designed and built a new high-performance, high speed aircraft, the King Kite, specially for the event. Three of these, plus Wills's Hjordis, and a Falcon III two-seater, which was to be used especially for duration prizes, would go to Germany. The King Kites were modern in appearance with shoulder gull wings and flaps, but the glider

135

was largely untried, since there had been little time to do any detail test flying or development work.

On 26 June the British team set off by boat from Hull with its trailers, and from Hamburg swayed off along the autobahns, reaching unprecedented speeds of 70 m.p.h. on these new straight roads, without quite leaving them altogether. The pilots chosen to represent Britain were Philip Wills, John Neilan, a brilliant young R.A.F. pilot, 'Willy' Watt, Joan Price (Meakin), G. O. Smith, Dudley Hiscox, and for the Falcon III W. B. Murray and J. S. Fox.

After their own happy-go-lucky clubs, everyone found the Wasserkuppe vast and organised. The British team was over-awed by the apparently suicidal nature of the surroundings, with no large smooth English fields, and by their temerity in getting involved in such expert competitions.

After a ceremonial opening, launching started, the rubber ropes being stretched with great strength and enthusiasm by Hitler youth. The first glider sank down into the valley. The second flew immediately into a thermal and disappeared, and the third, the first Englishman, Willy Watt, shot off the bungey launch and spun straight into the ground. The organisers were startled and the British dismayed except for the pilot, who stepped out unhurt. While the team rearranged itself Philip Wills struggled off to show what England could do. He started by following Hanna Reitsch, and then separated to visit what he thought was a better cloud. She went 361 kilometres. He 89.

The British team won no prizes, but the fortnight's regular soaring had been a luxury none of them had ever had before. It showed them increasingly throughout the meeting that opportunity for more flying, wider opportunities for getting launched at the right time, and particularly more aero-towing was what was wanted in England. The first British expedition into International Soaring was well worth while.

Chapter Sixteen

AEROTOWS AND EASTERLIES

By 1938 clubs were thriving all over England and, as in Germany, the newer pilots accepted as ordinary things which had seemed remarkable or even impossible five years before. A cross-country flight was no longer an achievement attainable only by an expert; it was within the reach of any club pilot. Downwind from Dunstable was no longer the great ambition, since so much more was now possible.

Two separate soaring meetings had been arranged for the Easter holiday. One was to be held at Ratcliffe aerodrome, near Leicester, almost in the centre of England. For the first time all launches would be by aero-tow from a flat site, making wind direction unimportant. Aero-towing would also be available at the other meeting, which was to be run by the Cambridge Club at Huish, a site which had the additional advantage that it was surrounded by hills suitable for slope-soaring in a number of different wind directions. From both sites record distances would be possible to the north, into East Anglia, and to Kent. Long distances were also possible by flying into Cornwall, but so far no one had succeeded in soaring effectively in the easterly winds of anticyclonic weather; the air was so often stable, and if cumulus did form, they were usually little flat plates high in a hazy sky which were quick to disappear. The majestic drifting castles that grew out of the north-west air following a depression were wonderful to look at against the deep blue, and exciting to fly with. Nevertheless, with just the right combination of temperature, humidity and wind, it was occasionally possible in the English spring to get wonderfully unstable air pushed along on a fresh N.E. wind.

The spring of 1938 brought just this weather. The air was like ginger beer, cumulus raced across the sky towards the land of high moors and steep valleys, sea breezes and Cornish cream. Since nearly every pilot who could manage to lay his hands on a glider turned up at these meetings, the British distance record of 104 miles, which had stood for two years, was in a shaky situation.

On 10 April John Fox, flying Collins's old Rhönadler, was launched into the N.E. wind at Huish to try to fly across wind to his home at Wellington in Somerset. Conditions were so good that he sailed high over the top of it, landing at South Molton 91 miles away. At about the same time as Fox took off Philip Wills had an aero-tow at Heston in his new German Minimoa to try to soar to Huish, 50-odd miles away, and was only a few miles short when he had to land. Doubt over anticyclonic weather vanished. Not only were the thermals good, but the wind and the weather appeared to remain uniform over long distances.

The north-easter went on blowing, so instead of staying at Huish Wills drove north during the Saturday night to join the Ratcliffe party. From here he would have a greater distance towards Cornwall, and a better chance of cracking the record wide open.

On Easter Sunday, the 17th, the anticyclone was firmly established, and the wind still from the N.E., so Wills drew a line on his map from Ratcliffe to Start Point. He was launched later than he intended, and found it more difficult than he expected to get up and away. As he worked his way from thermal to thermal along the line on his map, the clouds grew flatter, and the air more stable, finally forcing him to land near Bath, after 110 miles. He had beaten his old 1936 record by 6 miles, but an hour before he landed Kit Nicholson had flown a Rhönsperber 119 miles from Huish. Nicholson had been launched at 1115 hrs, and landed between Bigbury and Burgh Island off the South Devon coast on a strip of sand which was uncovered only at low tide. Although he had found the thermals good, the strong N.E. wind had been drifting him all the time towards the sea, and he had to fly inland across wind between thermals to avoid being pushed out over the water.

The anticyclone stayed put; the north-easter was still unstable. Philip Wills now joined the Huish contingent from Bath, having thoughtfully brought his toothbrush with him from Leicester.

The anticyclone was still roaring on Easter Monday. The steady cold wind digging the spring thermals out of the ground, and kicking them up like great balloons to drift on the wind. It was Dewsbury's turn to fly the Rhönsperber, which had been brought back overnight from Bigbury, and he was followed into the air by Wills and then by Fox in the Rhönadler. It looked as though Nicholson's record was to have a short life.

Early in his flight, Wills had an easy time and, on reaching the Blackmoor Vale in Somerset, flew all round the edge of it to keep to the higher and drier ground. Near Yeovil he nearly had to land, but managed to find a thermal at the last moment. By now he was much nearer to the sea than he had intended, and giving up the struggle to work across wind to Plymouth, arrived at the coast near Seaton. This seemed to make the prospect of achieving his goal distinctly remote, until he saw that big cumulus were drifting across Lyme Bay in the direction of Exmouth. He had no difficulty in latching on to one and, circling under its friendly umbrella, sailed across the bay several miles out to sea.

He managed to reach the land to the south of Dartmoor but found little lift, getting steadily lower over the small fields. The low sun was shining on the S.W. face of the great brown moor when, at 1,000 ft—below the tops of the highest tors—he flew over the lower slopes and found lift. With excitement he realised that, in spite of all his doubts, it was still just possible to beat the record. But the going was desperately slow over the broken country of S.W. Devon; sometimes he had to float over chunks of higher ground with only 200 ft to spare. Then at last Plymouth hove in sight, but it was impossible to reach the airfield, which was up on the hill high above him. There seemed little in the way of landing fields anywhere, except one which sloped steeply up from the railway line. The Minimoa was thankfully pressed on, rather than into, this field like a fly on a window. It would not have been possible to fly another 50 yards.

Wills's distance was 118 miles, not quite far enough. Meanwhile, John Fox, in the faithful Rhönadler, following the same route as Wills, had cut inland across Dartmoor, and arrived high over Plymouth at 4,000 ft, throwing a loop to celebrate. There were just five little clouds left in the dying sky, and from them Fox extracted another 3,000 ft, before he set off on a compass course into the haze. He had hoped to cross the Fowey estuary with plenty of height, but the sea breeze blowing inwards over the peninsula cut down his effective gliding angle with the result that he floated over the wooded banks with only 300 ft to spare, to land in a tiny field near the village of Golant. Here his reception was in proportion to the importance of the occasion—when he eventually succeeded in finding anyone to give him a reception at all. The Rhönadler had regained her old record of 1934. This time it was not 98 but 144 miles.

And so the Easter meetings ended, but not the northeasterlies. Everyone went home, and thought about this anticyclonic weather and ways of using it. Wills had been thinking about it longer than most, but when the opportunities had come he had been pipped on the post every time. Twice the record had been snatched from under his nose. But when on Friday, 29 April, the forecast gave 'same again', Wills mapped out a line which took him from Heston airfield (just west of London), across Salisbury Plain, round Blackmoor Vale, across Lyme Bay as before, and to Plymouth, which he declared as his goal. Taking a day off work he rushed to Heston to get an aero-tow. But it was after 1100 hrs before he at last got airborne, and then he almost finished his chances by enthusiastically releasing at 600 ft, when the tug jerked upwards in what he thought was a good thermal. Cursing himself, he just managed to locate the lift again before having to land. At Staines reservoir he was up to 3,600 ft, but near Farnborough the flight nearly ended again when he sank to within 500 ft of the ground; thereafter the lift improved and he was able to race along, discarding all but the strongest thermals. In one hour he covered 44 miles. After this, the flight became almost a replica of his previous one, even to having the same doubts about reaching Plymouth. But this time the thermals over the S.W. face of Dartmoor were better, and he was still climbing at 6,000 ft over his goal. Now it was difficult to decide whether to land there, or to go on flying as far as possible, but the realisation that the distance of 300 kilometres required for the new Gold 'C' certificate was a possibility decided him. He went up into the cloud, reached 6,900 ft, and flew on to land near the china-clay cones at St Austell. Once again the record was broken: it was now 209 miles. But on this day in 1938 Philip Wills's wife, Kitty, was also totting up mileage. Over the Easter holiday she had driven the car and trailer no less than 1,280 miles, solely on retrieves.

Since the first pilot from Dunstable had succeeded in working his way round London to the S.E., thoughts of one day soaring across the Channel to France had never been far away. In 1937 Wills had arrived at Dover from Dunstable in his Hjordis at a height of 4,000 ft, but this was not enough height to cross and he could find no more. In July 1938 Kit Nicholson had arrived in the Rhönsperber, also from Dunstable, but with only 2,000 ft. On 3 September Wills set off again from Dunstable climbing to 8,000 ft, which was high enough to cross, three times on the way. But there was no lift near the coast, and like the others he had to land with the goal in sight but out of reach beyond the glittering sea.

There were no further attempts till the next year. April 22 looked a fine unstable day with a strong N.W. wind gusting up to 40 m.p.h. and if the thermals were not torn to shreds by the wind, it was just the day to try to get across to France.

A young pilot, Geoffrey Stephenson, who had been trained at the London Club decided to make the attempt in an

141

English Slingsby Gull which he shared with his partner Donald Greig.

First of all, Greig and Stephenson tried to get an aero-tow from Heston, near their homes, so as to avoid having to drive all the way north to Dunstable and then soar all the way back again round London before setting off for Kent and the Channel coast.

But at Heston they were unlucky, so drove the 40 miles across the outskirts of London to Dunstable, hoping that the thermals would last, as it was already afternoon. Frantically they rigged the glider. At 1455 hrs with the strongest thermals of the day finished, Steve had a feeble winch launch which took him to 300 ft, barely level with the hilltop. He luckily flew straight into a thermal, and was even luckier when he never stopped going up until he reached cloud base at 4,000 ft. Without hesitation he set off to go eastabout across Essex to the Thames. Thinking of his partner driving the trailer back through London yet again made him hesitate before crossing the river, but an excellent thermal persuaded him that it was worth going on. The lateness of the day was worrying, but as first Canterbury and then Hawkinge were reached he stayed hopeful—if only just. When he arrived at the coast he was a mere 1,000 ft up. Then without warning he hit a new thermal. With great care Steve centred the Gull in it until he was climbing in the strongest lift of the thermal core at 10 ft/sec. As the Gull climbed, so the view widened. Looking hard like glass, the green-blue sea was dappled with shadows, and far to the south was the hazy line of France. The lift in his thermal grew even stronger, up to 20 ft/sec., and at 4,500 ft Steve went into the cloud. At 6,000 ft he came out near the top, and had a good look round. The Gull had drifted beyond the coast, and was well out over the Channel, which looked vast. He knew that the strong wind on his tail would never let him return, but he could see boats ahead. Eight thousand feet had always been reckoned as the minimum safe height for gliding across, but Steve was not dismayed with his meagre 6,000 ft. There was only one more cloud out over the Channel and he made for it, but there was no lift, only the strong sink of the finished thermal; so he sheered away and went straight off under the empty sky towards the far coast, still some 15 miles away, and looking like 50. The wind was strong and with its help he could soon see the fringe of the surf and white dots of houses, but it was going to be a near thing. Fortunately, five

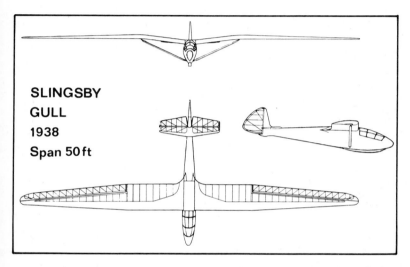

**SLINGSBY
GULL
1938
Span 50 ft**

FIG. 22. Slingsby Gull I, in which the first soaring crossing of the English Channel was made. Glide angle 1:23

miles off the coast the sink grew less, and he was still 2,000 ft up when he floated silently over the beach. Steve flew on into France looking for a field big enough for an aeroplane to land in so that he could be towed back; but they were all too small, and he touched down at 1735 hrs having flown 127 miles from Dunstable at an average speed of 48 m.p.h.

In England, as well as in Germany, the days of peace were vanishing. As this last summer before the war passed all too quickly, gliding seemed to become greater fun. The clubs had

143

more members than they could cope with; even new ones like Oxford and Surrey, were expanding fast. Almost every week-end gliders flew high over the land, new names in new aircraft. It was no longer possible to keep count: but so far no one had used wave lift in England.

After Wolf Hirth had explored the Moazagotl wave in Silesia, pilots in other countries discovered and used wave lift created by their mountains. In the British Isles there were mountains also which should produce waves. The year before, Dr Kuettner, who had gained record height in the Moazagotl, had written that he was sure that Cross Fell in the Pennines would produce waves up to 10,000 ft when the Helm wind was blowing. The Helm is a local wind which, coming from the east, pours in a torrent down the west face of the Pennines with such force that there are legends of cabbages being uprooted from fields and men being blown from their horses; it was given its name because of the helmet-shaped cloud which it produces. When the wind flows down the 2,000-ft drop of the west face it causes a wave to rebound through the air, the crest of which is usually marked by lenticular clouds. Noel McLean had discussed the possibilities of soaring in the Helm with Gordon Manley, a meteorologist who knew the area well. In June 1939 they sited a winch at what they hoped would be a suitable distance out from the hill to contact the wave. One of the pilots, Savage, was launched first in the Newcastle Club Grunau. He nearly connected with the lift, but, going just too far towards the torrent, was swept back to the ground again, having only just enough time to make a hurried landing. The next day the Helm still blew and McLean was launched at 1240 hrs. Profiting from Savage's experience he did not go so far towards the area underneath the odd-shaped cloud, and soon ran into lift. At once the air became extremely rough, so much so that it was almost impossible to keep control; McLean was thankful that he had a parachute. However, after a time the roughness died away quite sud-denly, and the lift grew stronger until it was greater than 20 ft/sec. when the indicator went off the scale. The altimeter needle moved round visibly, the bar cloud slid downwards. until it was far beneath the tiny glider, and the great mountains of the Pennines appeared flat. At 9,000 ft the lift died away, and the air became rough. Then quite suddenly the Grunau, bearing the astonished McLean, started rocketing up once more. At 11,140 ft the upflow again died away and McLean cruised around looking at the stupendous view,

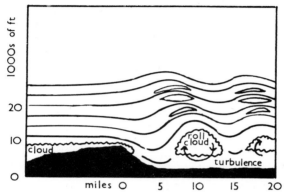

FIG. 23. Diagram of flow through a standing wave

almost to the Isle of Man, exploring the wave area, and trying to decide whether to hurry down to let someone else have a go, all at the same time. He decided on the last, but this was easier said than done. All his controls were stiff and frozen, and wherever he flew the lift pushed him up again. He tried diving, spinning and side-slipping, and eventually had to move back over the mountain and take the risk of getting caught in the waterfall of air which plunged down into the valley. In the two hours that he was airborne, the wind had increased to 40 m.p.h. which was greater than the flying speed of the Grunau, so almost the biggest problem was holding on to the glider once it was back on the ground, to prevent it being blown away.

McLean hoped to explore the Helm wave fully, but he was never to fly in the wave again. Even his record climb of

10,540 ft was not to stand long: On 1 July Philip Wills climbed 14,170 ft in a thunderstorm above Dunstable.

In September 1939 the gliders were packed away, and the cumulus clouds of the dying summer gave their beauty to the war.

17 (a) The Slingsby Petrel of 1938; its cost in 1939 was £266
    (b) The classic Weihe of Hans Jacobs, 1938; it was built in several
       countries in various forms immediately post-war

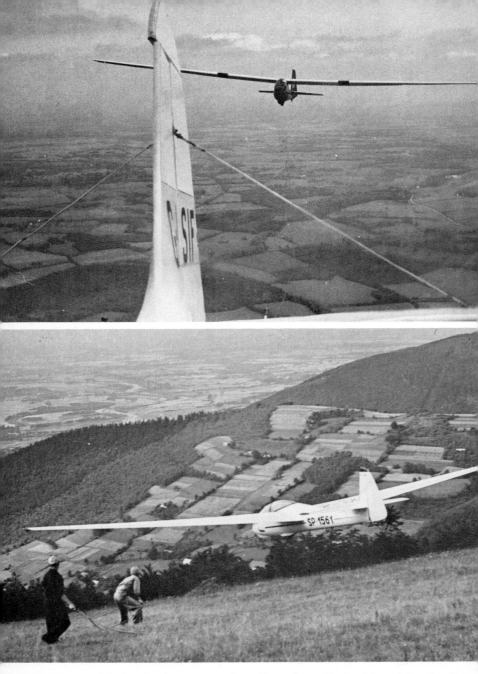

18 (a) Aerotowing was used as the sole method of launching in the World Championships in Sweden, 1950. In 1948 at Samedan both winch launching and aerotowing were used

(b) Bocian 2-seater being bungey launched from Zar in the Tatra Mts

Chapter Seventeen

THE SKY IS FREE

The difference between the enjoyment of flying a glider and of soaring is considerable. The first is similar to the pleasure that can be obtained from controlling any piece of equipment, such as a dinghy or a car, which involves both movement and co-ordination. But added to the pleasure of handling the machine, soaring provides an intellectual challenge which is greater than in almost any other sport.

It is probably the single-minded effort which this involves that makes the glider pilot prefer to fly alone. In the air, in a cockpit tailored to fit, he feels part of his aircraft. The one-man-one-glider urge is strong, and the finest design brains have always been lavished on the single-seater. There are good two-seaters, of course, but they are complementary, or useful, or fun, but not the same as one's own wings. In 1945, after five years of war, the idea of soaring alone in the summer skies was irresistible: the silence, the beauty, and the individualness of it, had been magnified in people's minds as the antithesis of war itself. But in 1946 there were almost no gliders to fly. Little remained anywhere in the world of pre-war organisation or equipment; there was enthusiasm, but even for people whom the war had taught to become able scroungers, few pickings. In one country some piece of army equipment could be changed into a winch, in another military spotting planes could become tugs, and in countries which had started teaching their pilots on light gliders there were some aircraft. But in general it was a matter of starting again to build new equipment, with a widespread lack of materials, fuel and tools.

There was, however, no shortage of pilots. Apart from those

who had been deprived of their gliding, there were many servicemen who wanted to continue flying. Their training had been extensive, tough and disciplined, so they had little difficulty in converting to the relatively simple glider. Such pilots progressed fast, and it was obvious that they would

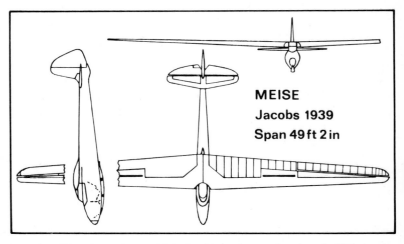

MEISE
Jacobs 1939
Span 49 ft 2 in

FIG. 24. The Meise, from which the Olympia was developed. Glide angle 1:25 at 45 m.p.h.

quickly teach themselves to soar well, once they could get their hands on some good machines.

In England, fortunately, this was to happen sooner than anyone expected. A furniture firm at Newbury, Elliotts, not wanting to sack its now redundant wartime staff, decided to build a hundred Olympias. These were modified and modernised versions of the Meise design, which had been intended for the 1940 Olympic Games. Had these aircraft not become available when they did it is likely that much enthusiasm would have been frustrated, and a source of experienced pilots lost at a time when it was badly needed.

As well as people who could fly, there were, of course, others who wanted to start gliding, particularly those who had been too young to get in on the war, or who had been unable to get themselves a flying job. For such pupils, getting airborne was quite difficult, since they still had to learn by the same slow method as in the 1930s, on single-seaters. However, in 1948, Slingsby Sailplanes started production of the T21, or Sedbergh, as it was called by the Air Training Corps. This was a strong, safe, side-by-side two-seater, which was easy to fly, and at last it became practical to change to dual training. But the change took place slowly, due to lack of money, a shortage of winches powerful enough to launch these heavier gliders, and—not least—tradition. The first to teach entirely on two-seaters were the combined Surrey and Imperial College clubs at Redhill, with a T21 affectionately called 'Daisy'.

Learning to fly in a two-seater, with an instructor, meant that hops close to the ground were no longer necessary; from the start the pupil could get properly up into the air, have room to make his mistakes, and see much more clearly what gliding was all about. He could be taught to fly accurately at the beginning, instead of having to find out for himself over the years, and so could start soaring more quickly. With the help of the Olympia, the T21, and unlimited enthusiasm, gliding in England was able to turn itself into a going concern just as quickly as in many nations which had subsidies to help them. It was not long before there were results.

In 1949 Philip Wills beat his own 1938 record of 209 miles, and in 1951 Bill Bedford, in an Olympia, broke new ground by flying northwards from Farnborough to Newcastle, pushing the record up to 257 miles. This flight particularly made England seem to be just a little on the small side. It was not surprising that the 22 miles of gleaming water between England and France once again began to acquire a peculiar fascination. This was, of course, partly because the Channel-crossing immediately opened up a wide and unfamiliar range of country, but also because the very act of making it involved taking an exciting decision, and then accepting the full consequences of it.

The problem was an interesting one to think about; it was not just a matter of gliding across 20 miles of water, but of getting to the other side high enough to be able to reach the thermals, which would not start to form for several miles inland. This almost certainly meant climbing in a big cloud on this side while it drifted out over the water, knowing that if control in it was lost, or if the glider came out going in the wrong direction, it might be difficult either to reach the far side, or to return to England against the wind.

In the late 1940s a number of flights were made with the hopes of repeating Stephenson's success of 1939, but as so often before not enough height was obtained to make a safe crossing. With each year that went by, finding a suitable cloud was made even more difficult by increasing air traffic control in this corner of England.

The ideal fair wind for France appeared to be between W. and N.W. If it were further north than this, clouds at the jumping off point near Dover seemed less good, probably owing to their having been born in the cool area of the Thames Estuary. It was a matter of arriving at the coast with the right wind, early enough in the day still to have time to fly a long way on the far side, but late enough for the cumulus to have grown sufficiently big to push the glider high. And the cloud had to be in the right place, because the Channel was narrow only at one point.

It was not until April 1950 that the meteorological fruit-machine turned up a jackpot; then two crossings were made in one day: Fl./Lt Miller went from Detling in Kent to Coxyde on the Belgian coast in an Olympia, and Lorne Welch soared from Redhill to Brussels (210 miles) in a Weihe.

Although this flight proved that it was practical to re-connect with thermals beyond the new coast, five years more were to pass before another glider would set out over the water. It was again Welch, but this time with Frank Irving, to make the first-ever two-seater crossing. They flew from

150

Lasham to Louvain (254 miles), creating a British two-seater distance record. Irving wrote:

For various reasons, all quite respectable, it was not until 10 a.m. that I crawled out of the bunkhouse at Lasham to see a sky which was already superb. At the same moment, Lorne appeared looking very wide awake, but speaking of dreams such as the Channel and goals far into the Continent. The next hour was a whirl: drinking a cup of coffee, buying some chocolate, sorting maps, grabbing a camera and writing a goal declaration which said Aachen. As always we got airborne in a rush with only the vaguest of lines on the map and insufficient paper in the knee-pad.

Derek Piggott in the Tiger Moth towed us off straight upwind, as we had requested, and we cast off in rather inadequate lift 3 miles west of Lasham. For the first 30 miles it was something of a struggle. Wally Kahn, who had been towed off in the Weihe immediately before us, was visible some miles ahead going well, causing us to think that we had got out of phase with the thermals since we always seemed to arrive at one just before it petered out.

Near Redhill we got near cloudbase and after this stayed well up with little difficulty. At Tonbridge we overtook Wally, and enjoyed a 'formation soar'—sometimes circling in the same thermal, sometimes cruising together under a cloud street. In general, the Weihe fared slightly better when climbing in thermals, and slightly worse when flying straight. One rarely sees a glider flying straight at close quarters for any length of time; it is a singularly beautiful sight.

In the meantime, we had started a debate—on the height to leave Dover. Being fairly pessimistic, the sums indicated that 7,200 ft would give a good chance of pressing on in France, an estimate which, in the event, would have been about right.

The general cloudbase had worked up to a little over 4,000 ft, but as we approached the coast we could see that over Romney Marsh and further east the clouds along the coastline had a curious appearance. Long streamers of cloud extended upwards from 3,000 ft to more solid clouds at the top. We wondered whether they were due to damp ground or sea breezes and whether they indicated lift.

After trying unsuccessfully to find lift inland from Folkestone to Dover we sank to below 3,000 ft. After a little discussion, we took Lorne's courage in all four hands and went to investigate the low wisps of cloud near the coast. The first two wisps gave vast sink, but the third was surrounded by strong lift and we went up at a great pace, half the circle in clear air and half in the wisp. At 5,200 ft, just inland from the coast, we entered solid cloud and went smoothly and rapidly up to 8,000 ft. Above 7,000 ft the cloud became progressively lighter, and we came out, on course, quite near the top. Dover harbour lay beneath, and after flying through the top of another cloud the Channel lay before us in clear bright sunshine. During the climb we had accumulated only a very small quantity of ice.

The French coast looked surprisingly close, but took quite a long time to approach, at our cruising speed of about 50 m.p.h. E.A.S. The rate of sink was almost normal ($3\frac{1}{2}$ ft/sec. average for the crossing). There was nothing to do but sit and wait, so we had a cigarette and some sandwiches, noted times and heights and indulged in a little photography. Nineteen minutes after leaving Dover, the French coast just west of Calais passed 3,700 ft below. I, at least, felt a slight sense of relief at having solid ground beneath again.

However, the nearest cumulus were still some miles away and their bases ominously low at about 3,000 ft, but we eventually found a little thermal at 2,250 ft. Thereafter progress was quite slow and we were able to inspect the French countryside closely. After staying near the coast up to Coxyde, we turned somewhat inland. Shortly afterwards we felt that this had been a mistake, as conditions deteriorated and we were at one time down to 1,550 ft, but after more struggles we eventually got up to cloudbase near Ghent.

There appeared to be a large expanse of flattened-out cumulus ahead and we began to think that Aachen had been an over-optimistic goal. West of Brussels we were up to cloudbase again and then flew on across the city. It looked a long way to the fields on the other side, and it was only when down to 2,800 ft, a little over half-way across, that we realised that the wind was now southerly rather than westerly. At this juncture Lorne observed that this was a funny height to be flying over someone else's capital city, but fortunately a little thermal appeared before it got too funny. This tided us over the forest east of Brussels, but was the beginning of the end, for, after nibbling at some elusive patches of weak lift we found ourselves quite low south of Louvain. The sky still contained cumulus, but little looked active.

We descended inexorably, trying to find a sensible field among the little strips. Finally we picked a long field near some army

19 (a) The Gull IV. Slingsby's answer to the Olympia, 1947; (b) Manhandling the Polish IS-1 Sep back up the hill. The prototype was built at Bielsko in 1947; (c) Geoffrey and Beryl Stephenson with the Slingsby Sky; the famous Dunstable Bowl in the background

20 (a) A Swiss Moswey soaring in the Alps near Samedan
   (b) A Slingsby Eagle scraping for lift in the Bowl at Dunstable

21 (a) One of the first hundred Olympias built by Elliott's of Newbury
(b) Finding a thermal low over Polish fields

22 (a) Prepared for any eventuality: equipment carried by competitor Nick Goodhart in Argentine, 1963; (b) End of a contest flight in France, 1956; Goodhart helping to farm his landing field

barracks. The field consisted largely of mud and we ploughed no mean furrow.*

In 1957 there were four crossings, three of which were successful in getting going on the far side. These were by Tony Goodhart, from Lasham to Vitry-en-Artois (188 miles), Anne Burns, from Lasham to Merville (165 miles), Philip Wills, Dunstable to St Omer, all in Skylarks; and Robert Cockburn, in a Sky, from Farnborough to Wimereaux.

Tony Goodhart's flight was unusual in that having left the English coast at 5,000 ft he found lift in a cloud half-way across the water which took him up to 9,000 ft. This was unexpected, as it had been thought that by the time a cloud had drifted 10 miles out to sea it would have become lifeless. He sailed over the French coast at 8,500 ft, with plenty in hand to fly on inland to search out more lift. The weather over France was very different to England: towering cumulus, whose bases were only 2,500 ft above the ground, were growing in profusion, and there was a great deal of showery rain. Goodhart stayed well above cloudbase for more than two hours, and reached 11,000 ft, but gradually caught up a blanket of medium-high cloud, which even produced snow. There seemed nothing good in the distance, so rather than plough on into this murk he landed. He wrote:

The airfield at Vitry is used by the Douai Flying Club and little else, but it has a caretaker who advanced upon me with much talk of regulations and insisted on ringing the gendarmerie before I was allowed to ring Lasham. There seems to be a hoodoo on telephones at Gliding Centres when calls from away landings are expected. The Lasham lines were first of all said to be engaged and then out of order, and it was not until nearly one-and-a-half hours after landing that I got my message through. By this time I was involved in making a statement to the gendarmerie.

'Is it that you have the need for an interpreter?'
'Is your interpreter young and beautiful?'
'No, she wears glasses and has a moustache.'
'I have not the need for an interpreter!'

* From *Gliding* (London), vol. 6, 1955, no. 2, p. 52. (Reprinted from *Flight*.)

By the time the statement was completed and the caretaker's wife had filled me with eggs and vin ordinaire, the sky had cleared and it was once again a glorious gliding day with towering cu. away to the west.*

Perhaps the nearest to a ducking was Philip Wills. He had taken off on 15 September from Dunstable at 1045 hrs and reached the Dover area without much difficulty, but under a dead-looking sky, with a thin layer of overcast. He had picked a field north of Deal, and was about to land in it when he flew into lift at 6 ft/sec.

The wind was fairly strong, and was now blowing from the N.N.W., and as I climbed away, a fascinating plan offered itself. It turned out to be the piece of cheese in the mousetrap.

Since the sea is uniformly heated, in the general way the air above it contains no vertical currents and a sailplane will descend steadily whilst flying over it. But for many years there has been a theory that, about the month of September, when the land has cooled more rapidly than the sea after the summer months, one might find up-currents persisting out over the Channel itself.

I now had a chance—the first time anyone had had a chance—of finding out if this theory was correct, and apparently without taking any risks. From Deal down to the South Foreland, the coast runs roughly N–S, and the wind, although strong, was blowing out to sea at a fairly narrow angle. I could therefore circle along in my lift, only gradually leaving the coastline as I gained height.

If the lift petered out, I could immediately turn inland again at any point; if the lift continued all the way, I would leave it as I came abreast of the South Foreland and fly back to land. Q.E.D.

The plan worked splendidly. Lift continued smoothly and over a wide area, and as I climbed the wind got stronger. The sky was grey and overcast, and underneath it a milky green sea heaved uncomfortably in the freshening wind. Visibility was perhaps 10 miles, so I could not see the French coast. Instead, I kept a watchful eye on the slowly receding coastline of Kent, and was still climbing well, at 2,500 ft, when the South Foreland came abreast of me, perhaps 5 miles to the west. I had circled and climbed steadily over perhaps 9 miles of sea—very interesting indeed. Undoubtedly the lifting air went on, but it was not for

* From *Sailplane and Gliding* (London), vol. 8, 1957, no. 5, p. 270.

me. I turned on to a westerly course towards the white cliffs of England.

And I almost immediately flew into eight feet a second—down.

It was as if someone had picked up a bucketful of the turbulent sea below and suddenly thrown it through my cockpit window over me. My first instinctive reaction was to wrench the Skylark around and back into the comforting up-current behind me. Next came a feeling of fury at my stupidity. For if in these conditions up-currents are to be found over the sea, then clearly one should expect compensating down-currents also to be found around them. And as I could not possibly guess how fierce and how wide this down-current was, it was now simply a matter of blind chance as to whether I could get back to the English coast or not, beating across the strong N.N.W. wind. The coast which looked so near, was, in all probability, cut off from me by an invisible cataract of descending air. If one must be a pioneer, at least let one be an intelligent one. But it had looked such an innocent little bit of pioneering!

The alternative both looked and felt desperate, but quick calculation showed it was theoretically the better one. From where I was, although it was invisible in the grey mist and greeny sea ahead, the French coast could not be more than 25 miles away at most. I was still climbing, around half a mile up, and with the following wind my gliding angle in straight flight was over 1 in 45. I only had to circle and stay where I was in the friendly air for a few minutes more, and if I could hold course thereafter and not find any more down-currents, I was there.

I went on circling and climbing gently until the land behind had faded from sight. Except for one or two ships ploughing short and faded furrows in the cloudy sea below, I was alone in a grey and misty sky. Slightly to the east of my track I saw a darker smudge in the dull overcast—I flew over towards it—and encountered good strong lift!*

This lift carried Wills to 3,500 ft, and after a short time the French coast appeared. He crossed it with great relief at 3,000 ft—having left England 30 miles away, at only 600 ft.

There were four more cross-channel flights before the spread of controlled air space stopped play. Those of Alf Warminger, Derek Piggott, Joe Croshaw, and Andy Gough. On 21 May

* From *Sailplane and Gliding*, vol. 8, 1957, no. 6, p. 316.

during the 1958 R.A.F. competitions at South Cerney, Gough set off in a Skylark, and landed at the Dutch–German border, near Aachen, 348 miles away. This was a new British record, and he achieved what everyone had hoped for—a really long distance.

By 1962 growing air traffic in the S.E. of England left little room for the enterprising soaring pilot, and the opportunities for crossing were reduced to a level where it was more practical to fly somewhere else. Up north the Irish Sea was crossed from Scotland by Charles Ross, using wave lift, and a year later, in 1963, the return crossing was made from Northern Ireland by Dimitri Zotov, also in wave. Both flights were made in cold winter, flying at heights up to 14,000 ft.

Now, for a long time, if anyone wanted to fly on the Continent they put their trailer on a boat: the Channel had been well and truly conquered. Loss of interest did not come only from increasing air traffic control problems, but from the cost in both time and money in getting back home again. Closed-circuit flying was just as much fun with its challenge to fly ever faster, and the pilot could be home in time for tea—or supper. Few even noticed the solitary Frenchman, Xavier Canler, who made the only crossing the other way, from Valenciennes to Ashford, 120 miles, in a Phoebus.

With the arrival of fibreglass and epoxy resin as prime constructional materials glider performance went up with a jump, giving the flying of big 300-km. triangles a high success rate, and lessening the attraction of straight distance. But to people like Philip Wills the pendulum was now swinging too far the other way, and the great freedoms of gliding—to explore, to navigate, and to decide where to go next—were becoming lost in the passion for speed. In 1974 he launched Competition Enterprise, intended as a week of contest flying in the old style, for pilots who preferred to wander gently through the skies. Initially looked at askance by the new pilots Enterprise found itself gaining adherents with each passing year until it led, in 1976, to new migrations. In the eighteen years which had passed since Gough reached

Aachen in his wooden Skylark, Britain had joined the Common Market, glide ratios were up to over 1:40 instead of the 1:30 of the early 1960s, and most gliders carried radio. With these new gliders, 500-km. triangles were becoming commonplace, and the possibility of being able to fly not just into Belgium, but to the heart of Europe was a new challenge. On 1 August 1976, three gliders set off. Mike Pope from Booker in a Nimbus 2 reached Yves-Gomezee, Belgium, after 11 hours, and Mike Carlton in the 2-seat Calif A-21 with Brian Spreckley made 394 miles (635 km.) to just south of Luxemburg, to claim the 18-year-old record from Welch and Irving. But the longest flight started from Competition Enterprise at North Hill in Somerset, when Justin Wills flew a Standard Libelle 443 miles (713 km.) to Trier in Germany. It was a flight in the classic tradition, as indeed was the son of Philip's account of it:

It was John Fielden who converted me to the feasibility of crossing the Channel: just start far enough upwind so that when you reach Dover cloudbase is high enough to get across in VMC. It sounded easy in 1974.

By 1976 I hadn't tried it even once. However, June 10 at Competition Enterprise showed how it might be done, despite London TMAs and other problems. So several of us decided to stay in readiness over the coming weeks for The Day.

Walks to and from work became dreamier than ever.

Late on Thursday, July 22, John Fielden rang and, risking merely our future employment and solvency, we rushed down to North Hill believing Friday would be It. It wasn't.

The weather map for Saturday, July 31, looked promising for a flight starting from the north. Despite Tom Bradbury's warnings I rushed to Dishforth to find a trough over southern England blocking the Continental route. Meantime, Tom Docherty flew past on his way to Ford to break the [British Distance] record at last.

Desperately we rushed to North Hill for the next day, Sunday, August 1. I took off at 10 a.m. with the next front already visible to the north. There were good cumulus overhead and to the west but nothing to the east on track. Down to 1500 ft over Yeovil, ballast burdening the gallant Libelle, lower still over Sherborne and then Sturminster Newton. Fifty kilometres in the first hour, 115 km after two hours. Gloom. Then, suddenly, thermals; and clouds; time to make a run for it.

Hurry, hurry. Over Folkestone at 13:45, the last 200 km in 1 hr 40. Straight into 8 kts and up to 7000 ft. Set compass course for France. It's not in view, hope nobody's moved it. Lots of ships below, their wakes suggesting they can't steer straight, currents or something. Crossed the French coast at 4000 ft and found the first Gallic thermal four miles SE of Calais. Conditions ahead looked tremendous, so radioed back to the others still over Kent. The next 150 km the stuff dreams are made of: 8000 ft cloudbase, shallow cu dotted evenly on track, 8-10 kts under each.

Nothing lasts. At 16:00 approaching Charlerois the sky ahead over-convected with wide areas of showers, and cloudbase down to 4500 ft. With the tailwind gone it was back to crawling along over the forest of the Ardennes. Flying from one sunny patch to the next we reached the Luxemburg border at 18:00, at 2500 ft. Dumping its Devonshire water the Libelle climbed gently back up to 6000 ft and then flew eastwards across Luxemburg towards Germany. Over that border lay another storm, but I arrived too late for it, and only caught the rain. However, a line of zero sink along the banks of the Moselle enabled me to reach Trier airfield, where I joined the circuit and landed at 19:15.

After $9\frac{1}{4}$ hours in the air I was hardly prepared for the onslaught of German efficiency which then swept over me: within ten minutes of landing I had (in descending order of importance) (a) found the Gents (b) completed all custom formalities (c) telephoned home my position (d) arranged for the Libelle to be hangared at the local gliding club (e) got some food and drink.*

* From *Sailplane and Gliding*, Oct.–Nov. 1976, p. 194.

Part IV

UP TO NOW

Chapter Eighteen

CHAMPIONSHIPS IN WOOD

Although soaring in a glider is a highly individual pleasure, competitions have always been popular, because they provide a yardstick against which a pilot can measure his personal performance. At the end of a wonderful, even record-breaking flight of several hours during which the pilot has been alone in the sky, he may consider that he has done well. But because of the variable conditions along the track, he cannot know whether or not he has extracted the maximum energy from the air, or made the fewest possible wrong decisions, unless others have attempted the same flight at the same time. This reason, is not, of course, the only one. Although individual in the air, gliding is a sort of mutual-aid society on the ground, since no one can launch himself. Gliding competitions have always had an easy companionship and are enjoyed for the chance to meet friends and talk.

After the war, the first international competitions (to be known in the future as World Championships) were held in 1948 at Samedan, Switzerland. Eight nations entered, among them the British, who went with a mixture of delight and apprehension: delight after the long years of shortage, and restriction, to be going almost as tourists to a land of cream cakes; and apprehension over how to learn to soar in the high mountains—obviously quite a different task to floating above the rolling downlands of England. The first glimpse of the airstrip of Samedan in its narrow valley between towering mountains on either side, was from the top of the Julier Pass. Although July, the temperature was freezing, and masses of cloud loomed over the mountains, so that through gaps the peaks appeared somehow to be directly overhead, leaning inwards far above the puny trailers standing on the pass.

Mountain flying is a mixture of hill-soaring on a gigantic scale—except for the fact that the wind twisting through the valleys may not hit the slope from the expected direction—and thermal soaring, in which the thermals appear to grow much more from the cold mountain tops than from the warm valleys. The difficulty lies in avoiding being caught out in sink, where it would seem obvious that there ought to be lift. But the flying is exhilarating. The first soaring, after the launch, is close along the face of some lower slope, gradually working up above the scented pines, and past grey lichen-covered rocks until level with the snow. By this height the thermals growing on the sunny slopes have gained strength, and it is possible to start circling in new strong lift. It takes little time now to climb above the highest peaks, and like the eagle, which may come to inspect the coloured intruder, look down upon the world. In one direction from Samedan it is possible to see far across the Maloja Pass, or the Bernina Glacier, to the dusky haze of Italy; in the other, far over a sea of jagged peaks to the Jungfrau or the Matterhorn. Above, the sky is the clearest blue, sometimes with cumulus still almost out of reach. But should the lift not work, or if the clouds sit like hats crammed about the ears of the mountains, escape is possible by flying into the valleys. The dark upper ravines with nowhere to land look terrifying, but the slope of their floors towards the main valleys and the neat safe fields is steeper than the glide path of the aircraft.

The 1948 Championships were small and personal by today's standard; and soaring in such superb surroundings gave them a delightful holiday air—until just before the end.

It was not practical any longer to fly only long distances, particularly among mountains, so on most days a task was set to give a flight over a specially arranged course, such as a race across the snowy rocks to Davos and back.

The task on 28 July was a pilot-selected goal, with a wind towards Italy. Only a single mountain range separated Samedan from the North Italian plains, and prospects were good for long flights; but the weather turned sour. By mid-afternoon most pilots had reported back, including four of the six British. Only Kit Nicholson and Donald Greig were still not accounted for. It was hoped that they had worked their way through the poor weather, and were now beyond Maggiore and Como, out over the open ground, far to the south.

Then over the telephone from Italy came a garbled account of an accident to Nicholson, and a car immediately set out to investigate. There was still no news of Greig. At midnight it was discovered that Nicholson was dead.

It was not until next morning that members of the British team, after searching the villages for information and climbing up the mountains to wreckage-covered rocks at 6,000 ft, were able to find out what had probably happened. There had been cloud covering the tops, but with a well defined base and reasonable visibility. Nicholson had flown over the Maloja Pass, and was trying to work his way south, slope-soaring on the ridges that lie along the west side of Lake Como. He was too experienced a pilot to go into a cloud stuffed full of rocks just to gain a few extra feet, even in a World Championship. He was almost certainly soaring in the clear a little below it when more cloud must have formed underneath and, rising in the hill wind, enveloped him.

In damp, turbulent air, patches of orographic cloud can form well below the general cloud, and, caught in a rising current, sweep up the mountain face. Nicholson would certainly have been on the lookout for orographic cloud, but could have got caught in some which formed unexpectedly fast. In trying to escape from it out into the clear again, he must have come face to face with the rocks on the crest, and pulling up to clear them, stalled on to the huge boulders. The death of Kit Nicholson was terrible, but worse was to come. On the same day, Donald Greig was found. He had been slope-soaring on the easterly side of the same mountain, when his Olympia hit an unmarked and invisible steel wire, a cable used to slide logs down into the valley from high up on the face where trees were felled. It cut off a wing, and he was killed immediately. The holiday was over.

Two years later, in 1950, the World Championships were held in Sweden. This was largely because a Swedish pilot, Pelle Persson, had won in 1948.

Eleven nations entered, and the event was well organised. Orebro, in southern Sweden, was quite flat, in a land of fields, forests and water. The only fumbles were when a pilot landed half-way down one side of a hundred-mile-long lake and discovered that his crew and trailer had gone down the other side!

The 1952 Championships in Spain were totally different from those of the northern land, of which one competitor had remarked 'This is not the country for me—it rains all day, and the sun shines all night.' The British team went to the brown summer of Madrid with new gliders, Slingsby Skys, and for the first time with radio in both gliders and retrieve cars.

Spain was remarkable. Perhaps it was that few countries had experience of running world events at that time, or perhaps that their small gliding movement had been diluted with helpers who did not understand the problems. The weather was wonderful, with dream skies of superb cumulus, but there was a strange reluctance to give competitors much flying. On the other hand, briefings were interminable, first in Spanish, then by a Venezuelan into English, and by a Chilean into German, and then also into French. By this time the briefing in Spanish would have started again, and to demonstrate that they were doing a keen job, other interpreters started up as well, until there were several meetings going on concurrently, all taking slightly different decisions.

For those pilots who had no radio, the problems were insuperable, because the telephones were not good. On several occasions it took more than a day to find and retrieve pilots.

The British team remained undefeated by the heat, or by confusions around them, and although frustrated by not being allowed to fly in soaring conditions almost unknown in England, they won. Philip Wills was now not only the top British pilot, but World Champion.

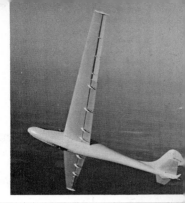

23 (a) Lorne Welch, first pilot to twice soar across the English Channel; (b) The Breguet 901, flown to victory by MacCready, 1956; (c) Skylark 3 crossing the finish line in Poland, 1958; (d) Paul MacCready, designer of the Gossamer Condor which won the Kremer Prize for manpowered flight, and, in 1979, the Gossamer Albatross which crossed the English Channel

24 (a) World Championships. Early morning, Leszno, Poland, 1958
(b) Vladimir Chuvikov in his Russian A-15

So the Championships came to England, and competitors came across the world to the peaks of Derbyshire, where it rained and rained and rained. In a minimal competition, Wills was beaten into second place by Gerard Pierre of France.

In contrast, largely because of the combination of excellent weather, and a big and varied land, the 1956 Championship in France provided some memorable flying.

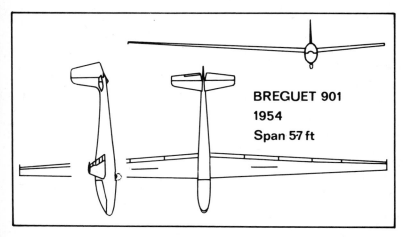

BREGUET 901
1954
Span 57 ft

FIG. 25. The French Breguet 901 in which Paul MacCready won the World Gliding Championships in 1956. Glide angle 1:35 at 50 m.p.h.

For years, pilots had dreamed of finding lift in the evening which would enable them to go on soaring cross-country after the day thermals had died away. Hill-soaring is not much use for this since the lift is restricted to its immediate locality, and does not go very high. On wave lift, however, it is possible to climb to a much greater height, and perhaps be able to glide on another 60 miles or more before landing. The only difficulties are that the mountains have to produce a wave which is working, and the wave has to be reached before the thermals die. The chance of such a combination of circumstances is obviously small; but in 1956 at St Yan it happened.

In Southern France there is a wind called the Mistral, which hurtles down the deep-cut valley of the Rhône and bounds upwards over the range of mountains on either side. This torrent of air sets up a series of waves which may reach up to 30,000 ft. Not a great deal of exploratory flying had been carried out in this region, and the French felt that if the weather was right during the Championships it would be a good idea to try to reach the wave from St Yan, and then soar in it. This would not only give excellent competition flying, but also provide a chance of finding out more about the wave itself. Having a number of aircraft flying in it separated by both miles and hours would provide a clearer picture of its extent.

On 3 July the forecasters declared that the classic conditions for the Mistral existed; so a race to the airfield of St Auban, 188 miles to the south, was set. Wills was one of the pilots to fly on that day:

The dish we were therefore offered was a royal Macedoine de Fruits, containing almost all the major forms of up-currents used by sailplane pilots: on the leg to Lyons thermal and cloud-flying, thereafter slope-soaring on a gigantic scale and wave-flying. Never have sixty pilots strapped themselves into their brightly coloured cockleshells with livelier anticipation.

The 60-mile flight as far as Lyons over the Monts du Beaujolais was a little more difficult than we had expected, but most of us survived it. At the base of many of the cumulus into which I circled I found large flocks of darting swallows feeding on the swarms of insects carried up in warm rising air from the sunny fields below; but the birds never followed the insects or me into cloud, being just as incapable as I would be to fly blind were it not for the additional powers conferred on me by the magic properties of the gyroscope. After Lyons, 40 more miles on a south-south-easterly course and I would reach the mountains, and all, I thought, would be well.

It was a struggle, but I made it, and the wide bowl of Valence opened up, of which the south-eastern part is boxed in by two walls of mountains at right angles to each other rising up almost sheer to over 3,000 ft. But something had gone wrong, the situation was far from classic after all. The meteorologists must have made some minute error in their forecast of the moisture-content of the air, for instead of ranges of mountains rising sharp and hot into clear air with puffs of white cloud far overhead, the view ahead on course consisted of sinister black walls rising up and disappearing into a complete sheet of grey and black cloud.

To offer oneself up to one of these frowning cliffs and be sucked up into, and possibly above, such a pervading and turbulent shroud would obviously be suicidal, since one would either fly blindly into one of the myriad peaks, or else get trapped over the clouds with no possibility of navigation and the eventual certainty of finally having to descend again quite lost, over virtually un-landable country.

Our course lay south-east diagonally over the mountains, but since this was clearly impossible, the only alternative was to try and keep to the westerly end of each ridge, within reach of the Rhône Valley, and whilst keeping under cloud, climb high enough on each face to enable one to dart over it or round it on to the one behind it. But this was not to be easy.

The lower half of each escarpment was densely clothed in trees, the upper part bare and jagged rocks, and there was no hope of landing at the foot, whilst the wind was so strong that, once pinned to the face, it was impossible to force one's machine any distance north again to reach kinder country. And each succeeding moun-tain-wall was partly 'in irons' from the one in front of it, so that if one reached it more half-way down there would probably be no lift at all, but a wildly turbulent cataract of air which would sweep one helplessly down to the rocky floor of the cleft below.

However, this was World Championship flying, not a Sunday afternoon at Dunstable, so after a lot of delicate juggling I got myself pinned against the first battlement and was rapidly swept up, a span or two away from the precipice, to the top. Towards the east the razor-edged ridge ran up into the cloud-sheet, but where I was there was perhaps a 300 ft gap through which I could peer downwind, over the precipitous valley of the Drome to the next range of Roche-Courbe, a 5,000-ft mountain towering up invisible and menacing into the ceiling of cloud. And now I saw something which put the lid on my troubles, and made me realise my cata-logue of woes had so far been incomplete. Over the valley of the Drome, looming and rotating like a gigantic garden roller, was the largest rotor cloud I have ever seen. . . .

These rotors can be seen by the naked eye to be rolling over and over at high speed, with rags of tortured cloud being flung over and out at all levels, and in and underneath them the air is tossed around with unprecedented violence. Last year in such a cloud in the U.S. an exploring sailplane quite suddenly literally disintegrated, in spite of strength factors higher than those of many aeroplanes, and the pilot had a miraculous escape by parachute. He found himself falling with the nose of the glider locked to his feet by the straps of his boots, but when he pulled his rip-cord the jerk was sufficient to pull his feet out of his laced boots and he descended to safety.

Now I knew that the formidable monster I could see was not likely to be such a killer, since the mountains over which I was flying were far smaller than those of the Californian Sierras, but in this case I was faced with the problem of flying under it whilst surrounded on nearly all sides by invisible mountain peaks, at an altitude insufficient to give me much chance of finding a safe landing place should I be forced down. I heard myself saying, 'And we do this for fun!' I decided to try out a trick I had practised earlier in the year on the smooth and friendly slopes of the Long Mynd. The plan was possible because of a miraculous little compass recently invented by a gliding enthusiast at home which is 'dead beat' and shows one's course instantaneously at all times. Keeping to the west end of my escarpment, where there was a small gap of clear air between the crest and the cloud I checked my compass course on each tack of my beat and allowed myself to be drawn up blind into the cloud.

Six minutes on 050°, turn, four minutes on 335°, turn, six minutes . . . all the time watching my rate-of-climb indicator like a fascinated rabbit. Green, up 5; green, up 3; green, up 3—rapidly and easily we gained a further 1,000 ft then, blind, turned and held a grim southerly course. The climb turned to a descent, two or three minutes went by, and we broke cloud over the Drome valley, safely south of the mountain I had just left.

Suddenly there was a jar and a shock, and my starboard wing fell into nothing. With full opposite aileron we hung and slid in space for what seemed an age. The next ten minutes were unforgettable. Seven pilots eventually completed this flight, and all of them confessed they had never experienced such wild turbulence before. Many were forced to land in the Drome valley, and Bill Ivans, the American holder of the world altitude record in the Bishop wave in California [1950], had his machine fall out of his hands at 60 feet into a rocky field—it was completely destroyed, and Bill cracked a vertebra and was laid up in hospital in plaster.

But my extra 1,000 ft stood me in good stead and a shaken pilot reached the Roche Courbe ridge in one piece, climbed, dodged round behind it over the Jabron to the Montagne de la Lance, and again over and to the valley of the Eygues.

Here patches of blue sky began to show between the mountains, and it became possible to try and mount through the rough air, up past the clouds to the wide smooth waves in the blinding blue air above. Since these waves would run due east, once attained any one of them would lead one in blissful smooth silence straight over the mountains to the goal in the valley of the Durance to the east.

And this is what happened. With the vulturine bald-headed Mont Ventoux to the south marking my position exactly, I struggled and slowly gained height in the wild air until quite suddenly I was over it, riding in silky silence whilst below me the clouds lay in enormous ribbon-like rolling masses from west to east like the warp-threads of an enormous loom.

I climbed to 10,000 ft and set course direct for the goal. The contrast between the struggle and the maelstrom I had left and this last leg of the flight was almost too dramatic to be real. It was nearly 7 o'clock and the sun was setting beyond the Rhône Valley to the west. To the south the clouds dissipated and the brown and grey parallel spines of Provence, like ranks of soldiers, led the eye on to a distant blue circle which was the Etang de Berre behind Marseilles. To the north-east cloud-piercing snowcapped mountains swelled up to Mt Pelvoux and the massif dominated by Mt Blanc. Below and to the north-west was my carpet of rolling cloud, dazzling white and glowing pink in the sinking sun. In absolute calm, in absolute peace, with a whisper of silken air over the wings, I flew at 10,000 ft and nearly 100 m.p.h. to the goal which had seemed so impossible to reach.*

* From *Sailplane and Gliding*, vol. 7, 1956, no. 5, p. 228.

Chapter Nineteen

THE NEED FOR SPEED

In the middle 1950s championship flying took on a subtle change. Quite suddenly the standard of soaring went up, not only with the few top pilots such as Heinz Huth of Germany, but widely. The events themselves grew larger, and competition became fiercer, although still as friendly. The reason for this was partly because the trained pilots who turned to gliding after the war were now reaching the top in some numbers, and partly because competitions included a much higher proportion of races. This forced the development of techniques which would give high cross-country speeds, so that a given course could be flown in the shortest possible time, notwithstanding the direction of the wind.

Although it will always be possible in a glider to fail to soar and to fall out of the sky, even on a good day, the competition pilot now had to concentrate on going fast and assume that he would be able to keep his glider in the air. The accent had changed. It was now speed, speed, regardless of all else.

The advantages of being able to fly fast had, of course, been appreciated in the mid 1930s, when although the main emphasis was on distance flying it was realised that the pilot who could get the most miles into each hour would go furthest in the soaring time available.

Apart from the obvious points like having a good glider, and not getting lost, high speed is achieved by using only really strong lift, and climbing up in it as efficiently and rapidly as possible. It involves operating at a height where the thermals are at their strongest, and not wasting time in any weak lift encountered on the way. The disadvantage is that the pilot may find himself lower than he intended because he discarded the last thermals as not being good enough: he is then either forced to land, or to waste precious time in climbing up in the only one that he can locate, however weak it is.

Although a good pilot becomes highly skilled in assessing when to fly really fast and when to proceed more warily, it is difficult to determine just how fast to fly between thermals.

In championships the risk of pressing on fast, and possibly failing to recognise good thermals before having flown right through them, is lessened because they are marked by other gliders circling in them. When a pilot decides to leave his thermal, he will fly off at high speed towards a gaggle of gliders that he can see in the distance, or towards his destination. If, on the way, he unexpectedly flies into good lift, and starts to circle, many of his original companions will almost certainly arrive in a flock to join him.

Since the margin of a winning pilot in a race of some 150 miles may vary by as little as 30 seconds, there is a risk in sheering off from what is obviously strong lift to plough a lonely furrow. The strain of gaggle flying is appreciable, since a stack may contain as many as twenty-five machines all circling round within feet of each other.

As a race nears its end, the pilot must consider just how soon he can afford to stop using lift, and glide straight and fast towards his destination, because getting this moment right will give him the shortest time for his flight. If he works it out correctly, he will start his final glide at, say, 5,000 ft, 20 or even 30 miles away from his goal, which may still be invisible in the hazy distance. The aim is to arrive at a height of only a few feet above the finishing line.

During the 1950s a number of people felt that the competition glider was becoming too expensive, and that the time had come to use cheaper aircraft, at least in some contests. Another school went one stage further and suggested that all competitions should use the same type of aircraft. This would have happened in the 1940 Olympic Games, had they taken place, when all competitors were to have flown the Meise.

After much discussion it was agreed that one-class international contests would be administratively difficult and further, that although cheapness should be the aim, it would be impossible to define cost as such. All that could be done was to decide which features of an aircraft were expensive and to restrict or prohibit these. The matter came to a head during the World Championships at St Yan, France, in 1956, when the Standard Class rules were formulated.

In the 1958 World Championships over the flatlands of Poland the results showed considerable progress in speed-flying techniques. The new Standard Class was won by Witek of Poland, flying a Mucha Standard, and the Open Class by the veteran, Haase, of West Germany in the HKS-III, a glider designed primarily to go fast and achieving its performance to a large extent from the very smooth surface that had been achieved with its wood-sandwich construction. This was not fully appreciated at the time because of the rumours that Haase was using secret thermister snifters to find the thermals for him. The equipment was carefully guarded from prying eyes, adding fuel to controversy ranging from unfair advantage to heated technical speculation—but it did not actually work.

To Germany in 1960, the Poles brought two new high-speed gliders, the Zefir, and the Foka. These were the first of the new generation fast aircraft to go into production, which meant that such gliders would now be available to many more pilots.

Polish gliding had always been enterprising. Even during the '30s it was technically nearly as far advanced as the Germans, although on a smaller scale. In reconstructing their country after the war, the Poles developed an efficient sporting flying movement, which included light aeroplanes, gliding and parachuting. This movement, which was subsidised, was unusual in that it concentrated on quality rather than quantity, and promising pilots could get a great deal of flying. Their flat country was ideal for cross-country soaring, and the combination of the two soon put them ahead in the develop-

25 (a) The Dutch Standard Class Sagitta designed by P. H. Alsema
    (b) The Breguet 904 2-seater which held the World 200-km. Triangle
         Speed Record of 84.5 km./h. flown by Barbera and Robert

26 (a) Chris and Philip Wills rigging the Skylark; (b) Polishing the Czech all-metal Blanik 2-seater. This one had just been towed over the 16,000-ft-high Andes from Chile

27 (a) Gerard Pierrre, France, World Open Class Champion 1954 with his crew;
(b) Dick Georgeson, New Zealand, winner of the 1976 F.A.I. Gold Medal; (c)
Billy Nillson, Sweden, World Champion 1950 on a Weihe; (d) Adam Witek,
Poland, First Champion in Standard Class, 1958

28 (a) The all-metal Jugoslav Meteor of 66-ft. span, designed by Obad and Cijan in 1955. It was still competitive enough to be entered in the 1968 World Championships; (b) The 64ft.-span HKS-1 of sandwich skin construction for improved surface finish. A later version, the HKS-3, won the 1958 World Open Class Championships; (c) The Czech VSM-40 Demant of 60-ft.-span which came third in the 1958 Championships flown by R. Mestan

ment of speed-flying. They also carried out a lot of soaring with the gliders flying in pairs or small groups, to see if by working together the luck element in searching for lift could be reduced. This team flying had other advantages as, for example, on one day in an international contest when six Foka pilots decided to fly together. It was a day of big cumulus, with widely separated areas of lift, so that it paid to climb in clouds to get enough height to cross the gaps. The six pilots went one after the other into the same cloud, and avoided collision by calling out their heights over the radio. By using air brakes as necessary to control their altitude, each pilot was able to keep adequate separation from the next. On another occasion, several pilots were being aero-towed back to Leszno, their base, at the end of a free distance day. They wanted to get back the same night, in order to have some proper sleep before the next day's contest, but the towing aeroplanes could not arrive over the airfield until after dark. On arrival each pilot pulled off from its tug, again using radio to make his invisible whereabouts known to the others, and landed on the airfield by the light of car headlights.

In the 1962 Polish Nationals, a triangular course of 500 kms was set for the first time ever in championships, and many gliders got round. In 1964 the weather permitted them to set the same task again, and thirty-four out of thirty-six gliders completed the 300 miles and more to land back at base.

In British Nationals the geographical limitations of the country made it more difficult to have such long competition flights as were possible in Poland, but in the 1964 Championships at Aston Down, a triangular course of over 300 kms was set for the first time, and completed by twenty-six out of forty-nine pilots. Because of the more erratic weather, with its generally weaker thermals, most British pilots preferred aircraft like the Skylark 4 and Olympia 419, which although not very fast could continue to stay airborne in poorer lift.

Soaring in England is so much a case of grabbing any opportunity that comes along that pilots have become extremely good at extracting the last ounce of energy from the air, even when conditions appear to be quite unpromising—as on the free-distance day during the 1959 Nationals at Lasham. The wind was southerly, and in a moment of optimism, with nothing to lose, Nick Goodhart declared Portmoak, the home of the Scottish Gliding Union, 360 miles away, as his goal; but the weather was poorer than expected, and after he had

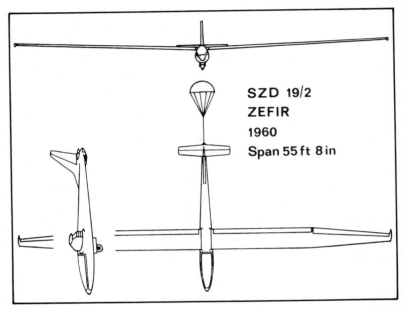

SZD 19/2
ZEFIR
1960
Span 55 ft 8 in

FIG. 26. The Zefir, Poland. Winner of the World Championships, 1963. Glide angle 1:35 at 59 m.p.h. Wing loading 5.9 lb/sq. ft

failed to get away from Lasham on two of his three permitted launches, he was so depressed that he went to have lunch. At 1303 hrs he took his third and last launch into a sky which now looked more promising, with cumulus forming into streets. Slowly he worked his way north, endeavouring to keep to the east of the Pennines. By 1600 hrs he had reached Chesterfield, and went into cloud, climbing slowly to 7,500 ft:

Coming out of this cloud I was immediately presented with a good growing cu-nim, but was above the base and had to enter it from the side; below me David Ince's red and white Oly 419 stood out clearly as he headed for the same cloud. Despite my entering from the side, I was soon able to find a core of lift which quickly built up to over 2,000 ft a minute. This was quite the roughest cloud I have ever been in; the turbulence was such that I was convinced

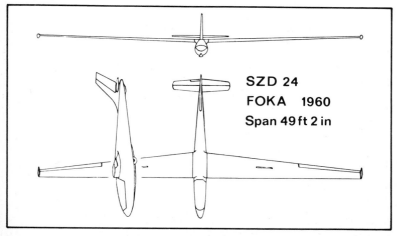

SZD 24

FOKA 1960

Span 49 ft 2 in

FIG. 27. The sleek and hungry-looking Polish Foka. Glide angle 1:34 at 54 m.p.h. Wing loading 5.5 lb/sq. ft

that I must be on the edge of the main lift area, but no amount of searching would show smooth lift but only succeeded in producing temporary interruptions in the climb.

Soon after passing 10,000 ft I realised that the climb might go quite high, so fished out my oxygen mask and turned on the oxygen. Fortunately the mask is easy to put on, so even in the extreme turbulence I was soon sorted out and giving full attention to the climb; but after a quarter of an hour and at 18,000 ft I could find no more lift, so straightened up on a northerly heading to come out of the cloud. It was at this point that I received a very severe shock through both feet where they were resting against the rudder cables, although in fact I had not seen much lightning.

Soon I came out of the side of the cloud and was in clear air. However, the ground was quite invisible through the murk below, and a huge anvil spreading out over my head made everything seem very dark and uncheerful. When I finally got enough of the canopy clear of ice to be able to see out properly, I could see that there was a very considerable load of wing icing of a most interesting but incredibly unaerodynamic shape, and if my instruments were right I was only getting a still-air gliding ratio of something like 1 in 14. One wonders under such circumstances what on earth is the best speed to fly.

Now that I could see a little bit, I realised that there was another band of cumulus 20 miles or so ahead, and I was able to enter this at just over 10,000 ft and get carried back to 15,500. On coming out of this cloud it was apparent that there was nothing further in the way of clouds out in front. The ground was still hidden in a layer of misty haze and the question arose as to which way to steer. I had not bothered to get any high altitude wind forecasts for this area, and it was over an hour since I had last seen the ground. For want of a better course I headed due north, and slowly as I got lower I began to be able to see something through the haze. At first I got the somewhat discouraging impression that I was over the sea, but luckily this was not so and by the time I was down to 8,000 ft I could make out that I was over moorland; and at about this height I was glad to say good-bye to the ice, which was so seriously affecting my performance. About 20 ft of this ice came off the port wing in one piece and I saw it sailing away behind me. A 20-ft ice spear may have come as rather a surprise to some enthusiastic moor walker.

At 4,500 ft I succeeded in identifying my position over a railway line 20 miles East of Carlisle, and at this point was very surprised to find very weak lift at about 50 ft per minute.

This lift was clearly of the wave type, and by heading just south of east I was able to keep in it and gain about 500 ft. However, try as I could, I could gain no more height, and was forced to set off again on what was clearly a final glide. Purely by chance, and trying to stretch my final glide to the limit, I happened into the valley which carries the Carlisle to Edinburgh railway just north of a place called New Castleton. The ground wind was obviously very strong from a point just south of east, and I was busily engaged in selecting myself a safe landing field when suddenly I found good lift on a windward-facing slope, the characteristic smoothness of which clearly indicated that it was of wave type.

Quickly forgetting all thought of landing, I started working this wave lift and for a while was actually getting 1,000 ft per minute out of it. By continuous trial and error I kept in the area of maximum lift, and to my intense surprise in some three-quarters of an hour I managed to reach 10,000 ft. Barring unforeseen circumstances, this was clearly enough to reach Portmoak, so I set off heading considerably east of north, and by taking advantage of a few minor waves I found myself crossing Edinburgh at 6,000 ft. Portmoak was obviously in the bag, but there was one major problem. I had never been there before and the site was not marked on my map. I had a reasonably strong conviction that it lay at the south-east corner of Loch Leven, but what it looked like I had no idea. I was therefore extremely glad of my excess altitude, knowing that I would have time to explore a little to find it. In the event this problem was easily solved as the field was very obvious indeed, due to the cable-retrieving track running the length of it, and the hangar in the corner.*

Goodhart landed at 1930 hrs, just as the hangar doors were shut for the night.

The 1960 World Championships in Germany was won by Hossinger of Argentina, and that country offered to run the next event. For the first time, it would be outside Europe, and also in the southern hemisphere. Because of the nature of the vast flat land of the pampas, which has few roads, some of them permanently varying between dust and mud, it was decided that all retrieving would be by aero-tow instead of with the pilot's own car and trailer. The prospect of championships in such entirely different surroundings was exciting, and since it was expected that the thermals would be strong, the newest and fastest gliders were brought from all over the world. The British team departed from the English snow, and landed into a temperature of 35° C.

It was quickly seen why the Argentinians had decided to provide aero-tow retrieves. There was not only more space between farms, people and telephones than anywhere in Europe, but even when found, the latter were often ineffective. Nick Goodhart, on a practice flight, landed on a farm, and

* From *Sailplane and Gliding*, vol. 10, 1959, no. 4, p. 187.

eventually finding someone, moved his glider to their yard so that it was the opposite side of a wall to the cattle. When he asked if he could telephone, he got a blank look. The Spanish-speaking farmer indicated with smiles that he could be taken on the back of a tractor, sitting in a farm cart, or riding on a horse. Engineer Goodhart chose the tractor, and they set off in a straight line across the rough grass, which was pitted with armadillo holes. After three bumpy miles they reached a fence and the farmer stopped. Goodhart's heart sank as he first saw no gate, and secondly lorries shimmering in the heat on what was presumably a road running along the skyline. He thanked the farmer, climbed the fence, and walked two more miles, convinced that the road was remaining just as far away. When, hot and thirsty, he finally arrived, it was not long before a lorry came along and offered him a lift to a village some five miles away. But when he got there it had no telephone. So back he went onto the road, and after a half-hour wait in the sun, got a lift in the other direction, to a town 25 miles away, where he was finally able to telephone his whereabouts to base.

Most of the pilots were, in fact, picked up quickly by the tug aeroplanes, which patrolled over the contest routes looking for gliders.

Free-distance tasks are, in many ways, still the most exciting in championships: although it is likely that most pilots will fly downwind, there is always the possibility of someone deciding to do something quite different, and if his theories work out, going further than anyone else.

As evening approaches, everyone is waiting for news of the few pilots who are still unaccounted for. Some who were unlucky, and landed early in the day, are already back, wondering how others whom they had been flying with had gone so much further. It is a time of peculiar excitement, particularly if there are some flying who are known never to give up until their wheel runs on to the ground. After this flight in Argentina, an American pilot, Dick Schreder, was not heard of until the next afternoon, because he had gone on over the empty land, quite simply because that was where the lift was. But no one who remembered a flight that he had made a few years earlier in the American Nationals was surprised.

On that occasion, the task had also been for distance. Downwind there was good country, but after a hundred miles or so, it changed, gradually becoming uninhabited, heat-stricken desert. When Schreder had reached this, he flew on, though buildings and tracks became less and less frequent. Even when, late in the day, the thermals weakened, he still flew on, quite straight, although signs of life disappeared. After all lift had died and he was only 2,000 ft above the ground, he passed over a single isolated shack, and went on, until after nearly 15 miles further his glider touched the ground. He had not turned, but simply continued along his line until he stopped.

As the evening light softened the harsh desert colours, Schreder walked the 15 miles back to the shack on a compass course. In it he found a Red Indian and after a long search in the dark a broken-down truck. It took him nearly a day to fix the truck. It was 50 miles to the nearest road, and 75 to the first telephone.

This flight won Schreder the competition.

The 1963 championships in Argentina were won by Edward Makula, Poland, flying a Zefir in the Open Class, and Heinz Huth, West Germany, Ka-6 in the Standard, but since neither country was prepared to take on the onerous job of host so soon again the organisation of the 1965 event was given to Britain. R.A.F. South Cerney became a world village, and 86 pilots arrived not only with their gliders but supported by more powerful base radio stations than ever before. In Spain radio had proved a much-needed aid in finding a pilot quickly and getting him back for a night's rest. Now it had blossomed into navigational and meteorological assistance seriously eroding the concept of a contest between pilots, a development countered the following winter by the F.A.I. Gliding Commission (C.V.S.M.) rewriting the rules to limit external aid to competing pilots. Now, right on the crest of their technological wave, and with five years of Foka experience and development behind them the Poles had the temerity to enter this little 15-metre glider in the Open Class. It won—flown by Jan Wroblewski, aged 25. The Standard Class was also won by a new slimline glider, the Siren Edelweiss, flown by François Henry of France. There was only one glass glider, the Bolkow Phoebus, although it was five years since the first fibreglass glider, the Phoenix, had flown in world championships, piloted by Haase. So far none had been placed. It was not that glass had failed to demonstrate its benefits in improving the surface finish, but that many of the more forward-looking designers were deeply involved in developing new gliders to the Standard Class rules, and had not yet been able to devote their full talents to doing it all in glass. And there was, of course, still some reluctance to change totally to a material whose life-expectancy, if nothing else, was still insufficiently understood. But there would now be a three-year interval before the next event—a return to Leszno. Here, a decade after the HKS-1 had proved in 1958 that good surface finish was essential to any appreciable improvement in high-speed performance, glass was to show its real worth.

It was, however, not only the gliders that were changing. Their improving performance altered the form of championships, the tasks that were set, and not least the work of those dedicated supporters, the trailer crews. Distance flying and long retrieves had been inseparable and, before the advent of radio, trailer drivers with skill and stamina were needed, and preferably possessing psychic qualities. Some crews, often wives, seemed intuitively to know the mind of their pilots and what decisions would be taken in difficult weather. With the minimum of telephone calls the trailer driver would unerringly locate his or her pilot perhaps 400 miles distant in a totally strange country. Other crews, of course, sometimes managed to end up a hundred miles further away from the glider than when they had started out.

29 (a) The AV-36, designed by Charles Fauvel. Tailless gliders have been tried
from time to time, but have never become popular; (b) The Polish Standard
Class Foka, winner of the Open Class in 1965, flown by Jan Wroblewski

30 (a) Steve Dupont photographing the task declaration board before take-off, Marfa, 1969; (b) Göran Ax, Sweden, 1972 World Champion, flying a Nimbus 2; (c) Waiting for thermals to start; Championships Director, meteorologist, and start marshal, South Cerney, 1965; (d) Hans Nietlispach, the Swiss World Championships pilot who incorporated a digital time display into his turn-point camera to give start and turn-point times

31 (a) The fibreglass ASW-17, one of which made the first 1,000-km. goal flight
in 1970 flown by Hans Werner-Grosse, winner of the 1978 FAI Gold Medal;
(b) Glasflugel's popular Standard Libelle. In 1970 Sue Martin, Australia, beat
the World Goal and Return Record for Women in a Libelle; (c) The Diamant
was the first completely fibreglass glider with no wood filler. Produced in
1967 by FFA of Altenrhein, Switzerland

32 (a) Standard Cirrus 75 dumping water ballast before landing, flown by A. Hammerle, Austria, in Finland, 1976; (b) the 64-ft.-span Kestrel 19 which set the first 1,000-km. Goal and Return Record in 1972, flown by Dick Georgeson; (c) Helmut Reichmann, W. Germany, World Champion in 1970, 1974, 1978; (d) Ingo Renner, Australia, 1976 Standard Class Champion; (e) Sighting frames and radar help check heights over the start line, Waikerie, 1974; (f) George Lee, UK, 1976 Open Class Champion

The arrival of radio in glider and car reduced fumbles, but the crew still remained basically drivers, navigators, and de-riggers. Wooden gliders needed protection from the weather and lived in their trailers between flights, but as they became heavier—weight being no longer so much of a disadvantage—crews had to be strong. The centre section of a Skylark 4, for example, weighed 200 lb. With the increase in closed-circuit speed flying, brought about by the cleaner, faster gliders, long retrieves became rare, so that there was much less driving; instead, with complex instrumentation, cameras, and tail parachutes, crews needed more technical skills if they were to look after their pilot properly. The advent of fibreglass gliders almost removed the de-rigging chore because they could be picketed down outside, but the need for great physical strength was replaced by plumber's work, filling the glider's water ballast tanks each morning.

It was a known fact that a heavy glider would go faster than a light one, so there was a lot to be gained in increasing the weight when thermals were strong, particularly if the weight carried was in some form, like water, which could be easily dumped when lift weakened. Filling up with water ballast—100 kg. or more—came into use with glass gliders as this material did not go mouldy, like wood. Frau Steinhoff, whose husband had been one of the four pilots to fly the first 500-km. flight in 1935 said to me in 1969, at the U.S. Nationals in which Ernst was flying, 'I do not understand my husband. All his life he has tried to lose weight to fly his gliders better, and now he has succeeded he fills it up with water.'

In the early days a crew of three for each glider was really needed in world championships, but now two could manage. Some crews even became addicted, and preferred looking after their pilot and his glider, rather than fly themselves; but most crews enjoyed doing both.

Chapter Twenty

CHAMPIONSHIPS WITH GLASS

The World Championships at Leszno, Poland, in 1968 had 105 entries, making this event the world's largest. But only one-third of the gliders were wholly or partly constructed of fibreglass, although they took the first six places in the Open Class and the first seven in the Standard. The first fibreglass glider in serious production, the Phoebus (twelve entered) came second in the Standard Class, flown by Göran Ax of Sweden, while the champion was Härro Wodl of Austria, flying a fibreglass Cirrus. But numerically the most popular glider was still the wooden Foka, with twenty-seven competing. The Open Class was won by A. J. Smith, U.S.A., flying a part fibreglass, part wood-sandwich Elfe S-3 with a dural spar. In other ways the 1968 Championships were unremarkable, apart from floods on the airfield and an attempt to prohibit cloud flying by limiting altitude. This did little except to show that barographs were inadequate for this purpose in championships. The Leszno results proved without doubt the superiority of fibreglass as a fine way of achieving better performances, and orders poured in to the German factories already geared for production. Rigorous test flying was of course carried out, but it was fully appreciated soon enough that the aero-elastic properties of this new material were quite different from those of wood or metal. Certainly fibreglass gliders were strong enough, but they lacked stiffness, and violent and unexpected flutter of the tail or wings occurred, often when diving across a finish line at, or occasionally a little beyond, the maximum permitted speed. It did not take much time for this new phenomenon to be dealt with, though in the meantime quite a lot of pilots frightened themselves, but managed to slow the glider and stop the flutter before it caused the aircraft to come apart. One or two pilots baled out when it did, and an equally small number were killed.

As a result of Andrew Smith's win the world went to Texas in 1970, to a Second World War desert airfield named Marfa, 5,000 ft A.S.L., and within sight of the Mexican border. For only the second time the championships were to be held in the sub-tropics, which could produce cumulus at 12,000 ft and high-powered thermals with which to reach them. Argentina in 1963 provided such weather, but neither the glider performance nor pilotage techniques were yet quite good enough to fully exploit it. Now, with fibreglass giving a jump in performance from around 1:35 to 1:45, and with 3–4 years' experience with the faster ships the strong weather expected at Marfa could be used to the full. This did not only mean that closed-circuit triangles could be larger than ever, but that much desert or other hostile terrain was no longer unacceptable for championships, because twenty miles of unlandable scrub needed a height of only some 2,000 ft to cross it—and less if flying downwind.

It was not only the improved glide ratio which was important, of course, but also that this performance was available at considerably higher speeds—because of the clean shape that fibreglass had made possible. At the same time stall speeds had not markedly increased, and widespread use of flaps enabled the lower end of the speed range to remain effective. The only fly in this excellent ointment was the frequent transitioning needed from high inter-thermal speeds to the slow flight best for thermal circling: it was too easy to fly right through the lift unless the glider was rapidly pulled up into a steep climbing turn on entry. This, certainly in competitions, increased the risk of collision although actual contacts remained rare. However, it was soon realised that when thermals were strong and frequent it was not actually necessary to circle at all, but simply to pull up as the thermal was entered, and then as the rate of climb began to reduce,

183

to dive through the peripheral downdraught and return to the selected inter-thermal speed. This technique became known as dolphin flying; a somewhat more dignified description than porpoising.

Marfa had the weather and the expansive terrain to fit the gliders which came, and its very success also showed the other side of the coin—that such large, exotic and expensive gliders might be less satisfactorily exploited in smaller countries with weaker thermals; in other words, that glider performance now exceeded that actually needed to provide top competition flying. This, to many, was a heretical concept; except to those pilots or countries which could no longer afford to go in to win.

Because of its weather and terrain, and the experience that the Americans had already gained in flying in such conditions, Marfa became the focal point for the changes in operational practices now becoming essential because of the increasing high-speed performance of the glider. Up to this time almost all turn points had been manned by human observers, but now they were often unable to get into position before the first gliders started arriving! Increasing use was being made of photography from the glider, but it was at Marfa that the efficient and highly effective system now employed was established. The use of photographs, however, brought another problem, in that the photograph did not state the time at which it was taken, and this permitted the possibly unscrupulous pilot to visit and photograph the first turn point before crossing the start line, and then 'achieve' a fast time by flying a shorter course. To make this impossible the R.T.I. (recognition time interval) was introduced, which required every pilot to present himself over the starting airfield at such intervals as would make it impossible to visit a turn point between take-off and any crossing of the start line. Cloud-flying was not permitted during the championships, and this was enforced by prohibiting the fitting of any blind-flying instruments; a rule that was also seen to work well.

Marfa had nothing for the spectator, who would in any case have had many miles to drive to get there, and provided little for the crews. It was a pilot's championships and as such showed that, hidden away among the complexity and the expense, gliding had not lost its essential charm; particularly to people like Wally Scott, who three weeks later was to break the world distance record high over his native Texas pairs-flying with his friend Ben Greene. Of Day 6 at Marfa, with a 221-mile triangle task, he wrote:

I didn't have any idea that my first start would count. I was going to test the [start] gate more than anything. I went through it and out toward a dissipating cu with one edge that looked like it was recycling and rebuilding. It gave me 800 feet per minute right up to cloudbase. It is very seldom you can get that good a start, so I just decided to go ahead. It looked real good out on course. I didn't have any problems at all. I got high—probably 12,500 feet about twenty-five miles this side of Van Horn.

There was good lift to that point, but it was clear blue from there into Van Horn and beyond towards Sierra Blanca. I was getting 600 to 800 feet per minute, and then out in the clear area I ran through a couple of thermals. They were giving me about 600 feet per minute, so I knew that there wouldn't be any problem; I just went bombing toward the turnpoint, took my picture, and worked the first thermal which was about 500 feet per minute beyond the first turn. Finally I connected the cu between Van Horn and Sierra Blanca and I would say that I was probably a good forty-five minutes too early at that point, but the lift was good, but very erratic and broken up, probably averaging about 600 to 700 feet per minute—one side would be 1000, the other side would be maybe 500. Then I contacted the good cu's about halfway back on the final leg.

It was so early when I finished that the team captain and I thought it might warrant another start. We knew the day would last long enough to [do another 221 miles] get back and who knows, maybe a cloudstreet or something like that would have enabled me to beat my first go-around with the second timing. I think it took me about fifteen minutes longer. What I wish is that since I went around twice today they would let one of them count for yesterday.*

* From *Soaring*, September 1970.

185

The 1970 championships were won by Helmut Reichmann, West Germany, flying an LS-1 in the Standard Class, and George Moffat with the enormous floppy winged 22-metre Nimbus top of the Open. But although he won by the considerable margin of some 300 points, the constant decision-making which so easily makes the difference between winning and losing was hard work, as his wife Suzanne comments on Day 7:

George didn't put in water ballast; the weather was supposed to be very weak. That turned out to be a big mistake. He should have carried a half-load of water. He started early because he assumed that with all the moisture from the last couple of days it would convect very early. But it didn't over-convect, and it wasn't weak.

As a result of starting too early and having to pussyfoot around a bit, he just didn't get fast enough time. I guess the others all caught him about at the turnpoint, and then he came back with the rest of them, but they already had ten or fifteen minutes on him from starting later in stronger weather.

His flight was just kind of slow and safe. He figured he had to finish no matter what. He doesn't have to win big, he just has to win, because he's flying from the top, of course. It's not the same as he would fly from 100 or 200 points behind, when he had to catch up. From the top you fly safely, which is what he was doing. He just flew a little too safely.*

From the hot Texas weather the scene changed in 1972 to the cloud-ridden skies of Yugoslavia; usually having good summers, this one bred disaster, not helped by the inexperience of the organisers in running a sophisticated and highly technical championships. They certainly did not appreciate that at world event level there was so much at stake, and that the prudence and caution of everyday flying did not make for winning; if the organisers declared a 300-km. triangle that is what every pilot gave his maximum to achieving. If the only lift available was inside a thunderstorm—and cloud-flying was permitted at Vrsac—then that lift would be used. The competition was intense, but not tempered, as in the distance flying of past years, with the

*From *Soaring*, September 1970.

freedom of manoeuvre to choose one's route. In this fortnight two pilots were killed—the first fatalities in world gliding championships for 18 years—and there was a collision in cloud which could easily have killed two more. Rain bogged trailers and flooded the airfield, but in spite of the enormous luck element introduced by the many confusions, the winners deserved their places. Göran Ax, Sweden, won the Open Class, flying a Nimbus II, while Jan Wroblewski, Poland, pulled off his second title to become Standard Class champion, flying an Orion.

1972 had been an expensive championships and there was serious doubt whether many countries would be able to raise enough cash to go across the world to Australia in only 18 months' time, instead of the usual two-year interval. It was probably thoughts of the sun in a northern hemisphere winter which spurred many of the sixty-seven pilots to go. Waikerie, north of Adelaide on the Murray River, had been chosen because of its known mixture of good soaring weather and acceptable terrain. It rained almost continuously throughout the practice week, the Murray broke its banks, the airfield on which take-off pads of real grass had been nurtured out of the arid ground for 18 months became a bog, and the forecasters were pessimistic. The first contest day came and went, as did the second, and it was not until 15 January that the first task, in very 'English' weather, could be set—a 269-km. triangle which no one completed. But after this the weather steadily improved until on the sixth contest day the largest triangle ever in world championships was set for the Open Class: 707 km. and rapidly nicknamed the Boeing. It would be a difficult flight, with the first 138-km. leg having a headwind component towards an approaching front; then downwind for 353 km., and finally a 216-km. race back against the wind, hopefully beating the front to Waikerie. At briefing surprised expressions quickly gave way to the concentration not only of how best to fly the task, but over crew strategy and tactics; because an outlanding could give a retrieve as long as those of the old

187

distance-flying, and with the same problem of getting back in time to fly the next day. The day did not brew early so it was noon before the start line became busy. There were still blue holes in the sky, and a premature outlanding would put paid to any chances of winning. Moffat in his Nimbus II did not start until 1156, but even this delay gave him a somewhat troublesome run to the first turn point, like most of the earlier starters, although Ragot, France, crossing the line in his ASW-17 just four minutes later had an easy journey, and a fast run all the way to the second point at Nangiloc. Now came the difficult part. It was not long before the massive cumuliform cloud bank that was the front closed in enough for its ominous shadow to kill off thermals along the route. But the front itself looked life-supporting— if it could be reached—and John Delafield, Great Britain, was one of those who managed it and got home. Meanwhile Moffat and Dick Johnson were working their way back together, but as evening approached Johnson was low. Moffat radioed to him that there was reduced sink under the front, but he could not reach it. As Moffat came into the final glide Ragot's ASW slid past, then the extra weight of the Nimbus showed and Moffat caught up, so that the two of them crossed the finish line together at 1845. Ragot's speed of 104.5 km./h. had beaten Moffat by just 1.2 km./h. over 707 km. Altogether ten pilots from eight countries finished this historic race: Ragot and Cartry of France; Grosse and Holighaus of West Germany; Moffat (U.S.A.); Ax (Sweden); Delafield, (U.K.) and Zegels of Belgium; Tarbert, Australia; and Hammerle of Austria in the only 19-metre span glider, a Kestrel. The other successful gliders were four 20.3-m. Nimbus IIs, two 20-m. ASW-17s and one 22-m. Kestrel 604.

For those who landed far from home help came from Waikerie Air, a patrolling Bonanza equipped to relay messages between pilots and crews, and in some cases to actually lead a trailer across desert country to the glider, as had also happened at Marfa. Waikerie Air finally landed that night at eleven o'clock, by a hastily rigged row of paraffin flares.

There were eleven contest days at Waikerie, the greatest number in any world championships. 239,460 km. in 3,691.4 hours were flown by the sixty-seven pilots*. Waikerie was one of the great contests. Its Director, Wally Wallington, had combined the organisation of South Cerney, where he had

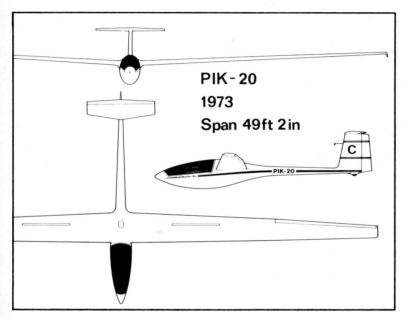

FIG. 28. The Standard Class Pik-20 from Finland which took four of the five top places in the 1976 World Championships

been chief meteorologist, with the updated control procedures of Marfa, while the Australian Gliding Federation members, who made up the very substantial workforce now needed to run a championships, gave it great enthusiasm and good humour.

The Finns' case for holding the 1976 event was that although

* And both winners had done it before. The two schoolteachers, Moffat and Reichmann, repeated their Marfa placings.

they could not produce sub-tropical thermals, the land of the almost-midnight sun gave an 18-hour flying day which should more than compensate. So in the coldest June the country had experienced for 100 years eighty-five top pilots settled in to their portacabins in the land of woods and lakes. Like Waikerie the first contest days were cancelled because of the weather, but unlike latitude 30° S. it did not recover itself sufficiently to give more than a minimum, and difficult, contest. The rule change that now allowed water ballast to be carried in the Standard, as well as the Open Class, often achieved little more than double the artificial rain which fell on the airfield while pilots were struggling to stay airborne. A more serious problem of ballast, that of overloading the glider beyond the limits of its certificate of airworthiness, had been causing rumbles of discontent and suspicion for some time. At Räyskälä this problem was firmly taken in hand, and largely overcome by spot-weighing gliders on the grid immediately before take off.

In Finland there were two entirely new winners. George Lee gave Britain its first win for 20 years with his ASW-17 in the Open Class, and Ingo Renner, presented Australia with their first world title. He was flying one of the Finnish Pik-20s which took four of the first five places in the Standard Class.

After so much travelling around the world, and having to adapt to extremes of weather—much of it locally quite unexpected—the prospect of the comfortable centre of France for 1978 produced sighs of relief.

In Europe 1978 was a bad summer, cold, wet, and windy—except at Chateauroux. Over the smooth countryside of central France the sun shone and the eleven championship days equalled the record of Waikerie in 1974. But, as with the South Australian rain which ceased flooding the airfield only as the competition began there was fortune also in France. Each day the Meteosat photographs received on the airfield from space showed depressions to the north, thundery cloud originating from Spain to the south, and a cloud-filled

Atlantic to the west. Only over the task area and to the east was the weather good. In these eleven days five tasks of over 500 km. were set, although not always completed.

It was the first championships with three classes: Open, 15 metre Unrestricted, and Standard Class. This posed no organisational difficulties from the task point of view as there were no less than 67 turning points, so all triangles—there were no other tasks—could be satisfactorily graded for size for the 3 classes over routes which did not clash. Launching was no problem either with the 79 gliders line astern on the long runway, and 20 Rallye and Robin tugs to get them all airborne in 30 minutes.

There was only one sadness with these championships, and that was the absence of the well-liked pilots from Poland, and other Eastern countries, because of the presence of pilots from South Africa. Anti-apartheid rumblings had been increasingly evident in gliding events, as in other sports, since 1970 when India entered but did not come. At Vrsac the South Africans did not enter to avoid trouble for the organisers, and at Waikerie they were refused visas at the last moment, though their telegram of good wishes was well received by competitors. In Finland they were correctly invited, in accordance with the F.A.I. Statutes, and arrived, but the Finns had financial support withdrawn as a result. At Chateauroux South Africa accepted, and the Eastern countries pulled, or were pulled, out by their governments, including the Finns who entered with private money but were stopped at the last moment. Other countries, like Britain, had state support for the national entry withdrawn. It was not that glider pilots were pro-apartheid, or for that matter concerned with the political activities of any other country, but simply that they did not see why sport should be made the tool of politics. People could get to know and better understand each other in friendly competition, and this surely could not be bad.

The weather on the first task day at Chateauroux was hot with an inversion at about 1,000 metres, and many thermals dying before they even reached this high. There were no cumulus and no relief from the heat over the 336, 309, and 272 km. triangles that were set. As a result gliders congregated in great sagging gaggles, as many as thirty-three being counted in one thermal. These gaggles, naturally, proceeded steadily around the triangles, feeding into a common final glide path to arrive over the finish line at maximum speed and minimum height. Two pilots, Rantet of France and Urbanjic of Argentina, flying in each other's blind spots, touched without realising that they had collided. Unfortunately Urbanjic's wing caused Rantet's tail parachute to open, so that he just failed to cross the finish line; an insignificant happening but one that gently repercussed for days. The Director, Yves du Manoir, discovering that no fault lay with either pilot gave Rantet the same finish time as Urbanjic, but this led to a protest to the effect that a glider not crossing the line cannot be given speed points. It was not that Rantet should be done out of his points, but if he had been given no points his team manager could have protested and then everyone could have voted that he should have the points. It seemed a small matter magnified, but in reality it was a way of saying that the competitors should retain their freedom to continue the generosity of spirit to their fellows that has been such a long standing tradition in gliding championships.

The days went by with a high level of operational efficiency, but increasing fatigue among pilots as the big triangles followed each other in monotonous succession. Challenging tasks were fine in principle, but were now only producing repetitive results as the same type of survival flying was demanded every day. From Day 5 on the top pilots in each class had stayed the same; only in the Standard Class did the second and third pilots, Brigliadori, Italy, and Recule, France, change places just before the end. Although for the last two days smaller, speed, triangles were given, which made some changes in the Day positions, it was already too late to affect the overall results. One pilot, Helmut Reichmann, achieved the distinction of winning on every day, finally to become the only thrice times champion. This time he had forsaken his LS-3 for the variable geometry SB-11, the first glider to be specifically designed for the new 15 metre Class, and full advantage had been taken of the term unrestricted. The SB-11, created at the Akaflieg Braunschweig, which in 1971 had produced the 29-metre span SB-10, was made almost entirely of carbon fibre. It weighed only 270 kg., in spite of the full span chordwise movable extension to the wing. This varied the area from 10.56 m.^{2} to 13.2 m.^{2}, reducing the wing loading with a 75-kg. pilot from 32.7 kg./m.^{2} to 26.1 kg./m.^{2}, or with full water ballast from 45 kg./m.^{2} to 35.75 kg./m.^{2}. Its main advantage over more conventional craft being its ability to circle slowly in small thermal cores, and at 60 km./h. Reichmann had no difficulty in outclimbing his competitors by going straight up through the middle of them. It was the cost of the SB-11 which worried people more than its actual performance. At 90,000 Deutschmarks for the materials alone the SB-11 looked like making entry into the 15 metre unrestricted class a mighty expensive exercise.

Chateauroux was a good championships. It was happy and it brought pilots from seven countries to the top nine places overall. In the Open Class George Lee, Britain, retained his title won in Finland. In the 15 metre Class Reichmann had stiff opposition from Karl Striedeck, U.S.A., the only pilot to have soared 1,000 miles, but in his first international championships. From Day 3, when he flew his ASW-20 into second place he relentlessly crept up on Reichmann until at the end he was only 44 points behind out of a possible total of 11,000. Another newcomer, 23-year-old Baer Selen from the Netherlands, won the Standard Class flying a new ASW-19. Thought likely to die when the new 15 metre class was introduced the Standard Class flourished at Chateauroux: the object of contest flying is, after all, to obtain close and satisfying competition between skilled pilots. It is not to achieve ultimate performance.

Chapter Twenty-one

THE BIG WAVES

For more than ten years after pilots learnt to soar on the hills little thought was given to what the air might be doing downwind of them. It was known that in the immediate lee of the hill, curl-over of the wind would quickly dump gliders in the rough, but that was all; the idea of the air having inertia and a springing system was too big an intellectual step.

The first wave system to be discovered and used was the Moazagotl, which has already been described, as has the experimental flight in the Helm wave by Noel McLean. After this, some degree of wave lift was found and used at several gliding clubs whose sites were in hilly country. For a while the strange lift which appeared from time to time was thought to be a sort of evening thermal, because it turned up more often in stable air late in the day. On other occasions a wave created upwind of the gliding site would augment, or destroy, the ordinary hill lift to a disconcerting extent. As more experience was gained by flying in them, the waves became better understood. However, these systems, even to some extent the Moazagotl wave, were small fry compared to those which existed in the regions of the big mountains of the world. Not much soaring was done in these giant waves until after World War Two, when exploratory flights were made in the Bishop wave in California. Here there is a wide valley, about 4,000 ft above sea-level, lying just to the east of the Sierra Nevadas. These mountains rise 10,000 ft, while on the far side the White Mountain range reaches 8,000 ft above the ground. The air pours down the lee face of the Sierra Nevada, and the upwave through the air produces huge lenticular clouds over the east side of the valley. The airfield at Bishop is about 20 miles to the north of the narrowest part of the valley. For a long time, all flying in the wave was done by expeditions which based themselves on this field.

By 1950, heights of over 20,000 ft had been reached by eight pilots, one of them, Bill Ivans, beating the world record for absolute altitude with a flight of 42,000 ft on 30 December 1950.

It was fortunate that such people as Ivans, and Bob Symons, a local flyer, had the experience and energy to exploit the wave properly, for this was no Sunday afternoon stuff. Soaring in the big waves could be magnificent, exhilarating, but to the careless or unwary it could be lethal.

Wave lift is characterised by the silky smoothness of the air, and once in it, the glider is borne swiftly upwards, without a ripple to disturb the peace. But outside the wave, and with no visible separation from it, the air is no longer organised, and this turmoil of flow and gust can produce turbulence of shattering propensity. So the glider has to be strong, and the pilot experienced enough to fly on tow, keeping station with an aeroplane possibly flying near the limit of its own controllability, while it is searching for the best place to start the flight.

Once released from the tug, the pilot must find the upflow as soon as possible, and keep clear of the down-going torrent of air. Once in the lift the glider will gain height perhaps at over 1,000 ft/min. while the view steadily widens and, above, a dark blue sky is splashed with the harsh white elipses of the lenticular clouds themselves.

Sometimes these clouds can be reached, and flown through, or instead it may be possible to slide upwards close to the dazzling cliff, overwhelmingly impressed by the huge power loose in the sky. At 6 or 8 miles above the earth, in surroundings of unbelievable colour and beauty, the flight can take on the quality of a dream—in theory. In practice, it is far from this.

At 15,000 ft most people need to start supplementing the thin air with bottled oxygen. Above 20,000 ft this is essential.

Above 35,000 ft they not only need a pressure mask, but even with it they may become less efficient. Above 45,000 ft it is pressure-suit country, with all that this involves in a tiny glider. Then there is the cold; at 20,000 ft the temperature is $-25°$ C, at 40,000 ft $-55°$ C, sometimes even lower. In this cold the pilot can take no exercise to warm himself, and must rely on whatever protection he has started with—as many suitable clothes as he can get on, and electrically heated socks, warmed by a small battery. Even the magnificent view can fade, literally, into insignificance behind the ice crystals which increasingly thicken on the canopy, sealing the pilot into the tiny world of an instrument panel and his own frozen feet.

As the glider continues to rise past 40,000 ft it is easy for awareness to decline, for cold and lack of oxygen to take over at a time when it is essential that action must soon be taken, and that decisions must be right, for the wave may go on up to 50,000 or 60,000 ft, and only a needle on a dial can tell the pilot that now he must break away, now he must fly out of the wave into the down-current, and before it is too late, return to the warmth, and the thick air below.

Flying high in the big waves of the world is exciting in a different way to soaring far across country. Both have their own intellectual challenge, and their own delights, but flying to great heights makes an additional physical demand on the challenger, and for the pilot who explores the dark sky alone, 8 miles above the earth, there is a special satisfaction.

The present world's absolute altitude record for gliders is 46,267 ft, held by Paul Bikle of the United States in a Schweizer 1-23E from Mojave in California, 150 miles from Bishop.

Bikle was equipped with a low-pressure oxygen system, with a pressure demand mask, but had no pressure suit. From tests in decompression chambers he knew that he could remain competent at high altitudes. On 25 February 1963 he was towed off at 1455 hrs and promptly sank to within 1,500 ft of the ground. Then he saw sand blowing from a dry lake being drawn up into the air. Bikle flew over to it, and soon found strong lift. By the time he had reached 25,000 ft he was above the huge lenticular cloud, but could only see a gleam of sunshine through the frost-covered canopy. He was now rising at a vertical rate of up to 2,000 ft/min. (nearly 25 m.p.h.), and found that by heading into the wind at between 50–60 m.p.h. he could maintain his position in the wave. After a while the rate of climb slackened, but at 43,000 ft it started once again to increase. When he had passed 46,000 ft above sea-level, and was still going up, Bikle decided that this was enough. The temperature was –65° C, colder than it is ever likely to be in the high Alps on a winter night. So Bikle opened his air brakes, flew back into the down-going part of the wave, and 2 hr 10 min. after take-off landed back at Mojave.

Far on the other side of the world, in the comparatively small country of New Zealand, there is also a big wave system. It is of such magnitude, that on occasions it overwhelms almost the whole of the two little islands that bear it.

In a westerly wind, millions of tons of air from 1,000 miles of sea hits the mountains of the Southern Alps, and is forced upwards. This affects the following air well out to sea, and this air tends to flow up over the air which has already reached the ramparts of the land. Beyond the high crest this air pours earthwards again, and in doing so, sets up a powerful and extensive wave system. The New Zealanders began tentatively to explore the air in the early 1950s, whenever the magnificent cloud of the North-West Arch appeared in the sky. The first flights, mostly by Dick Georgeson, and often in school gliders, slowly pushed the heights they were able to obtain from 7,000 ft up to 22,000 ft. But as Georgeson and others grew to understand their massive wave system better, they discovered that as well as gaining vast heights, they could use it to fly cross-country, even to the extent of crossing the straits between North and South Islands; instead of using only thermals, they would fly on wave. It would need a different technique but this was a matter of flying and learning, of taming the waterfall of air.

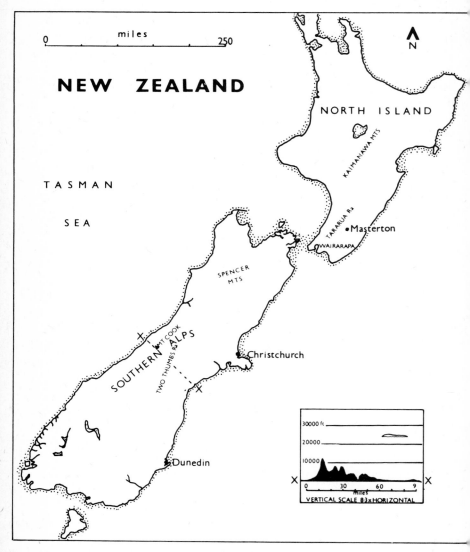

Fig. 29. New Zealand: the country of the big waves

198

Since Christmas 1957, meetings have been held at Wairarapa, 30 miles east of Wellington, and large numbers of exploratory flights made. Cross-country flights are, of course, flown at considerable heights, with oxygen as a necessity, but with the difference that big distances can be done at high speeds. Because the air high up is thin, the actual true airspeed will be increased. For example, at a height of about 40,000 ft, the true airspeed is double the indicated speed. When the glider departs from the wave lift, and flies downwind, its speed over the ground will be supplemented by the wind speed. This may be anything from 60–100 m.p.h. or more. In such circumstances, if a glider flies downwind at 100 m.p.h. indicated, at 40,000 ft, with a wind on its tail of 100 m.p.h. it will be actually travelling over the ground at 300 m.p.h.

In October 1957 Keith Wakeman flew 270 miles from South to North Island, and averaged 95 m.p.h. At Christmas the same year, Gordon Hookings flew 329 miles using both wave and thermal, reaching 23,000 ft. He had worked out that the only way to get his 500 km. Diamond 'C' in such a narrow country was to fly across wind along the wave for perhaps 80 miles or so, then return along this track, and finally set off in the original direction, sliding along the wave until it disappeared. After this he would hope to pick up thermals until the day ended. He succeeded, although when he took off he was quite unprepared for the flight he hoped to make:

On the morning of Friday, 13th December, I failed dismally to recognise that the big day had arrived. I considered that such clouds as appeared overhead from time to time were normal convection cumulus, and the fact that none appeared further to the west than about 2 miles from Masterton I attributed to the probable existence of an extensive area of down-draughts in the lee of the mountains. What must have been the cap cloud, I told myself was orographic cumulus. Consequently after extremely leisurely preparation for flight, I took off at 1130 for a pre-luncheon thermal reconnaissance. I released at a rather stupid 1,000 ft and dropped to 800 ft before centring on a strong but narrow thermal.

By 1139 I had reached 3,500 ft and the top of the thermal, so headed upwind. Because of the extremely rough nature of the turbulence, the most sickening I think I have ever encountered in free flight, I began to suspect that waves might be present in spite of the complete absence of any lenticulars up aloft to confirm the suspicion. Sure enough, by 1152 I was at 10,000 ft and hastily dressing myself in a pair of socks over the top of a scarf wrapped around the left foot, and a balaclava wrapped round the right foot. The left sandal would not fit over this unorthodox footwear, so I had to go shoeless, and it later became most surprising what a difference even an open sandal makes to the warmth of one's feet at 20,000 ft. Already I was regretting the folly of not wishing to appear foolish by dressing in sheepskin in midsummer for a short thermal flight!*

Another fine flight was one by Dick Georgeson, who flew 200 miles out-and-return in a Slingsby Skylark, remaining above 20,000 ft the whole way. Invisible from the ground, and over some of the wildest mountain country in the southern hemisphere, he was on oxygen for $4\frac{1}{2}$ hours unbroken time, except for a 30-second tea break!

Three years later, on 15 December 1960, Dick Georgeson took off early in the morning to try to get his 500 km. Diamond. The official observer, Warren Denton, left his sheep-shearing to tow him off, but in just over an hour, Georgeson was back on the ground again.

Just before 2.0 p.m. the weather looked better, and he had another tow; but conditions still seemed marginal. An hour later the glider had only reached a height of 5,000 ft, and was still in more or less the same place in rough air, flying under an overcast sky.

It was growing disappointingly clear that the chances of 500 km. distance was non-existent, when quite suddenly the Skylark flew into weak wave lift, and started to rise gently in smooth air. Georgeson realised that whatever may have happened to prospects for a distance flight, there appeared to be an increasing chance of going very high indeed.

The smooth climb continued to 25,000 ft, still under the high cloud, which was causing a dazzling glare. Fortunately, Georgeson knew the clouds of the great North-West Arch

* From *Sailplane and Gliding*, vol. 9, 1958, no. 2, p. 86.

well enough to realise that he was in the lee of its associated clouds. If he could work his way upwind of the great cloud itself, the lift there would carry him even higher, so he ploughed forward through the massive down-current, and then another area of lift. Quite suddenly he was out in the sunshine on the west side of the Arch, and able to look up at this extraordinary cloud, which stretched so far across the sky, and was 3 miles high.

Georgeson did not want to enter it, but where he expected lift, in the clear air, there was none, so once more he flew back under the cloud to gain more height. Then he flew fast upwind, immediately underneath the base of the monster itself. As, once more, he burst into the clear, clean sunshine, the Skylark began to rise. In silence the little red and white glider flew alongside the cloud wall, which was almost frightening in its sheer magnificence and grandeur. At 30,000 ft the deep blue of the sky contrasted with the white cloud in a purity of colour never possible with mere paint. Far below lay the mountains, flattened by their insignificance, and growing blue-black in the 100-mile shadow of the cloud. At 35,700 ft, Georgeson, still excited by the beauty and unbelievable magnificence of the gigantic cloud which had been forming alone in the sky since the beginning of time, left the wave to return to the shadowy earth far below. At this height he was above the cirrus, and as he sank through streams of this flimsy cloud, ice crystals whispered in with the draughts, until he was covered with a snowy glitter.

He landed on the airfield in the pink evening light and climbed out, stiff, cold and still remote. Denton, and another pilot who had been flying on that day, Westenra, took out a barograph, covered thick in snow, which had ticked on faithfully recording the evidence. He heard that Westenra had not been able to use the wave, because the turbulence had pushed his head through the canopy of his glider.

The evening air was warm and soft, but even an hour later the metal fittings of the glider still gleamed with frost.

During the next ten years the New Zealanders learnt more about the habits of their majestic wave, using it not only for its own challenge but to break distance records. In January 1965 Georgeson raised the world goal and return record to 460 miles in his Slingsby Dart, and in September 1972 to a magnificent 622 miles (1,001 km.) in his new Kestrel 19. This sort of flying needed good organisation and preparation, and was never easy:

I had a slow but steady progress [he recalled] arriving over Lake Coleridge powerhouse at about 15,000 feet at 0905 hours. The wave pattern, although not marked by clouds of any sort, seemed to disappear and eventually I was forced to turn downwind and ended up a little south of Snowdon Station at about 7000 feet. At Snowdon Station lives Lucy Wills, a cousin of Philip Wills. She once drew me a picture of a peculiar cloud which sometimes sat in the vicinity of Mount Hutt and which had a spiral which went up a number of thousand feet and then leant forward into the wind— almost like the top of a witch's hat. I had also seen this cloud once and tried to fly a sailplane in the vicinity, but it was too violent. Today, I struck turbulent, rough lift. Bearing in mind Lucy's picture, I circled and did not bother to treat it as a wave and rose rapidly at over a thousand feet a minute, and as I climbed, the aircraft drifted forward into the wind and eventually ended up at about 15,000 feet some two miles further upwind than I had originally started.

Progress was slow and hard as I continued south in the lee of Mt. Hutt, there not being much in the way of indications even of roll cloud. The process of travelling was that of imagining where the wave might be lying. crabbing along the imaginary wave and if the rate of lift fell off, turning first into the wind, and if it continued to fall off, turning sideways to the wind and drifting back to where one imagined the wave was lying. The process seemed to require continual effort and vigilance and one always appeared to be losing the wave.*

For over 16 years now Bikle's altitude record of February 1961 had stood unchallenged. No one else took on the world's giant waves simply to go as high as possible. The soaring emphasis was towards speed, and still more speed, and the

* From *Soaring*, December 1972.

complication and cost of pressure suits and all the paraphernalia needed to beat Bikle's record was a deterrent in itself. In any case the astronauts and cosmonauts were collecting the altitude honours, and a mere 9 miles up seemed puny by comparison. Not until 1977 did interest seriously begin to return, mainly at a new soaring site in Colorado, and right under the tertiary wave emanating from the Indian Peaks range. Within months five flights to over 40,000 ft had been made, and on one of them Jim Munn was still climbing at 45,000 ft A.S.L., but did not think it was wise to continue. There were now eyes on the 10-mile-high barrier.

But not all wave flying is done to beat records. In many countries, in the Alps, the Tatras, and in Iceland there are wave systems with their own challenge and special beauty, explored by club pilots. In Scotland, Pam Davis reached 19,000 ft on a cold March day to gain Diamond Height:

All the advice everyone has given me filters into my mind and I look around for the lenticular cloud. Sure enough there it is alongside me.

So I begin to tack into wind up and down the long soft white cloud. Every movement is made as gently as possible. This is a tender way of flying, a seeking and searching, slowly and cautiously feeling for the best lift. Along the cloud, a slow turn as the lift falls off, back again, another turn and always going up. The ground gradually recedes but not noticeably, not frighteningly. As I get higher I begin to look around. Away to the west the gorgeous Cairngorm mountains covered with snow, gleaming so dazzlingly, an unforgettable sight. To the east the city of Aberdeen and the sea beyond. Below me there are two little lochs and the bowl of Tarland, with its lovely flat fields to land in, and just nestling in the bend of the river Dee lies the site I have left and to which I must return. The higher I go more and more comes into view; it seems that the world is stretched out around me. I am alone in the sky in my safe little glider going upwards, alone with the sun warming one side of the cockpit, and ice crystals forming on the other. There is no taste, no smell from my switched on oxygen, but my faith in the system is absolute. The glider is flying normally, but there is this magic feeling of stillness and quiet.

As I reach the top of my cloud, away to the west I can see other lenticulars forming and reforming, so, taking my courage in both hands I shoot across the clear gap. The variometers go quiet and the altimeter goes down, down, down. Will there be lift where I expect it? The anxiety and apprehension of leaving my safe patch of lift for the unknown give way to relief and enormous satisfaction as the variometer sings again. I've made it. . . .

After several hours I realise that it is getting late as I watch the full glory of the setting sun. The great ball goes down the sky and I am above it, but the ground is darkening below and I think that this is possibly the greatest moment that I will ever experience in flying. A moment up there alone in the evening light, a moment that makes all my training worthwhile. I know now what the poet meant when he wrote:

> Above the clouds the airman finds his peace
> Where he can call the boundless skies his own.

Chapter Twenty-two

A THOUSAND KILOMETRES

Today most soaring flights, either in competitions or just for fun, are over a pre-determined course, or as far over it as the weather holds out, or the pilot continues to make no wrong decisions.

Distance-flying has not been forgotten, it is simply that flying to some point and returning home again is a more practical use of the time available, and less expensive in terms of possible retrieves. But the hope of flying further than ever before is still there, waiting for an opportunity to occur. To many, flying for hundreds of miles whilst navigating over unknown country is the ultimate in gliding. Long beforehand there is an idea slowly formulated into a plan. Then the day comes, often unexpectedly; there is panic to get ready, to get into the air. The moment of release from the aero-tow on such a day is like stepping into a different world.

Between 9 and 10 in the morning, in the cool air, the lift is rare and weak, and it is prudent to fly with care, sniffing out the thermals and exploring the feel of the day. Too much boldness at this moment could spoil everything, for the glider can be so quickly back on the ground. As the sun climbs slowly up the sky, its warmth creating strong thermals and a million cloud castles, it is possible to race on fast to try to get 60 or 70 or even 80 miles into each of the best hours of the day—usually between 2 and 4 o'clock. All the time while flying the glider with great care, one must work out speeds, calculate averages, measure what is left to do—and possibly eat something. All too soon, the sun once more begins its downward slide and the air quietens, although the clouds stay big. It is a warning that the life of the thermals is now limited and they will weaken, and then die. With regret one must start being careful once more, careful to stay high so as to use the lift a mile above the earth, which still exists when no more thermals leave the ground. It is a time of hanging on to every ripple that supports the glider, while gently drifting on, hoping that each thermal will not be the last. And yet, one knows when this moment comes; from feeling alive and bubbling, however gently, the air suddenly sighs and the lift is quite gone. From now on, flying in air like silk, the last miles can come only from the sheer performance of the glider, and the accurate lightness with which it is controlled. Perhaps by now the sun will have left the deep valleys, and the higher fields and towns have a golden look. The pilot now knows exactly how many more miles he can go. Ahead he can see the village, or the farm, where the glider will come to rest. He has never been there, nor knows a soul, but within minutes he will be their uninvited guest.

The first really long flight that a pilot is likely to achieve is that for his Diamond distance, 500 km. (311 miles). But in small countries like Britain flights of even this length are difficult. There has never been, therefore, the challenge which has existed in bigger countries of trying to fly 1,000 km. (625 miles) in a glider.

The first thoughts that such a distance might one day be possible, came when the Russian pilot Olga Klepikova flew 749 km. (465 miles) in 1939, but were promptly overwhelmed by the war, and forgotten for almost twelve years. Then in 1951, a young American called Dick Johnson beat this record with a flight of 861 km. (535 miles), and it was realised that 1,000 km. was no longer an idea, but could be achieved.

Johnson had had his eye on the distance record for some time, and intended to start from Odessa, Texas, to fly north-wards as far as he possibly could over the great central plain of the United States. Here was wide country, with almost ideal weather: in summer the cloud base might go as high as 15,000 ft, with perfect cumulus stretching across the sky.

On 8 August 1951 there was a good southerly wind of

about 20 m.p.h., but thermals did not materialise as early as hoped, and it was 1030 hrs before Johnson could start on his way. At 1915 hrs, after 8¾ hours of concentration, he landed at Salina, Kansas. The glider he flew was the RJ5, a fast experimental aircraft that he had designed and built himself. He knew that to beat the record at all, he could not afford to waste a single minute, and the loss of the best part of an hour's soaring in the morning must have been infuriating. Once on his way, however, he managed to work up his speed, so that by alternately circling, and racing on straight at up to 80 m.p.h., he was able to average just over 60 m.p.h. for the whole flight. He used thirty-seven thermals, and nibbled at several others, which he quickly discarded as useless. His total circling time was 3 hr 6 min., during which he climbed in lift a total of 63,300 ft, which gave him an average rate of climb of 342 ft/min. The distance: 861 km. (535.5 miles).

These figures showed that if Johnson had been able to start soaring at 0930 hrs, as he had hoped, and gone on until 2000 hrs, which would not have been unusual, the 1,000 km. could have been achieved. It did not need a better design of glider, a finer pilot, nor a stronger wind. All that was needed now was the opportunity, that often unexpected moment in time when all parts of the whole suddenly come together.

It was not, of course, only in America that 1,000 km. plans were being made. The Poles had drawn a line from the west of their country to Kiev. This meant crossing into Russia, but glider pilots know each other all over the world, and the barrier although difficult was not insuperable. On several occasions pilots arrived near the frontier having flown 600 km., but calculated that there was not enough time left in the day to make the likelihood of 1,000 km. worth the complications of crossing. This would be a fascinating flight, first over the vast green plain of eastern Europe to the Pripet Marshes of school geography, and on through the hot afternoon, finally seeing the ancient city emerge imperceptibly from the distance.

Further west in Europe, other lines were drawn on other

maps: from north France towards Spain, or eastwards into Germany gave possibilities, but an even greater chance existed in flying from Germany across France, using the north-easter on the fringe of a big anticyclone.

In Australia and South Africa long enough distances existed, but the problem was complicated by empty desert, or inhospitable bush. Johnson's record was not beaten until June 1963, when three Germans flew 875 km. (544 miles). They had taken off neither with the intention of beating any records, nor of flying together. On 2 June the easterly winds were too strong for flying round a triangle, so pilots at the gliding clubs at Teck and Hahnweide, near Stuttgart, declared goals some 500 km. away in the area of Paris.

The first to take off was Karl Betzler, who had a winch launch at 0930 hrs, in an attempt to reach Beynes, 520 km. to the west beyond Paris. Rudi Lindner, in the Phönix that he had built himself, had an aero-tow from Hahnweide at 1000 hrs, to try to reach Bordeaux, on a line which would take him well to the south of Betzler. The third to go, Otto Schauble, had a winch launch also from Hahnweide at about the same time, declaring Tours, 680 km. away. Over 250 other pilots from Germany set off towards France to use the wonderful weather offered in the forecast.

But it was not as easy as it seemed. In the Vosges mountains Schauble was down to within 500 ft of the ground, and had to soar on a slope to keep himself airborne at all. By 1040 hrs. Betzler had reached Strasbourg, and was in a thermal over the cathedral. But he also had trouble getting through the Vosges.

The gliders had radio, and from the chatter of all the pilots flying came discouraging comments from some who could find no more lift and were having to land. West of the mountains, however, the weather cleared, and some seven or eight pilots were left to start working their way slowly across central France, checking on their maps the names of Epinal, Chaumont and Montargis. As the afternoon wore on the voices over the radio grew fewer as one glider after another sank to earth. By 1700 hrs, only Betzler, Schauble, Lindner and a pilot called Röhm, who was high in a thundercloud, were left. From the clarity of the reception, it was clear that the gliders were not far apart, and on giving their positions, three of the pilots discovered that they were all using the same thunderstorm, some 60 km. west of Orleans.

The possibility of beating the record now existed, and the three realising this decided to continue the flight as a team. Quite soon they could see each other, and flew on along the storm front close together, searching out the best lift from the confused mass of cloud.

Slowly, over the great watershed of the Loire, they approached the Atlantic Ocean. As they neared the sea the weather worsened, with poor visibility and cloud which grew steadily lower. The wind swung round from east to west, and rain showers became frequent. Then quite suddenly through the murk they saw water below. They had reached the coast, at the mouth of the Loire. Further distance was possible by flying parallel to the coast N.W. towards Brest, but a raging thunderstorm in their path decided them, and they went in to land on the airfield at St Nazaire. So that they would share the record, Betzler landed on the near side of the airfield, in order to cancel out the slightly greater distance he had flown from his starting point, compared to Schauble and Linder.

Of all the gliders which flew into France from Germany on this Whit Sunday the record had been broken by three.

The 1,000 km. was still the challenge, but now there was only another 78 miles to go, and the pace was getting hotter. Instead of another twelve years it was less than two months later that the distance record was beaten again, but since the pilot did not carry a recording barograph the flight could not be recognised. Far from the sea, this flight started in Sun Valley, California, and went almost 900 km. (557 miles) to the N.E., to Swift Current, Saskatchewan. The pilot was Paul Bikle, the glider a small 15-metre span Prue Standard, and the date 24 July 1963:

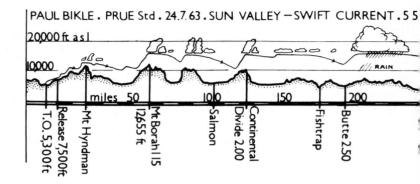

PAUL BIKLE . PRUE Std . 24.7.63 . SUN VALLEY −SWIFT CURRENT . 5 5

20000 ft a s l

10000

RAIN

miles 50   100   150   200

T.O. 5,300ft
Release 7,500ft
Mt Hyndman
Mt Borah II 5
12,655 ft
Salmon
Continental
Divide 2.00
Fishtrap
Butte 2.50

I selected a take-off time shortly after noon and left to nurse my cold while John and Alan made the sailplane ready. Actually, I felt more like going to bed than flying, particularly as I could only see a flight of, perhaps, 200 miles across 12,000-ft mountains with a good chance of landing in isolated terrain with a long and difficult retrieve. This is rough country; the airport is at 5,300 ft and the valleys along the course are at 6,000 ft or higher. The weather information indicated to me that I should head north over the Continental Divide and across 300 miles of mountains, trying to stay west of the thunderstorms associated with the front.

At this point my primary concern was one of seeing that adequate clothing, food and water were placed in the sailplane. Also placed aboard was a bag of cough syrup, cold tablets and nose drops, as well as maps covering the area some 400 miles to the north and east. It never occurred to me to include a barograph. Actually, I have not carried a barograph for years except on record attempts (and then I carry two) because I had long ago achieved all of my F.A.I. badge flights. Certainly, this day did not look like a record-breaker to me.

Shortly after 1100 hrs, small Cu. began to form over the airport. I changed my take-off to 1152 hrs and had my crew bring the Prue Standard N9730Z, up to the take-off line. Actual take-off was at 1157 hrs and release was at 1205 hrs over the ridge about 3 miles south of the Hailey Airport near Bellevue. Release altitude was 7,500 ft. Things went well right from the beginning as I worked to the top of the 8,000-ft mountain, picked up a thermal and climbed to 10,000 ft. Immediately heading for the higher mountains I was soon at the 12,000 ft cloud base working my way past 12,000 ft

210

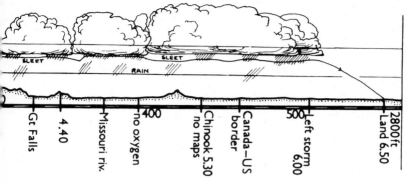

Fig. 30. Paul Bikle's unofficial World Distance Record flight

Mt Hyndman some 18 miles out on course. As the air poured over
the mountain crests through the small gap between the top of the
lift and the crest of the ridges, the sailplane was tossed almost out
of control. On the lee side, vicious down-currents dropped me
hundreds of feet at a time.

For a time it appeared that I would never reach the next valley
and the Twin Bridges airstrip in the pass beyond Mt Hyndman
might well mark the end of the flight. Over the mountains to the
north, a tight, vicious thermal carried me back to 11,000 ft and I
was assured of at least reaching the next valley. Again, strong
down, and I was soon down to 10,000 ft; 4,000 above the valley
floor. But ahead were large cumulus building high over Mt Borah,
the highest peak in Idaho. The lift was entered 5 miles before I
reached the mountains. Gaining a few thousand feet here, I then
moved forward over the face of the mountains and circled in strong
1,500 ft/min. lift to over 16,000 ft. Bob Moore had just left the
clouds above me in his 1-21. This was more like it. Cloud bases
were at least 3,000 ft higher than anticipated and cumulus dotted
the area to the north and east.

It was 1.15 p.m. Moving north along the ridge at high speed I
again encountered sufficient turbulence to require full control
deflections to remain upright. The lift appeared to be more upwind
of the mountains; over the mountains and in the lee, the air was
rough with plenty of down.

Soon the Salmon river was reached. Turning east across the next
valley, strong lift again took me to cloud base as I reached the
mountains south of Salmon. Another dash north along the mountains, then east across the next wide valley, and I am high over

211

the Continental Divide about 15 miles north-east of Salmon. It is now 2 p.m.; just 65 miles in the last 45 minutes.

My plan had been to press on north from here towards Missoula. There was no landing field for 59 miles in this direction. Of even greater concern, it appeared that the clouds also stopped further north. To the east the cumulus were still scattered across the sky but isolated thunderstorms were already in evidence as it had been forecast for that area.*

Ahead there was a large storm, and in the absence of other good lift Bikle used it, reaching 16,500 ft in sleet. He flew at 100 m.p.h. to avoid being drawn up into cloud. Some 50-odd miles ahead was another even larger storm, and as there was nothing good in between Bikle went for it, arriving in its lift, and soon reaching base at 17,000 ft. The storm stretched as far as the horizon to the north and west but was growing on its eastern edge:

I followed this to the north and then to the east. Oxygen was getting low so I began to ration myself. It was 4.40 and I was over a small airport about 40 miles east of Great Falls. Soon I crossed the Missouri river and again was out over country with no roads or people. The storm continued to build but now to the north and I swung north, still under the dark leading edge, flying between 15,000 and 17,000 ft at airspeeds between 70 and 100 m.p.h. as the lift varied in strength. Great clouds of dust were blowing along the ground below, both from the east and west, and then lifting into the storm above. To the west the base of the storm dropped to a much lower altitude, rain and lightning obscured the ground. I was flying through intermittent sleet and rain. The freezing level was right at 15,000 ft.

Now I was completely out of oxygen so generally limited my altitude to 15,000 ft. I had also flown beyond my sectional charts back by the Missouri river but I did have a road map of the Western U.S. which extended a bit further. My north heading was again bringing me back to populated areas. The mountains below turned to flat land, and dirt roads appeared.*

At about this time Bikle realised that there was a possibility of exceeding the world record, and perhaps even the 1,000 km. He began to curse himself for bringing no barograph. Mile

* From *Soaring* (U.S.A.), September 1963, p. 5.

33 (a) Lenticular clouds over St Auban in the French Alps
    (b) New Zealand, waiting to take off for a wave flight

34 (a) (b) Dick Georgeson flying his Skylark 3 seven miles high, close to the lenticular cloud of the N.W. Arch in New Zealand

35 (a) Bill Ivans, U.S.A., who beat the World Altitude Record in 1950 in a
Schweizer 1-23; (b) Paul Bikle, holder of the World Altitude Record, in his
Prue

36 Dick Georgeson soaring his Eagle in the Southern Alps

after mile the storm continued, its powerful lift forcing him to fly continuously at 100 m.p.h. to keep out of it:

Flying on and on for almost another hour in this dream-like situation it was obvious that the border had been crossed and that the flight must have extended many miles into Canada. I was in no mood to press on when the terrain below changed from open fields to low, wooded hills. Although it was only 6 p.m., the light was fading rapidly and the visibility was quite restricted. Never having flown over this country before, it was my rather provincial impression that all civilisation in Canada lay in a relatively narrow band just north of the border. Still at 15,000 ft the sailplane was turned away from the storm and headed north-east along the most northerly fields in sight. Fifty minutes later, a landing was made in a plowed field beside a highway and a railroad. This last glide added only a minimum distance as the wind was blowing out of the east into the storm at 35 to 40 knots.

The high surface wind caused immediate concern for the safety of the sailplane after landing. The storm was an awesome sight stretching from the southern horizon to the northern horizon as it moved slowly east. Sharply defined lips or rolls extended ahead of the base and the whole mass of clouds rose to great heights. Leaving the sailplane, I ran out to the highway and tried to flag down a passing motorist. After seven cars drove by at high speed, the eighth stopped only because I stood in the middle of Trans-Canada Highway No. 1. I tried to explain that I had landed a sailplane in a field just over the hill by the road and needed help in making it secure before the storm struck.

Bikle was retrieved by his crew of two who drove the car and trailer 930 miles in 22 hours, crossing the Canadian border overnight. All the driving was done by his son John aged nineteen, and the navigation by his son Alan, aged ten.

Almost exactly a year after this flight of Bikle's, on 24 July 1964 another attempt was made on the 1,000 km. by another American, Al Parker.

Parker was not a person to let opportunities slip by; a year previously he had beaten the world goal-flight record with a flight of 487 miles. His glider was the elegant Sisu, with which he felt nothing was impossible, and of which he once wrote: 'The Sisu N-1100Z would gain back in one 360 degree chandelle the altitude lost at 120 m.p.h. I.A.S. between cumulus, which were about 20 miles apart. This breath-taking performance went to my head and I almost flew into the ground near Sitka, Kansas, but luck did not desert me and from 1,200 ft I climbed back in a real hurry to 10,500 ft.'

On 24 July Al Parker took off from Odessa, Texas, at 0945 hrs, having declared a goal of 1,013 km. (630 miles) to try to regain the record recently taken from him by Wally Scott. Like Johnson he flew north with a tail wind of 20 m.p.h. Steadily in the warming sun the base of the cumulus rose to 10,000 ft, and the thermals were strong enough to let him fly between them at over 100 m.p.h. Late in the afternoon the fine cumulus grew into thunderheads, which Parker used, but they barred him from his original goal. At 2015 hrs, 10½ hours after the take-off, he landed at Kimball, Nebraska. He was 1,036 km. (633 miles) from Odessa; the magic distance had been achieved.

Only a little over thirty years before, in 1930, Wolf Hirth had circled with a hawk in his Musterle and shown that it was possible to fly across country without an engine. In the year that Parker was born, the world gliding record was less than one kilometre. Now a glider had flown a distance more than half the way from Mexico to Canada, more than the distance from London to Turin, using only the clouds, the wind and the warmth of the sun.

Chapter Twenty-three

A THOUSAND MILES

It did not take long for the magic of Parker's flight to fade. Like the 4-minute mile, once it had been achieved by one human, others could more easily follow. Pilots everywhere looked at their maps once more, drew long tenuous lines and dreamed of landing at Kiev from Leszno, or Biarritz from Belgium. For many the problem was not one of crossing land frontiers, but of being able to use the 'grain' of the weather, particularly in a westerly direction; by flying the same way as the sun the thermal day would be lengthened by perhaps an hour, or another 100 km. Europe was better for this than the United States, because anticyclonic north-easterlies blowing across West Germany and France could provide both good thermals and excellent terrain. In the U.S.A. and Australia few good days came on a large-scale easterly wind, so although thermals might be stronger and cloudbase high, there was no free ride. But it was not of course necessary to do your 1,000 km. in a straight line. The fact that it had been done this way merely opened the way to new challenges, such as goal-and-return or triangles—where little wind was a positive benefit if you could fly really fast.

But although now known to be possible there was no repeat performance for six years. This time it was less far than Parker's distance,* but it was a goal flight and it was in Europe; using a northeaster flowing round an anticyclone centred over Southern Scandinavia. On 4 June 1970 Hans Werner-Grosse flew 1,032 km. from his home at Lubeck to Angers, in France, just a few days before leaving for Marfa to take second place in the World Championships Open Class.

* Parker's flight was finally homologated at 1041.52 km.

His 1,000-km. eminence did not last long. Within a month of the end of the Marfa event two Americans, Wally Scott and Ben Greene, in two ASW-12s, jointly beat Parker's distance record with 1,153 km. from Odessa, Texas, northwards to Columbus, Nebraska. This lasted just two years when Grosse took it back again; in Europe on 25 April 1972.

This time the anticyclone was centred over Northern Ireland with cumulus base expected at over 6,000 ft and strong thermals. Grosse took off from Lubeck at 0820, having declared Nantes, France, as his 1,100 km. distant goal. Ten minutes later another German pilot, Klaus Tesch, left Boberg, 50 km. further to the S.W. with the idea of beating Grosse's two-year-old goal record. He had declared Ancenis, near Nantes, a distance of 1,050 km. being unaware of his rival's longer declared distance. Shortly after setting course the two heard each other on the radio and discovered that they had a contest on their hands. Slowly the weather strengthened from 4/8 cumulus at 2,400 ft with light snow showers to 5,000 ft in the Rhineland and only 1/8 cu. The wind had shifted from N. through E. and back to N.E. where it settled, blowing at about 30 knots. The two pilots kept radio contact until west of Paris, when Tesch called that he would be able to reach his goal. Grosse's goal was now also possible, but conditions were still good enough to go on and try for the pure distance—provided that he could work across wind enough to keep inland from the coast. At 1945, after nearly 11½ hrs in the air and 12 min. before sunset Grosse found one more thermal. It took him to the airport at Biarritz with 2,000 ft in hand, but as it was now after eight in the evening and growing dark he landed. His distance was 1,460 km.; but his wife, Karin, had to drive 2,250 km. with the trailer to reach him.

With straight distance now approaching 1,500 km. it was time to try something different—like the goal-and-return record, still standing at less than the tempting 1,000.

It was back in 1968 when Karl Striedeck started to seriously explore the Appalachian mountain chain for distance flying. Ridge lift extended the soaring season with thermals unessen-

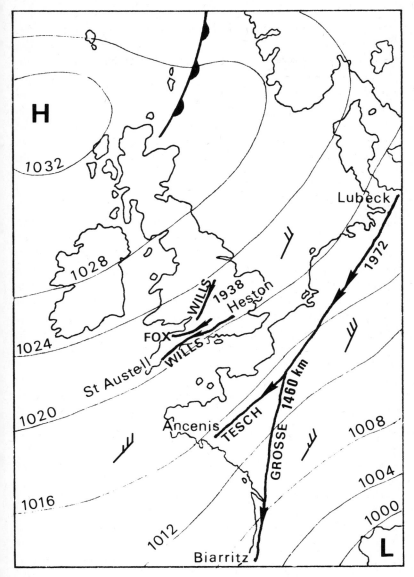

FIG. 31. The north-easterly weather situation in which Philip Wills broke the British Distance Record in 1938, and the 1,000-km. flights which were made in the 1970s

tial, and the flying could be done with inexpensive gliders. In March that year Striedeck startled the traditional gliding world with a world goal and return of 476 miles (766 km.) in a light Ka-8 trainer. But on the other side of the world the New Zealanders had their Southern Alps with its wave system, and it was Dick Georgeson's goal-and-return record of 460 miles in a Slingsby Dart on 6 January 1965 that Striedeck had taken. Now Georgeson aimed to get it back. But before he could do so Bobby Clifford in South Africa and Wally Scott in Texas had pushed the record to 488 miles (786 km.) and 534 miles (860 km.) on conventional thermals, and Striedeck had taken it once more on the ridge in cold November, pushing it to 913.3 km. in his new ASW-15. This now gave Georgeson a double challenge—the record and 1,000 km.

On 7 September 1972, now with a 19-metre Kestrel, Georgeson set off from Hanmer in South Island with Mossburn to the south as his turn point. It would not only be a long flight in distance but in hours, and the last miles were beset with difficulties. Bruce Drake and Helen Georgeson had taken off in a Cherokee to try to find him in the mountains in approaching darkness, as they reckoned he would be in need of help:

The wave system appeared to have completely disappeared; there was no evidence of wave, nor was the blue wave which I had been following for some time providing lift any further. I could hear Christchurch radar giving Bruce Drake his headings to pick me up and I was amazed how long it took him to catch me. However, he was under the impression that I was a good deal higher than I was. When he finally picked me up, I was down to 7000 feet down-wind of Hanmer and sinking at 1000 fpm. Things now looked bleak. It was almost the time to be looking for a safe paddock and landing while there was sufficient light. The only thing left to do was to turn downwind and hope that a lee wave existed some 20 miles downwind of the ranges.

Bruce headed for the Hurunui River, an area where Bruce had previously found wave. I was down to 4000 feet when he called back that the wave was working. I was not far behind him and soon I was in it, climbing. At 8000 feet I decided I could not afford

218

37 Designers as pilots: (a) Paul Bikle flying the T-6 he designed; (b) Ernst Haase, co-designer of the HKS series and winner of the Open Class in 1958; (c) Klaus Holighaus, designer of the Nimbus and holder of the 100-km. Triangle Speed Record of 159.24 km./h. in 1973

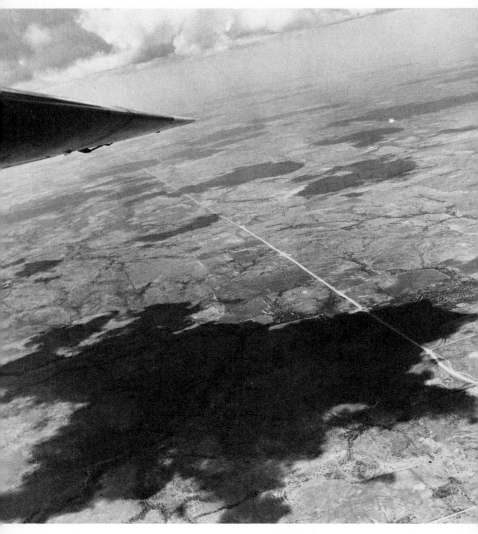

38 The flat plain of S.W. Texas where cumulus shadows dapple the arid ground from cloudbase at 14,000 ft. The country of the 1970 Championships

to wait any longer due to the approaching darkness, and at 1610 I started the final glide into Hanmer. Bruce had found a track in that gave reduced sink, and was desperately searching for lift further upwind. He had his nav lights on and it was easy to pick him up. The reduced sink held well and I was able to box along at about 80 to 85 knots. However, I was not at all confident that I had enough height to get through the gorge, which was probably about half a dozen miles long, into Hanmer. Bruce then called up to say the Cherokee was losing altitude fast and that there was heavy down toward the gorge. I had no option but to continue. I felt the light was not good to attempt a landing and the point-of-no-return had been reached.

Bruce called to say he had found a rotor, that it was very rough, and that it was giving tremendous lift. Shortly afterwards, however, he said it had broken up and he had lost it. I reminded him that if this sink continued, which had suddenly gone up to 1000 fpm, I would be in serious trouble. The air became violent and very unpleasant. The sink continued and I was pushing the aircraft along as fast as I dared, somewhere between 90 and 100 knots, to try and get through the down. Down to 2000 feet, or 1000 feet above the valley floor, the light was very poor indeed, and to the west I could no longer clearly see the ridge. And I still had some six miles to go.

I seemed to go on and on and on . . . violent up, violent down . . . the vario going from one extreme to the other. The cameras were all around the cockpit . . . also the maps. I had even lost one mike over my shoulders. The situation was beginning to look a bit sick. I turned east on to the ridge, the violence continued, but the sink stopped. Just then I rounded the corner over the Waiau Bridge, and smooth hill lift ensued and the next minute I was quietly going up. The relief was incredible.

Terry Shannon, my official observer, called on the radio saying to stay where I was until the flare path with cars had been laid out. This gave me the opportunity to tidy up the cockpit in preparation for landing. At 1825 Terry called me and said all was clear. I made a big sweep of the field and came in to a straightforward and easy landing with the wind blowing about 25 knots.*

The distance was 1,002 km. (623 miles), he was in the air for 11 hrs 55 min., and he held the record for just a month.

* From *Soaring*, December 1972.

219

On 7 October Striedeck climbed out of bed at 0500, launching at 0804, a delay caused by drizzle. Heading off along his now familiar ridges he found cloud on the ground at Altoona, so hung about for 35 minutes until it lifted, then at Bedford, less than a quarter of the way to the turn point, there was a 45-minute wait in order to gain enough height to cross a gap. But then it became easier and by 1030 he was into Maryland with cloudbase up to 6,000 ft. The turn point was reached at 1318, and with no problems on the return journey he landed at 1818 with 1,035 km. in his pocket. Two days later, with ridge conditions still good, he set out to beat his own record. This time he not only failed but lost what he already had to Jim Smiley, who had started from the opposite end near the point at which Striedeck had turned. Smiley's distance was 1,056 km. at an average speed of 73 m.p.h. (118 km./h.).

Six days later Striedeck got his record back again with 1,098 km., having set out with Bill Holbrook flying his Libelle 301. It was a difficult flight, as Striedeck reports:

We took off at 0700 with Jeep tows from my wife, and it was soon apparent that the winds weren't as strong as we had hoped for but nevertheless enough to provide 80 to 90-mph cruise speeds. The Altoona gap nearly shot me down, and I dropped my water as I contacted ridge lift near the bottom of the ridge. At Bedford, Bill beat me across the gap by going west and contacting wave action. We met again at Cumberland after both sighting the same golden eagle about six miles west of Bedford.

It was slow going to Petersburg, but we straggled along in weak wave flight and then got going again as the ridge improved. Near Seneca Rocks I blew 20 minutes when I got out of ridge lift and had to make a save. By this time Bill was miles ahead and I wasn't able to catch him again until Tazewell, Virginia.

From there to the turnpoint there was no wind, and we were reduced to using the very poor thermal lift that was available. We only had about 1500 feet of working altitude, and at one point I announced that I was giving up and turning around. However, the thought that Bill was going to the turn for his Diamond distance and therefore had a chance of completing the task, much to my embarrassment, made me change my mind. We both made the turn at about 1315.

Holbrook landed short, though with his 1,000 km. and his eye on a future record. All that winter he planned, aided by Chuck Lindsay of the National Weather Service, and he made his first serious attempt on 19 March. It ended with the Libelle sitting in three inches of snow by the Altoona shopping centre before seven o'clock in the morning. But on 5 May

The alarm clock was set for 0430. When we awoke the wind was blowing about 10 to 15 knots and it was spitting snow, exactly as forecast.

Release was over the east end of runway 27 at 0607. Away I went down Bald Eagle Mountain at 100 knots in comforting bumps about 100 ft above the trees. . . .

I reached Altoona in one hour and flew into a wave to top out

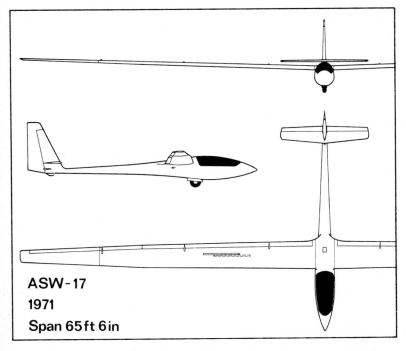

ASW-17
1971
Span 65ft 6in

FIG. 32. The Alexander Schleicher/Waibel-17 had flown over 1,000 km. fourteen times by the end of 1977

at 5,000 ft. I dropped down through the breaks when the wave quit and on to Bedford.

After a couple of turns and a false start the biggest gap in the ridge route was crossed at 0752, not far enough behind schedule to worry about . . .

The turnpoint was made at 12:07 p.m., exactly six hours after release, but four minutes behind the flight-plan ETA. I made three turns over the intersection of US Route 19 and Alternate US 58 at Hansonville where two pictures were taken with each camera, and then I started back to Lock Haven in booming conditions—so booming that I could not get down on the ridge, but stayed from 1000 to 2000 feet above and slowed to the rough-air yellow line of 90 knots.

Holbrook landed at 1803, concerned as an airline pilot with being 4 minutes behind his schedule, but with the record raised to 1,260 km. And he kept it for three years until Striedeck, now with a new ASW-17, and Roy McMaster jointly claimed it back with 1,289 km. on 17 March 1976. This was another difficult flight with both water ballast and drinking water freezing, snow showers, low cloud, and turbulence giving $+5$ and -6 g on their accelerometers.

During these feverish battles for the goal-and-return record Hans Werner-Grosse was considering how to get back his straight goal record which he had lost to Tesch. In April 1974, again in the spring north-easterlies, this time with the High centre over Scotland, he set off from Lubeck for Marmade, France, in his ASW-17. He achieved the 1,231 km. declared and then focused his attention on the still unattained 1,000 km. triangle, for both closed circuit distance, and speed. Unlike straight flights where the wind could provide, free, perhaps 250 km. worth of distance in the 10–11 thermal hours available, a triangle usually loses more from wind than it might gain, so speed, hard-earned from strong thermals—or an extra long day—is essential. Grosse chose June in Finland for his first attempt. Taking off from Nummela, near Helsinki, at 0828 on the 6th he flew the 1,012 triangle in $11\frac{1}{2}$ hours; faster than he expected.

He now held four of the five major world records, all over

39 (a) The Sisu, first glider to fly 1,000 km.; (b) Karl Striedeck, with 2 flights over 1,000 miles and 5 over 1,000 km.; (c) Wally Scott of Texas, with a World Record and 2 1,000-km. flights; (d) Malcolm Jinks (outside cockpit) talks to Ingo Renner; (e) Hans Werner-Grosse, with 3 World Records and 10 1,000-km. flights

40 Variable geometry experiments to increase the speed range: (a) The BJ-4 of South Africa's Pat Beatty showing maximum area; (b) Sigma, the British design which could change its aspect ratio from 36 for fast flight to 26 for circling; (c) Any wing, to be efficient, must be absolutely clean

1,000 km.; but if the big triangle could be achieved in cool Finland, even bigger ones could surely be flown in Australia in those magnificent strong thermals which had given him third place in the previous year at Waikerie. *And* it could all happen during the European winter, allowing him to be back home for the northern summer. So he returned to Waikerie but not immediately to success. Three times he set off and failed, although twice exceeding 1,000 km., but on 6 February his persistence was rewarded. His new record triangle of 1,040 km. was flown at a speed of 111 km./h., and would be hard to beat. It was 9 hrs. 50 min. of well-spent time.

By the end of 1976 thirty-one flights of more than 1,000 km. had been made, but none of the record-breakers could leave it alone. In May, Striedeck had flown 1,616 km. on his beloved turbulent ridge and so been the first to break the 1,000-mile barrier, but it had not been accepted as a record because of incorrect turn-point photography, so a year later in May 1977 he did it again.

January 1977 found Grosse back in Australia once more compulsively after his own triangle record. This time he raised it to 1,063 km. over the desert to the north of Waikerie, having released at 0828; very early for speed flying in thermals. But he was now to soon lose his four-year-old goal record and this time not just to a single pilot. In January 1978 Dick Georgeson, Bruce Drake, and David Speight with a formation of three Nimbus IIs flew 1,254.26 km. from Tower Peak Station in the south of South Island to near the top of North Island in 12 hrs. 20 min.

The 1,000 km. is still a great challenge. In the 14 years since Parker's flight it has been flown thirty-six times, but by only seventeen pilots. Apart from the mundane but essential demands on time and money, the determination, skill, and stamina needed will keep it as one of the pinnacles of achievement for a long time yet.

Chapter Twenty-four

ADD A LITTLE ENGINE

It is not difficult to get the impression that all glider pilots have moved into a mould, with their desires and hopes focused only on more and more speed. Such an impression has been fostered by continuous rounds of competition and championships which have left out of the glare—and the mainstream—those many soaring pilots whose enjoyment lies elsewhere. The motor glider enthusiast is one of these, and he is none the less a true soaring pilot for having a little motor, though still considered by some to be 'cheating' or polluting the purity of 'pure flying'. In the wake of this attitude has come the fear, which time has proved quite groundless, that the motor glider will turn soaring pilots into mere aeroplane drivers. As a result, the motor gliding enthusiast consorts with his own kind and develops his own brand of flying fun, instead of always remaining fully integrated with soaring as a whole—as is the sailor with his auxiliary engine on the sea. Only in training, where time and money can be directly saved, has the motor glider been fully accepted.

The first motor glider was probably the modified FSV-X of the Darmstadt student, Hans Gutermuth, intended for the third glider rally on the Wasserkuppe in 1913. It never took the air with its motor, nor is there evidence that this was ever finally installed. It was flown at the rally as a glider and did badly, because the special strengthening and streamlining that had been built in made it too heavy. And so was discovered, though for many years not fully appreciated, the basic problem of the motor glider; that there was little point in adding the weight of an engine to a poor-performance glider.

In 1924 an attempt was made to include motor gliders in

the Rhön competitions, and several, such as the Roter Vogel, Strolch, and Karl der Grosse of the Darmstadt Academic Group were satisfactorily flown, but enthusiasm was short-lived and not much happened until 1928 when Fritz Stamer, the Wasserkuppe chief, had an 80-second flight in one of Lippisch's earlier creations which was fitted with a rocket. Hissing and smoking it shot Stamer smoothly into the air and promptly blew up, setting the aircraft on fire. Stamer hastily dived back to earth, extricating himself with two large holes in the back of his coat. After this another ten years passed before a more amenable power plant appeared, in the form of the Kroeber M4 engine of 18 h.p. It was installed variously in a Grunau Baby, a Mu 13d, and a Condor, but more importantly in two aircraft specially designed as motor gliders. They were the C 10 of the Chemnitz Akaflieg and Wolf Hirth's Hi 20, the latter having the engine also coupled to the main wheel to aid acceleration. They were defeated not only by the headlong passion for long-distance soaring which consumed those last few years before 1939, but by the war itself.

When peace came the difficulty was just to find a glider to fly, and there was no time to bother with motorised versions. In any case any engines available were more likely to be nearer 1,500 h.p. than 15. But by 1955 there was a little engine: the V.W. of the famous Beetle car. It was too heavy and far from ideal, but enough to help the idea once more on its way. There were other engines too, from motorbikes and chainsaws, that were lighter and smaller, but none warranted the design of a motor glider. Instead they were mounted on a few existing gliders, either conventionally in the nose or on a pylon above the centre section. But the basic problem still existed; gliders still had not that reserve of performance to enable them to carry a motor without ceasing to be effective soaring devices. But, particularly in Germany, the idea would not go away. The mid-1960s produced the Scheibe Motorfalke 2-seater, underpowered by a 20-h.p. Hirth engine—as temperamental as all two-strokes. It was not a very satisfac-tory aircraft, but led directly to the excellent SF-25 Falke,

with a Stamo or Rectimo V.W. conversion, and later to
become the training workhorse of many gliding clubs.
Schleicher followed with the K-14, a pretty single-seater with
a retractable undercarriage and the Hirth engine in the nose,
and this was followed in 1970 by the Scheibe SF-27M, a
Bergfalke-like single-seater with the Hirth engine retractable.
With reasonable performance at last available for soaring
pilots to try out, a more objective assessment was possible.

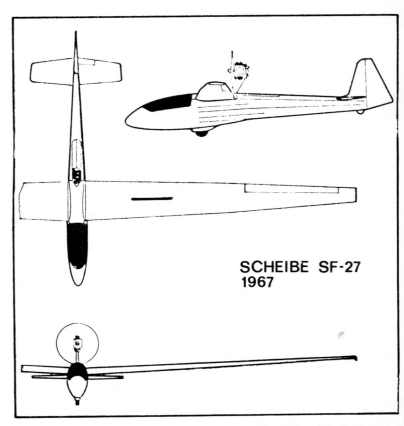

SCHEIBE SF-27
1967

FIG. 33. The Scheibe SF-27M with retractable 26 h.p. Hirth 2-stroke
engine

Many pilots returned to their pure gliders but others found
that, for various individual reasons, the motor glider had
something to offer them. It might be only a matter of time—
the difference between spending a whole day at a distant
gliding club, or having an hour's soaring after work at a nearby
airfield. For others it was the real satisfaction of having a
mechanical device to tinker with—and to be able to fly as
well. The motor glider gave a sense of independence, it
allowed greater freedom of cross-country wandering—because
you could take off again when the weather picked up or after
camping for the night. So at long last it began to collect
adherents. One of these was the American, Jack Lambie:

The idea of flying the condor paths [first] took hold while riding
my bicycle down from the Pinos Condor Observation point. My
brother and I and the rest of the gang had slept out overnight in
the freezing cold of the 8,800 ft peak to watch for condors in the
morning. Now, years later, I climbed out of the morning haze over
Rubidoux's Flabob airport to the quiet putter of the VW engine,
folded up the wheel and headed west to the Sespe Condor Range.
The fog and smog hung thick in the L.A. Basin but it was smooth
flying at 115 mp.h. in the featherweight Fournier.

At the apex of a gulley, Cow Spring, I think, a raven circled. I
glided over with the motor turning slowly to join him where the
sun-warmed rocks were heating the air enough to send a thermal
skyward. It was good lift. 500 FPM is good enough to shut off
the propeller even though the canyon is steep and unlandable. I
had gained 800 feet when the flash of feathers and movement
caught my eye. Could it be? Impatiently I waited for the Fournier
to get around its circle so I could see below again. A giant black
winged creature had moved into our thermal. Its tips were like
black bamboo leaf rakes.

A California Condor, of course. I turned wide to stay out of the
thermal core so it could move up with me and soon we swung in
silent circles a few hundred feet apart. We circled even with one
another for three full turns before he slowly climbed above by
moving his wings forward and pulling up in the better parts of the
thermal. Once from directly behind I could see the multiple
slotted effect of his pinions, then, as I moved alongside, I saw him
look nonchalantly at his fellow air creature. His thick feathered
body seemed hunched over his wings and in general looking

remarkably unlike the golden eagles, turkey vultures and hawks
I have soared with. The condor somehow looks much more archaic
with its long floppy feathers and white-marked wings held straight
out.

Although it has always been one of my treasured dreams to be
in the same thermal with a condor, right now it seemed most
natural and matter of fact. . . . The big bird was so damned
indifferent to me I was disappointed. . . . When about two hundred
feet above me the condor flexed his wings and sailed over to the
north edge of the canyon. I was surprised how much his wings
flopped around in the fast glide. It reminded me of a Rogallo hang
glider. He swung up into the next thermal. By staying behind for
a couple more turns I could be at his level as I caught up with my
30 m.p.h. greater speed. The pattern repeated as we moved down
the valley with the bird moving on ahead, me staying for awhile
and then catching up so we could circle around and around
together.*

Back in Germany a motor glider competition meeting was
being organised by Gerd Stolle at Burg Feuerstein, a curvaceous
hilltop strip among the pine woods and striped fields of the
Frankische Schweitz. Response was encouraging, and from
the experience gained a more formal event was held in June
1971. It attracted ten aircraft, nine of them two-seaters. Two
ex-world soaring champions, Haase and Huth, came to fly,
and although the weather was not very good there was a
determination to make Burg Feuerstein an annual event. By
1972 there were thirty-two entrants divided into two performance groups and further subdivided into single- and two-
seaters. Aircraft ranged from the production Falke and
Fournier RF-3 to a Swiss Diamant glider with a Microturbo
Eclair jet, and a standard Ka-8 fitted with two minute and
unacceptably noisy Stihl chainsaw engines. With such a mixed
bag competition was somewhat uneven, but Burg Feuerstein
was not, and never intended to be, a mere copy of gliding
contests. It was also a meet, a get-together, for the exchange of
ideas and for marvellous engine-tinkering sessions in sunshine
and beautiful surroundings. Nearby was the castle, converted

* From *Motor Gliding.*

to a hostel, where everyone could stay at no great expense. By 1978 Burg Feuerstein had gone international, attracting entries from the U.S.A., U.K., Austria, Switzerland and Denmark, and with three classes. Scoring was simple with time penalties on use of the engine. So diffidently, although not always quietly, the motor glider came to stay. The new fibreglass Nimbus and Pik-20E with cleanly retracting engines lose little of their soaring performance and offer greater opportunities to explore the sky. But the disciplines demanded from the pure glider pilot are not lessened, as Steve Dupont found out. He once tried for his diamond distance in a homebuilt motorsoarer, but when crossing the mountains thermals became erratic:

The moment of truth comes even in a motor sailplane and the time had come to admit it and to abandon my Diamond for another day, to fire up my vitamin capsule that quietly waited under the flush doors of the fuselage and go home. I was circling in barely zero sink, violently rough, occasionally flying into the narrow lift, then out again. I was turning very tight, in seventeen seconds. I could tell by the altimeter that I was hardly holding my own, the variometer zero having drifted and it being impossible to be sure from that instrument. The airspeed needle was all over the panel in the turbulent air. I speeded up and steepened my bank.

The crucial moment was now and I cranked the life-giving little crank six times to extend my folding motor; ugh! Like pulling the spoilers on! My speed fell off and the sink increased. I had to push the nose down to keep the speed up safely above stall in this tight bank and violently rough air. I pulled the choke, grasped the starter rope and enforcing discipline upon myself, counted out eight careful pulls over compression still thermalling as best I could in that narrow chimney of rising air. I opened the throttle one-third, closed the choke, snapped the ignition switch and hit the starter switch. The little jewel barely turned over! It slowly carried over compression, helped by the air dragging the propeller, hanging up on each compression stroke, then jumping around against the next stroke, but it didn't fire! Oh, for that twenty minutes of climb back at Truckee-Tahoe that would have put new life in my battery! The battery withdrew from the present struggle. I grabbed the recoil starter handle for a hand start. It must be pulled with two hands to properly spin the little engine. I held the stick between my knees and yanked for all I was worth, pulling the handle diagonally across the cockpit. The button-strap of my sleeve caught the joy-stick and the *Motosoarer* did part of a snap roll! I was terrified of the low altitude, the rocks and the near disaster. I straightened out and back into the tight circles, sinking badly because of the drag of the stopped propeller and the motor. Again I yanked. I lost the thermal and again the motor didn't even fire. I nearly stalled the sailplane and then got back into the circle still sinking. I recentered the squirming thermal, my heart beating as if it would pop out through my jacket. The rocks were so close I could smell them. I must get rid of the drag of this engine and propeller and try to thermal out of here. Carefully trying to hold the center of the lift, I pulled the propeller vertical with the hand starter, set the propeller brake, reached for and turned the little crank six times and the engine slid back into the fuselage. The drag of it gone, the ship felt lighter and I recentered the narrow column of rising air that was my life.

I reached for the fuel valve to shut it—to turn it—to turn it off—the fuel valve—*the fuel valve is already off*! I'd forgotten to turn on the fuel! Well, no time now to go through the routine all over again! I've only one chance left, to rely upon thermalling out or be dashed to pieces amongst those damnable devil's clinkers!*

Although the motor glider has been in existence almost as long as the soaring glider it has remained only a small part of the whole. Glider performance is now more than adequate to carry the extra weight, and there is increasing interest in the production of small, lightweight, and quieter motors, but having a little engine is still regarded by many glider pilots as polluting the purity of the sport. Certainly it can make a difference to the way in which a pilot flies, but it can also increase the amount of flying he gets. Outside gliding championships and record attempts the motor glider is just another means of exploring the air.

* From *Motor Gliding*, October 1973.

41 (a) Wolf Hirth's Hi-20 motor-glider of 1936; (b) The clean ASK-14 of Schleicher powered by a 26 h.p. Hirth 2-stroke; (c) Motor-glider experts Gerd Stolle, chief of Burg Feuerstein, Hans Zacher, and Seff Kunz, late President of the CIVV motor-glider committee; (d) The Finnish Pik-20E, with an Austrian Rotax engine and glide ratio of 1:40

42 (a) First competitions were for spot landings. The rolled-up kites
have already flown and are waiting to go back up the hill
(b) Gannet landing area

Chapter Twenty-five

EVOLUTION OR REVOLUTION

The fibreglass glider is probably the most highly developed, specialised and sophisticated piece of sporting equipment that exists. It performs better without an engine than do many aeroplanes with 150 horses at full stretch. To those who love this beautiful creation, it is the love of their life; but to extract its full worth the degree of dedication and skill needs to be high, and as specialised as the aircraft itself. But for many pilots, and for many reasons, the high-performance fibreglass glider and the full benefit of its great performance are out of reach. It is too expensive, it is difficult to land neatly in fields without regular practice, and it is costly and time-consuming to mend. Its very complexity discourages short flights in non-soaring weather, and its enormous potential is increasingly frustrated by the spread of controlled airspace plus the radio and other regulatory requirements which follow in its wake. By the late 1970s the structural pyramid of the sport all over the world had largely exchanged its broad base for the attenuated pinnacle of an Eiffel Tower. There was almost no other sort of gliding except championships, and no dinghy class, even in prospect.

Outside this race to the top there were, of course, still plenty of people who wanted to fly. They had no interest in becoming aeroplane pilots, soaring as a bird was physiologically impossible, but owning a 20,000 dollar glider just as remote. Hope did not disappear but was of little value without substance or technical ability. It ultimately became reality from an unexpected quarter, when Francis Rogallo designed a free-flying kite—which might have a possible use for the recovery of space vehicles. This structurally simple device could

231

obviously support man, and it could be made at home cheaply
from easily obtainable polythene and bamboo. It was unimportant that flights on such primitive aircraft would not last
more than seconds, made from the top of any little hill or dune
to the bottom. Here was the chance to have your own wings,
and in California's soft climate it was quickly grasped. Few
people spent any time wondering why such a simple aircraft
had not appeared before, nor appreciating that sailwing
aerodynamics were more complicated than they seemed: it
needed advanced technical understanding to produce an aircraft of such ultimate simplicity. Copies of the rogallo were
made from photographs, while those with a feel for history,
such as Richard Miller, imitated the 1896 stick-and-string
biplanes of Octave Chanute. All these aircraft flew, slowly or
badly, and sometimes uncontrollably, but they flew, and they
were taken into the air often by people who had never flown
before. In a world that had come to lack much in the way of
personal challenge the modern Daedalus, or Icarus—and there
was only a thin dividing line between them—caught the eye of
the press.

Brian Wood, who later became British Champion, saw
newspaper pictures of hang-gliding and eventually found the
address of a manufacturer. All his life he had wanted to fly so,
without hesitation, he ordered a hang-glider. Then it was a
matter of waiting with growing impatience until it came. At
last it arrived. He took it straight to a hill not far from his
home, walking to the top with the rolled-up wing on his
shoulder. He had arrived early so that there were only a
couple of people about, as he wanted to get his first flight over
before more spectators turned up. As in a dream he put on his
helmet and lifted the wing above his head, wobbling about in
an ungainly manner. 'I had that sort of sick feeling like I
wanted to go home, so I just ran. My eyes were watering so
much I couldn't see a thing; all I wanted to do was get back
on the ground. When I landed, I wished I was still up there'.
So he picked up the wing, and almost running, made his way

breathlessly up the hill for another flight. Other first-timers did not do so well.

In this new and exciting way of flying the hang-gliding of Lilienthal, Gutermuth and Pelzner was almost forgotten, but it had never in fact died. Far from the public eye individuals over the years had built themselves simple gliders with which to take off and fly like the birds. Mostly they had kept quiet about it for fear of ridicule. One of these was an American, George Congdon, who built a hang-glider in 1932. He had found some plans in a popular magazine, altered them to suit his own ideas, and used spruce, wire, cheap muslin, and stove bolts to hold it all together.

Came the day to try it out. It was important that we picked a windy day as we were not exceptionally fast runners. The glider was assembled at home and a small wagon type trailer made so the glider could be towed down the road sideways behind two bicycles. The site we had chosen was a gentle grassy slope about 100 ft high.

We excitedly hauled the machine about half way up, not wishing to take too many chances right off. The ship was a biplane with a hole in the bottom of the wing for the pilot and a leather strap to help carry his weight. I got in position and started down the hill, first running slowly to get the feel of it. I found myself running on my toes as the machine gained lift. I didn't get off the ground this time but was highly inspired with the fact that the thing really wanted to fly. The next try was more like an extended broad jump. Finally I decided to go to the top of the hill where the wind was stronger. After much perspiration getting it up there I was ready for the big leap. I started down the hill running as fast as I could. At the moment I thought I had enough speed I threw my weight to the rear and Wow, I was in the air about three feet off the ground. I sailed along twisting and turning to keep the machine in flying attitude. I must have flown over 50 ft [distance]. I really felt like a bird this time. I was so excited I could hardly talk.*

By the middle '70s there were 60,000 hang-gliders and as many pilots scattered across the world. In the United States alone some forty manufacturers were in business making not

* From *Low and Slow*, issue 2.1, 1971.

233

only aircraft but instruments, specialised pilot harness, parachutes, and all the bits and pieces needed by a thriving industry. The performance of the early rogallos was such that they could stay off the ground only if the take-off hill was really steep, but by the late '70s the glide ratio was up to around 8:1, a performance adequate for soaring. This was as well, because hang-gliding had not developed without its accidents, and many of these were the result of pilot exuberance overtaking common sense. It was not only that the limited performance, combined with the intense personal satisfaction of such flying, encouraged the more experienced pilot to exceed the hang-glider's limitations with aerobatics, but that there was no benevolent parentage. Just as the early gliders of the 1920s and '30s had been derided by the light-aeroplane pilots of the day, so the hang-glider was mostly spurned by conventional gliding. It was felt to degrade its quality and its disciplined approach to flying, and it received little help from its senior relation. So it stood on its own feet early and had to pick up much of its learning the hard way. This only added to the fierce and anti-bureaucratic independence of its adherents. Their flying needed no crews, trailers, launch equipment, airfields or rules. The complete aircraft could be carried to a mountain top by its pilot, who could take himself off and explore the sky and all that it contained. Tom Peghiny was one of these, flying from Mt Washington.

My first flight of the day was a long mellow ride to the landing area. The view was incredible, and the Fall New England foliage magnificent.

For the second flight, Terry Sweeney and I rode the Cog Railway up together, planning on a formation flight over to the South Bowl for a long traverse. Once Terry and I had set up, the soarable winds stopped, of course. Terry was content to wait for the winds to pick up, but I was afraid they would become less, so I decided to launch. The blue and yellow kite floated me into the Fall air. The Vario indicated lift, but not soarable, so I began a run of the ridge towards the landing area. As I approached the Cog tracks, the little coal-burner engine came into view. The wind was so calm that the smoke from the engine formed an almost vertical plume.

The plume looked interesting as it slowly drifted towards the peak of the mountain. I wondered what would happen if I flew through it, so I headed for the engine. Wow! I thought the Vario must be broken.

I began making 360° turns to stay in the plume. By the 11th or 12th turn, the kite was 1,000 feet and possibly 1,500 feet above the take off point, and I could see a very tiny Terry Sweeney jumping up and down and screaming. I continued the turns and lost count before the thermal petered out.*

Sometimes the single-minded independence did not limit itself to the exploration of soaring possibilities, but was carried too far by a few who trespassed onto private hills or left open farm gates. This merely lost sites for everyone else, and encouraged bans and prohibitions. Freedom there should be, but it could not be total. This was something that did not exist any more. But it took time to be appreciated.

Some restraints were both sensible and needed; it was more profitable to be taught to fly by a good instructor than to cast yourself from the nearest cliff. Schools came into being and in their teaching got across the disciplines essential to any flying. Competitions complete with rules came on the scene, and talks with aviation authorities took place to retain the essential freedoms in exchange for self-regulation. It was no longer quite the personal dream of the pioneers, but it had not strayed too far. And it was still the cheapest form of flying by a long way.

But as with gliding, after the first rush of followers to a new way of flying, there was a pause in the headlong growth. It was not difficult to soar on the hills; updraughts along the ridge were capable of supporting the poorest-performance hang-glider with its noisy rustling sail, and the technique was easy to learn. Newcomers had a grandstand view of experts flying the hill, often close enough to talk to. Soon the length of flight was limited only by daylight hours—and the physical

* From *Ground Skimmer*, June 1975, p. 20.

stamina of the pilot—and any hill worthy of the name chalked up tens and soon hundreds of one-hour flights. But again, as with early gliding, the better pilots soon wanted freedom from the hills, to fly high, to reach the tantalising cumulus that floated overhead; and eventually to land in some strange and distant field in the long shadows of evening. But this was more difficult. Certainly much was known by conventional glider pilots—how to find a thermal, to circle up fast, to maximise the inter-thermal glide, and so on; but there were few still around who remembered what it was like to work a thermal half-way up a hill in distorted lift, bent or broken by the friction of bushes or the slope itself. So the hang-glider pilot, too low to circle with any degree of safety, and not quite knowing what he was looking for, reached for the sky often frustratingly in vain. In countries with grander hills than those in England, like the U.S.A. or Austria, it was not so difficult because you could fly from the hilltop far out over the valley to pick up thermals at a height where they had become stronger and larger. So it was only to be expected that the first real cross-country soaring flights would take place in California though, again, as in the '20s, there was to begin with not always complete freedom from the hills.

Chris Price flew one of the first cross-country flights from a long ridge called Daughterey's Slide in Oregon—$13\frac{1}{2}$ miles:

About 2:30 the wind started to shift. By 3:00 the dust devils were whipping into the cliff and I was ready to go. Carol and I had worked out elaborate plans for her to find me in case I disappeared in one of those dust devils and turned downwind. As the wind started to increase, Carol let go of my nose wires and once again I was soaring. I knew as I caught the first thermal giving me a 1,000-foot gain that if Bob Wills were along he would have walked the three miles to the south end of the ridge—enhancing our chances of breaking the distance record. When I reached the steepest, tallest part of the ridge I flew away from the ridge into a visible dust devil and gained a thousand feet in about two minutes, leaving me 1,400 feet above my takeoff point. I decided to stay with the thermal as it blew over the ridge and ride it downwind. But as soon as the base of the thermal was blown over the top I lost the lift and had to penetrate back into the ridge lift. Slowly working my way back up into the wind I waited 200 feet above the eagles that were soaring down against the ridge for a dust devil that would give me enough altitude to clear the first major break in the ridge.

After about ten minutes I could see a dust devil that had a cylindrical core. As soon as it came within reach, I flew out straight into it. Going in was a little rough, but once the variometer needle was reading 500 up, everything smoothed out. I made a quick 180 downwind when the variometer started to drop. I kept on flying downwind and when the lift quit I was 1,200 feet above take off with easily enough altitude to clear the first break in the ridge.

I flew over it high enough that I could not even feel it was there. By the time the variometer needle stopped reading down I was well past the distance to the end of the ridge I had flown the day before. I also had another gap in the ridge to clear and did not see any dust devils nearby. Just before the gap, I slowed the kite and started to turn back into the wind to wait for a dust devil when a thermal moved the vario needle to 500 up just long enough to get me over the gap. Once again I was on my way downwind bobbing up and down in the lift with a ground speed of close to forty miles an hour.

The ridge, by this time, was next to nothing. The wind was blowing into it at such a poor angle that I was barely able to maintain altitude, and once again there was another gap to jump. Without any help from a thermal I just blasted across the gap. On the other side of the gap I found myself below the vertical portion of the ridge with only the part that gradually slopes up below me. With my wing tip two feet, and my body six to ten feet, from the rocks I skimmed along in ground effect with a speed of 30 miles an hour. I would gain a little, lose a little more, and so on for about a mile. With another gap coming up and just enough altitude to swing back into the wind, I landed.

After 14 hours of driving home I once again could smell the smog of Los Angeles. I wondered then as I do now if I ever really landed or ever will. It is as if the part of me that really counts—the part that hopes, wonders, aspires is not still above that ridge with the eagle, soaring in that particular moment forever.*

Although the lift was the same as that used by glider pilots,

. * From *Ground Skimmer*, November 1974, p. 14.

and the basic techniques of circling at a slow speed and flying fast between thermals was no different, just about everything else was so new and fresh. The hang-glider pilot was totally exposed to the air, the cold, and the chilly wet interior of even small clouds, without any protecting canopy. Almost without instruments, other than a variometer, usually audio and moaning gently in his ear, his flying had a physical aspect long since lost to the glider pilot. But it also demanded the same decision-making processes. Flights might be nearer 100 km. than 1,000 km., but the intensity of the experience could be even greater. Trip Mellinger, flying 24 miles from Sylmar to Palmdale, California, describes this well:

On March 4, 1976, the weather at Sylmar was incredible. The lapse rate was great and cumulus clouds were forming over the mountain range. Those enticing weather conditions found Rich Grigsby, Jerry Jacobson, Joe Greblo and myself assembling our gliders at the Sylmar 1,500 foot launch site.

It was comfortably warm, but we all knew low temperatures existed above us, so gloves, parkas and long underwear were added to our flight gear. I noticed a familiar sight next to me as Rich attached a barograph to his king post, adding to the atmosphere of cross-country possibilities.

Shining in the bright sun was my new Phoenix VI-B, awaiting its maiden voyage. While attaching my variometer to my glider, I looked up through the soaring windows and saw cumulus clouds drifting across the sky. Anticipation increased as I thought about learning to fly the new glider in such great conditions. Everybody was excited, like when you know the soaring is excellent and your feet are still ground-bound.*

The four took off and were quickly going up at 500 ft/min. Trip was soon at 6,500 ft–5,000 ft above take-off. The mountain range looked flat and, unused to being so high, he had difficulty in even locating his take-off place. Rich Grigsby was flying nearby and suddenly disappeared as they were both enveloped in the cloud that their thermal was generating:

I left the cloud and began heading east toward Mt Wilson. Miles and miles of snow-covered mountains lay 3,000 ft below. My first

* From *Hang Gliding*, May 1976, p. 40.

238

problem occurred when the batteries went out on my vario several miles downrange. Well, if the gods had decided the flight would be on sensory, so be it. Beautiful. I was sailing in a sea of clouds on currents of lift. Circling in each thermal, I would leave it as soon as cloud base was reached. Departing each cloud, I was surrounded by tumbling, swirling white mist that defined the areas of sink. Corridors of sunlight separated each cumulus and would deal out rolling punches of sink when flown through.

Over the mountains I encountered a large area of strong sink. Eventually, I was forced to leave. Flying low, I turned downwind into the Santa Clarita Valley. Much-needed altitude was retrieved as I circled in a thermal that seemed to come from a farmer's field. Once again I was at cloud base, perhaps about 6,000 ft above ground level.

It was spectacular! The whole Santa Clarita Valley appeared to be popping cumulus clouds. Large cloud shadows were cruising the flatland and were surrounded by brilliant sunlit areas. The 'go for it' signal flashed, and I began heading for the northern horizon.

Mile after mile fell away as I flew across the large valley towards a group of mountains separating it from the desert. Moving dots followed freeway lines, and occasionally a plane would fly under me, accentuating my altitude. I knew the valley went for miles in a northeast direction and most of the clouds were over the valley floor, so my flight path changed northeast, more or less the same direction as Highway 14. My goal was then decided. 'Avenue S' is a popular flying site for our northeast winds and is located just past the end of the valley I was flying over. Looking ahead, and 5,000 ft below, I spotted Rich circling what looked to be very close to the ground near Aqua Dulce Airport.

I encountered heavy sink near Aqua Dulce and my altimeter began giving up precious feet. It was really getting critical and landing sites were being chosen. Sylmar was to the rear on the distant horizon and there was satisfaction in getting as far as I had, but there had to be a thermal somewhere. Was I going up, down, maintaining? My vario was silent and I waited out the minutes as the ground began encompassing my environment.

A hawk! It was love at first sight and I joined him in what I hoped was lift and not a final approach. We both entered a bomber thermal that snatched us up several thousand feet into a cumulus cloud. I assumed the hawk was flying with me for amusement and he was a welcome companion. The country we were flying over had

239

snow on the ground and the temperature at cruising altitude was well below freezing.

A few minutes later Rich and Trip were together again, joining in a final search for lift to get them to Palmdale. Suddenly a small break in the clouds allowed areas of the ridge to become bathed in sunshine:

I left Rich to look for lift along the sunlit ridge. Working weak areas of intermittent lift, one final thermal lifted me over the top of the ridge. My goal had been reached. I began circling down. Which way was the wind blowing? I was too cold to care and finalized down a paved road that dropped away at about 10 to 1. Of course it was down wind and my frozen feet scrambled back to life as I tried to keep up with my glider. A new environment closed in around me. Earth, ground, walking; they seemed foreign. Different muscles reluctantly responded as I tried to adjust to being once again on the ground.

Rich Grigsby landed his Cumulus Vb nearby, and the same distance from Sylmar. It was the first official distance record for hang-gliders.

In smaller European countries with less good weather the opportunities for soaring cross-country were much less. The very slow flight and small turning circle of the rogallo enabled it to make use of little thermals, but it did not have the glide performance to range far for further lift with cloudbase at only 3,000 ft or so, nor could it penetrate into any but the lightest winds. By 1977 the longest distance in Britain was 24 miles, by Robert Bailey, flying a large-size Wills Wing Cross Country with a Colver variometer. He got into a good thermal shortly after taking off from Carlton Moor, near Newcastle. This took him to 3,975 ft A.S.L. He entered cloud several times, side-slipping out, and then going straight downwind. The next thermal was picked up at 2,000 ft, after which he subsided to 800 ft above the ground, then retrieved the situation with another good thermal to 3,000 ft. But now lift became patchy and without the glide performance to wait for it to improve there was not much chance of continuing. A weak thermal to 1,400 ft added another mile and then it was over. Bailey landed in a field, and tucked the rigged hang-glider behind a hedge while he went to telephone his position. He returned to find a policeman with his helmet and harness. We've got your gear, lad,' he said, 'but we can't find your horse.' In 1979 Bailey flew the first 80-km. distance in Britain.

Meanwhile, in the Californian summer the high cloudbase, strong thermals, and conveniently high mountains from which to launch were opening up possibilities which, less than five years earlier, would have been unthinkable on 160 sq. ft of dacron and a few tubes. Trip Mellinger again:

On Saturday morning cumulus clouds were forming over the mountains and conditions looked great. We flew twice that day, but were unable to go any further than 16 miles. We did have the

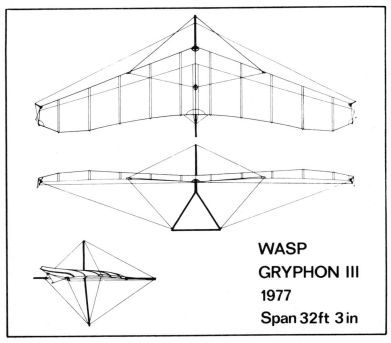

WASP
GRYPHON III
1977
Span 32ft 3in

FIG. 34. The Wasp Gryphon III, designed by Miles Handley

241

pleasure of watching a sailplane fly over us at Cerro Gordo travelling up-range the way we wanted to go. Disappointed, yet still satisfied with a great day of flying, we camped out in the Owens Valley and looked forward to the next day.

We woke up Sunday morning to a beautiful cloud street that was developing along our planned route.

At take-off, dust devils were breaking off the cement slabs left from the abandoned mine shafts and a large cumulus cloud was forming rapidly over our heads. Periodically we could hear the wind rumbling up the canyons toward us.

Barographs were sealed by our observer and mounted out of reach of the pilot on the glider. Survival equipment and other instruments were also mounted and final pre-flight was carried out. Gene and I both wore heavy clothing even though it was fairly warm on take-off and almost 95 degrees in the valley below. We knew that at cloud base it would be close to freezing.

Gene in his Phoenix 6B, was the first to take off at 12:30 PM. He immediately gained 2,000 ft over Cerro Gordo, and turned up range. I was unable to follow because of sudden downwind conditions until nearly 20 minutes later. I lost nearly 2,000 ft of altitude soon after take-off. My heart was sinking along with my glider until I caught an 800 ft f.p.m. thermal and gained almost 6,000 ft to cloud base!

Now directly underneath the cloud street, I pulled the bar in for more speed and began cruising from cumulus to cumulus toward New York Butte. It was there I met Gene circling in a thermal with an eagle. We both climbed to 14,000 ft then sped downrange under the clouds.

Our technique for covering as much distance in the shortest time was to mark average cloud base on our altimeters. When that altitude was reached, we would fly as fast as possible through both lift and sink until we had reached 12,000 ft. We knew we could always find a thermal from that altitude. Sometimes we were able to fly for several miles full speed without losing any altitude at all!

The view was incredible. The Owens Valley lay nearly 10,000 ft below us to the west and the Saline Valley 12,000 ft below to the east. Some clouds we flew over, some under, and some we went right through, flying as fast as we could. Cloud base seemed to vary between 13,000 ft to 14,000 ft. One time I saw Gene circle up and disappear into the base of a cloud. He told me later that the cloud was not all that big and he wondered what it would be like to ride the lift to the end. He kept on circling and circling in light grey limbo until rays of sunlight began shining through. Suddenly, he popped out the top and found himself looking down on the cloud! The shadow of his glider on the cloud was surrounded by a circular halo caused by the sun's rays.

The turbulence we encountered was not too strong. What tired us the most was flying at 14,000 ft. We could definitely feel the lack of oxygen and our breathing had to be consciously controlled to help prevent hypoxia. Concentration at this altitude sometimes would become difficult, but flying down to 12,000 ft would help clear our minds.

Mile after mile fell away as we approached our goal. Reaching cloud base at 14,500 ft under a large cumulus, I recognized Westgard Pass just ahead and Big Pine to our left. We didn't have to come down and more distance could have been covered, but we found ourselves flying out into the Owens Valley toward Big Pine. We were tired and cold, and both of us had had enough. We landed at 3:30 p.m. outside Big Pine about one mile apart.*

Only months later this record was beaten by George Worthington with a 95-mile goal flight on an ASG-21, hand-painted like a butterfly.

So now there were two glidings and two soarings, polarised at each far end of the performance spectrum. And there were two almost unrelated families of pilots, but using the same sky for the same reason and the same pleasure. As the conventional glider became more specialised, sweeping its pilots further into competition for speed, so those whose ideas about flying were less specific went to the other extreme; a common factor in any revolution. The problem now lay, not in all the flying that was being done, but in the emptiness between the two. Apart from a small number of vintage gliders, lovingly restored, and light gliders, such as the Ka-8, used almost exclusively for training, there was nothing between the 800-dollar hang-glider and the 18,000-dollar glider. A few individuals were building rigid aerofoil hang-gliders like the Mitchell Wing, or complicated light gliders, some with trap-doors for the feet, but that was all. Conventional gliding was geared to launch fast and heavy aircraft and pilots were

* From *Hang Gliding*, November 1976, p. 20.

generally unenthusiastic about slow aircraft with poor relation performance. At the other end the hang-glider pilot was not too enthusiastic about rigid wings like the Quicksilver or Easy Riser. They lived uneasily with the roll-up, one-man portable flyable hang-glider because they lessened the intensely personal independence that was held so dear. What was needed was something in between for those people who wanted to fly an aircraft less physically demanding than the hang-glider, but simpler and less expensive than the high-speed glider. There was room for an ultralight weighing more than the heaviest hang-glider, about 88 lb. (40 kg.) but substantially less than the conventional glider—say, a top limit of 220 lb. (100 kg.). It would not draw many of the pilots already committed to the love of their choice, but widen the opportunity for the many who waited.

The Mitchell Wing was certainly a candidate for an ultra-light category, although a genuine hang-glider. In return for its rigidly constructed wing and stable aerofoil section, which provided it with a glide ratio double that of the flexible wing, it gave away one-man portability, and it could not be quickly rolled up and safely put away if the wind on the hill became too strong. But its design had development potential and its better performance gave it the penetration needed to fly against the wind or reach more distant thermals. In the hands of a pilot, George Worthington, who flew both gliders and flexwings, the Mitchell Wing set up the world's first goal-and-return record for hang-gliders:

The Mitchell Wing, once you've really gotten used to it, is a very safe easy hang glider to fly. However, it seems very fragile in comparison with flex wing kites, and overly susceptible to major damage on minor ground loops and crashes. So, even though it is easier and safer, I worry more about take-offs and landings due to the likelihood of time-consuming and expensive repairs in the event of a minor crash. Consequently at the time of launch I was particularly taut and tense.

The take-off went well, though I would have liked more than the 4–5 m.p.h. upslope wind I was getting. At 8,200 feet above sea

43 (a) Deep billow hang-glider, 1974
   (b) Bob Wills, the first great hang-glider pilot, killed in 1977 by helicopter rotor downwash
   (c) Manta Fledge 2 Class III competition hang-glider, with tip draggers for turn control
   (d) The first International Champions. Dave Cronk and Roy Haggard, U.S.A., returned home with first and second places at Kössen 1975

44 (a) Vulturelite Emu: span 35 feet, nose angle 140°, aspect ratio 6.3, weight 52 lb, 1979; (b) Bennett Phoenix 8, glide ratio 8:1, 1977; (c) Strong wind flying at Perranporth, Cornwall. The Gryphon is airborne, held only by its wires

level hang-gliders need 16% more speed to lift off than at sea level. I headed for the valley, full of confidence that I'd soon be on the ground.

Three minutes later, after a loss of 400 feet I caught a smooth powerful thermal. The steady gain in this one thermal was 8,500 feet. As I circled in the thermal I noticed that I was being blown southward, although very slowly—perhaps five miles per hour so that my outward journey was going to be upwind.

My first thermal peaked at 17,000 feet. I left my program of continuous right hand 360°s and headed north. It was bitterly cold, and I was grateful for the ski type blizzard pants. But even with their extra warmth and protection I was beginning to shiver. And that was one of the two main themes of the flight—cold! The other theme was the almost constant fear of being sucked up into the black overcast above.

After gaining 8,500 feet in the first thermal and losing 3,000 of it in a 9 minute straight glide, I figured that the plan would be to find thermals, get up high, and glide down hill till I found another etc., etc. But it wasn't like that. The overcast, with rain just ¼ mile east of the spine of the mountains, was sucking the air up the west slope of the mountains and allowing me to fly straight ahead 60% of the time. The other 40% I would circle in lift to gain a few thousand feet.

I could clearly see Peak 13559 about 8 miles ahead and the picture was changing. The lift grew relentless and pressured me into increasing speed (and sink rate) to 50 m.p.h., which is still full forward. (I can't conveniently move my weight forward or backward at all once I'm in my hammock seat.) I searched the sky for an escape route should the lift push me unwillingly into the cloud. It was my feeling that a turn directly out toward the valley would lead me to air which wasn't going up as rapidly. But I was still going up slowly and was worried. For 9 miles I kept up the 50 m.p.h. speed at about 14,500 feet and shivering with the extra cold that the added speed brought. I felt that I might possibly be in a trap and it would spring closed at any time. And there is a difference between the Mitchell Wing and flex wing rogallos in the event of being sucked up into a cloud. Rogallos are inherently stable machines. If you close your eyes and hold your body in a cruise position the kite will stay up-right and make only mild turns. But the Mitchell Wing, in the same circumstances will turn, pick up speed and enter a grave-yard spiral. You won't know, with your eyes shut or in a cloud which way it is turning.

245

I headed toward the turn point, snapped my picture and wondered if I'd get back. The lift situation had changed because I was lower and because I was beyond the mountain temporarily. It was like crossing a gap in a cliff when you're ridge soaring.

I moved in close to the mountain and was losing a little altitude as several miles passed by. Then a thermal, a 2,000 foot gain and I was up again into the strong lift bank, and close to that same threat of being sucked up into the clouds.

For the next 22 miles back to the launch site, it seems to me I flew a straight course, varying my speed depending on the lift and maintaining at right around 14,500 feet. I was still very cold! When I was about 5 miles from take-off I began trying to lose altitude. Full speed produced about an average of 300 feet down per minute. The rest was easy.

The landing was greatly aided by the smoke flare I released at 500 feet. Without the flare I would have had no firm and accurate idea of the wind direction. The smoke bomb gave it to me and allowed me to make a picture perfect stand up landing. The flight had lasted 2 hours and 25 minutes.*

The hang-gliding revival was born in the warmth of California, so it would have been strange if the States had not continued to lead the way. But it also lost no time in spreading fast across the world. The Australians went for it as airborne surfing, the Danish authorities built a hill from tipped rubbish for training, some Poles saw a photograph and built what it looked like, but misinterpreted the scale so that their first hang-glider was far too big, and the Swedes taught themselves tow launching on snow-covered fields. In New Zealand a 50-mile coastal ridge was found, perfect for soaring. But everywhere there were problems. Hang-gliders were so easy to build or buy, and all that their owners wanted was to get into the air. In the absence of trained instructors and operational standards, together with the lack of the single-minded devotion and thought that so often safeguard the first pioneers, there were accidents. It did not take long to collect a reputation for hazard; which like all reputations remained with it longer than was justified. Conventional

* From *Hang Gliding*, December 1977, p. 48.

246

gliding, fearful of being considered any sort of a relative offered little or no help. Something was needed to draw everybody and their ideas together, to create an opportunity not only for exchanging talk, but for flying in that best of schools— friendly competition.

During the winter of 1974 word got around that a world event was being arranged in some obscure village in Austria. It all seemed a bit unbelievable, but such was the enthusiasm and the need to get together that in March 1975 nearly 300 pilots from twenty countries turned up at Kössen, when only fifty had been expected. They arrived as individuals and flew a simple task: straight from a tramped strip in the snow on the Unterberg mountain 540 metres down to a target landing they came on noisy, rustling wings, some barely achieving their vaunted 1:4 glide ratio. There were great arguments on what constituted a good landing, there was lots of accident-free contest flying, the Meister of the Kössen band wrote a fanfare to be played at the opening and prizegiving, and at the end two Americans, David Cronk and Roy Haggard, and an Austrian, Christian Steinbach, stood to be garlanded and photographed.

In September 1976 the world returned to Kössen for the first official F.A.I. World Championships in hang-gliding. This time there were 150 selected pilots in teams from twenty-six countries, divided into three Classes: Standard Rogallos with a nose angle of 90°; second generation sailwings; and a Class III which was open to rigid wings and hang-gliders with aerodynamic controls. Tasks were again target landings, but now with points for soaring up to a limit of 10–15 minutes' duration. Again it was a great get-together with talk far into the night on control and performance, competition tasks, training, accident causes, instruments; all the material, in fact, with which to forge a new technology.

This time it was not the Americans who won. The Austrian Steinbach brothers, as expected, took Class I, but in third place was a 16-year-old Australian, Ricky Duncan. The Class II Champion was not much older, Terry Delore, 17, from New

Zealand, and neither was the Class III winner. He was another Australian, 18-year-old Ken Battle.

A long three-year gap before the next World Championships resulted in the world trekking back to Kössen in September 1978 for the first F.A.I. European Championships. 175 competitors arrived, forty-two from countries as far as Brazil and Japan, even though they could not be eligible for the title of champion. But in just three years the change was remarkable. On elegant and silent wings pilots soared, set off cross country to strange landing fields, or flew distance over a series of markers laid out in the valley. There were still target landings, but with so many pilots finding it easy to gain the maximum score interest was starting to wane. It was the exploratory delights of cross country flying that was fun. Again, results were surprising; not only was it a European championships but it was Europe's turn to take the honours in straight contest. Of the top nine places in the three classes, Austria and France gained 3, Britain 2, and W. Germany, 1. Kössen will hold more championships, inevitably run, as all have been so far by Sepp Himberger, and the world will return to this little Tirolean village with its painted houses, because Kössen is now a part of the fabric of hang-gliding, much as the Wasserkuppe was to the early glider pilots.

The second F.A.I. World Hang-Gliding Championships in 1979 were held among the great limestone cliffs of the western edge of the Alps near Grenoble, attracting 181 pilots from twenty-five countries. There were thirteen consecutive days' flying, no accidents, and over 3,000 contest flights, but sadly no long cross-country task was set through waiting too long for perfect weather; inevitably it turned sour during the last few days. Wings were now becoming increasingly sophisticated, a few with floating cross-bars permitting asymmetrical deformation of the sail to improve turning; while deflexers, those early high drag aids to sail control, were fast disappearing. Variometers with audio were standard. Some pilots now had flown 1,000 hours on hang-gliders, and it was hard to even remember the first world events of 1975 when great rustling sails sank rapidly down the face of the hill.

But could this rate of progress be maintained; or should it be? With talk of using water ballast, drag chutes, and radio, was hang-gliding not fast becoming just another high-technology aviation sport, and losing its essential simplicity? Maybe the thought crossed a few minds but competitive soaring was the thing and the solitude of the old pioneers theirs to keep. High in the hot sunshine of France pilots flew who had seen far horizons, who had learnt their skills on the wind, and who now only wanted to fly with it on invisible thermals just as far as it was possible to go. Such a great exploratory migration had occurred once before, in the 1930s in Germany, and until it was satisfied there had been no reason to think of any other future.

As with any other sort of flying, hang-gliding is as safe or dangerous as its devotees make it. But it took time to discover what standards or teaching, or administration were needed. There could be no instructors until enthusiasts had first become pilots and gained experience, and pilotage standards could not be introduced until pilots themselves had demonstrated what sort of flying was practicable. Airworthiness standards still live in a state of breathless pursuit of new aircraft which a week earlier could have been no more than a pencil sketch. But for all the turbulence of its arrival hang-gliding, in less than a decade, brought into the air an overdue injection of new people, ideas, and a fresh approach to the delights of flying. It revived the dream.

And so gliding came full circle. In the eighty-eight years since Lilienthal set aside the feathers and started to build gliders which flew, the evolution of the human bird has been great. But like other birds it is subject to the pressures of an overcrowded world with just the same risks of becoming an endangered species. It must fight to survive.

Appendix 1

SOME MAJOR WORLD RECORDS FOR SINGLE PLACE GLIDERS
Initial and current (1979) records in each category

DURATION

30.8.21   Klemperer, Germany, Blaue Maus, Wasserkuppe   13 min.
3.8.33   Kurt Schmidt, Germany, Grunau Baby, E. Prussia
   36 hrs 36 min.

Duration records were discontinued in 1937 following an attempt which ended in a fatal accident after 40 hrs 55 min.

ALTITUDE

18.8.22   Martens, Germany, Vampyr, Wasserkuppe   108 m.
25.2.61   P. Bikle, U.S.A., Schweizer 1-23, Bishop   14,102 m.

DISTANCE

4.9.20   Klemperer, Germany, Schwarzer Teufel, Wasserkuppe
   1·83 km.
25.4.72   Werner-Grosse, W. Germany, ASW-12, Lubeck   1,460 km.

DISTANCE AROUND A TRIANGULAR COURSE

18.1.77   Werner-Grosse, W. Germany, ASW-17   1,063.53 km.

GOAL

8.3.35   Hans Fischer, Germany, Darmstadt-Saarbrucken   140 km.
14.1.78   S. H. Georgeson, B. L. Drake and D. N. Speight, N.Z., Nimbus 2s, Tower Peak, Te Araroa   1,254.26 km.

GOAL AND RETURN

14.4.38   Heye-Straatman, Germany, Hirschberg-Liegnitz-Hirschberg   85 km.
9.5.77   Karl Striedeck, U.S.A., ASW-17   1,634.7 km.

APPENDIX 1

SPEED ROUND 100-KM. TRIANGLE

22.7.48   S. Maurer, Switzerland, Moswey   69·6 km./h.
8.7.74   K. Briegleb, U.S.A., Kestrel 17   165.35 km./h.

SPEED AROUND 1,000-KM. TRIANGLE

18.1.77   Werner-Grosse, W. Germany, ASW-17   98.54 km/h.
17.2.78   Werner-Grosse, W. Germany, ASW-17   109.71 km./h.

HANG-GLIDERS

Distance in a straight line: G. D. Worthington (Mitchell Wing),
2 July 1977. U.S.A.   153·61 km.
Straight distance to a goal: G. D. Worthington (ASG 21),
21 July 1977. U.S.A.   153·61 km.
Out and return distance to a goal: G. D. Worthington (Mitchell Wing),
23 July 1977. U.S.A.   76·38 km.
Absolute altitude:
Gain in height: Jerry Katz (Alpine 2), 23 July 1977. U.S.A.   2,987 m.

Appendix 2

WORLD GLIDING CHAMPIONSHIP WINNERS AND BRITISH PLACINGS

1948	Samedan, Switzerland, 37 entries	P. A. Wills, Gull IV	10
	One class, 7 contest days	L. Welch, Meise	14
	Per-Axel Persson, Sweden, Weihe	R. C. Forbes, Weihe	17
		P. Mallet, Weihe	21
1950	Orebro, Sweden, 29 entries	R. C. Forbes, Weihe	15
	One class, 6 contest days	L. Welch, Weihe	24
	Billy Nilsson, Sweden, Weihe	P. Mallet, Gull IV	25
		P. A. Wills, Weihe	27
1952	Spain, 56 entries	P. A. Wills, Sky	1
	Single seater (39), 5 contest days	R. C. Forbes, Sky	3
	P. A. Wills, Gt. Britain, Sky	L. Welch, Sky	9
	Two seaters (17), 5 contest days	G. H. Stephenson, Sky	11
	Juez/Ara, Spain, Kranich		
1954	Camphill, Gt Britain, 43 entries	P. A. Wills, Sky	2
	Single seaters (34), 4 contest days	G. H. Stephenson,	
	G. Pierre, France, Breguet 901	Olympia 4	14
	Two seaters (9), 4 contest days	L. & A. Welch, Eagle	7
	Rain/Komac, Yugoslavia, Kosava		
1956	St Yan, France, 58 entries	G. H. Stephenson,	
	Single seaters (45), 6 contest days	Skylark 3	6
	P. MacCready, U.S.A.,	P. A. Wills, Skylark 3	10
	Breguet 901		
	Two seaters (13), 6 contest days		
	Goodhart/Foster, Gt. Britain,	Goodhart/Foster, Eagle	1
	Eagle		
1958	Leszno, Poland, 61 entries	H. C. N. Goodhart,	
	Open Class (37), 6 contest days	Skylark 3	2
	E. Haase, W. Germany, HKS-3	A. J. Deane-Drummond,	
	Standard Class (24),	Olympia 419	7
	6 contest days	G. A. J. Goodhart,	
	A. Witek, Poland, Mucha Std.	Olympia 415	7
		P. A. Wills, Skylark 2	18

1960	Butzweiler, W. Germany, 55 entries Open Class (20), 6 contest days	H. C. N. Goodhart, Olympia 419	4
	R. Hossinger, Argentina, Skylark 3 Standard Class (35), 6 contest days	A. J. Deane-Drummond, Skylark 3f	13
	H. Huth, W. Germany, Ka-6	G. A. J. Goodhart, Skylark 2	24
1963	Junin, Argentina, 63 entries Open Class (25), 7 contest days	J. S. Williamson, Skylark 4	8
	E. Makula, Poland, Zefir Standard Class (38), 7 contest days	H. C. N. Goodhart, Skylark 4	11
	H. Huth, W. Germany, Ka-6	A. J. Deane-Drummond, Olympia 463	15
1965	South Cerney, Gt. Britain, 86 entries Open Class (41), 6 contest days	J. S. Williamson, Olympia 419	6
	J. Wroblewski, Poland, Foka 4 Standard Class (45), 6 contest days	H. C. N. Goodhart, Dart 17	7
		G. E. Burton, Dart 15	5
	F. Henry, France, Edelweiss	A. J. Deane-Drummond, Olympia 465	9
1968	Leszno, Poland, 105 entries Open Class (48), 7 contest days	G. E. Burton, SHK	7
	H. Wodl, Austria, Cirrus	H. C. N. Goodhart, HP-14c	16
	Standard Class (57), 8 contest days	J. S. Williamson, Dart 15w	22
	A. J. Smith, U.S.A., Elfe S-3	D. Innes, Dart 15w	30
1970	Marfa, U.S.A., 79 entries Open Class (39), 9 contest days	G. E. Burton, Kestrel 19	4
	G. Moffat, U.S.A., Nimbus 22	J. Delafield, ASW-12	7
	Standard Class (40), 9 contest days	A. W. Gough, Std Cirrus	17
	H. Reichmann, W. Germany, LS-1	C. Greaves, Std Libelle	24
1972	Vrsac, Yugoslavia, 89 entries Open Class (38), 7 contest days	H. C. N. Goodhart, Kestrel 19	4
	Göran Ax, Sweden, Nimbus 2	G. E. Burton, Kestrel 19	6
	Standard Class (51), 6 contest days	J. Cardiff, Std Libelle	25
	J. Wroblewski, Poland, Orion	B. Fitchett, Std Cirrus	32
1974	Waikerie, Australia, 67 entries Open Class (28), 11 contest days	J. Delafield, Nimbus 2	10
	G. Moffat, U.S.A., Nimbus 2	G. E. Burton, Kestrel 19	12
	Standard Class (39), 11 contest days	B. Fitchett, Std Cirrus	4
	H. Reichmann, W. Germany, LS-2	J. S. Williamson Std Libelle	25

1976	Räyskälä, Finland, 85 entries	G. Lee, ASW-17	1
	Open Class (39), 7 contest days	B. Fitchett, ASW-17	18
	G. Lee, Gt Britain, ASW-17		
	Standard Class (46),	G. E. Burton, Pik-20c	3
	5 contest days	R. Jones, Cirrus 75	12
	I. Renner, Australia, Pik-20		
1978	Chateauroux, France, 79 entries		
	Open Class (24), 11 contest days	G. Lee, ASW-17	1
	G. Lee, Gt Britain, ASW-17	B. Fitchett, ASW-17	4
	15 metre Class (32),	S. White, ASW-20	11
	11 contest days		
	H. Reichmann, W. Germany, SB-11		
	Standard Class (23),	Entry withdrawn	
	11 contest days		
	Baer Selen, Netherlands, ASW-19	No entry	

HANG-GLIDING

International Championships	(Best British Placings)	
1975	Kössen, Austria, 98 entries		
	D. Cronk, U.S.A.	A. Beresford	13

First F.A.I. World Championships

1976	Kössen, Austria, 145 entries		
	Class 1 (44), 7 contest flights		
	C. Steinbach, Austria	A. Beresford	6
	Class 2 (61), 7 contest flights		
	T. Delore, New Zealand	L. Cruse	21
	Class 3 (40), 7 contest flights		
	K. Battle, Australia, Moyes	J. Carr	10

Second F.A.I. World Championships

1979	Grenoble, France, 181 entries		
	Class I (146), 17 contest flights	J. Carr	2
	J. Guggenmos, W. Germany,		
	Wings		
	Class II (35) 16 contest flights	R. England	10
	Rex Miller, U.S.A., Fledgling III		

Appendix 3

GLIDER DATA TABLE (metric)

Name (with designer/constructor)	Year	Span (m.)	Wing Area (m.)	Aspect Ratio	Empty Weight (kg.)	Flying Weight (kg.)	Ballast Capacity (kg.)	Wing Loading (kg./m².)	Best Glide Ratio (km./h.)	Best Sink m/s. (at km./h.)	Max. Speed (km./h.)	Aerofoil
AUSTRIA (Kupper)	1930	30	34·97	25·7	364	482·4	—	13·8	—	—	—	Gö 642 mod
ASW-12 } (Waibel/Schleicher)	1968	18·3	13	25·8	320	430	—	31·8/33·10	47/90	0·48/70	200	Wortman 62 K131
ASW-17 }	1971	20	14·7	27·2	405	570	100	32/39	48/62	0·52	240	Wortman 62 K131
BOWLUS BABY ALBATROSS	1932	13·6	13·9	13·2	114	226	—	16·2	20/54	0·69	105	Gö 535
BREGUET 901	1954	17·3	15	20	230	415	—	28	35/80	0·65/70	220	NACA 63
DART 17r (Slingsby)	1964	17	13·9	20·4	248	355	—	26·6	35/83	0·64/70	—	NACA 643 618
FAFNIR (Lippisch)	1930	19	18·6	19·4	200	280	—	16·6	25	0·76	—	Gö 652/535
FOKA SZD-24 (Schneider)	1959	15	12·16	18·5	225	312	—	25·7	34/86	0·66/75	260	63-618-4415
GRUNAU BABY	1933	13·57	14·2	13	170	250	—	17·68	17/60	0·85/55	150	Gö 535
GULL 1 (Slingsby)	1938	15·3	14·86	15·8	172	284	—	19·1	24/67	0·72/59	129	NACA 4416
HJORDIS (Buxton)	1935	15·55	11·5	21	141	216	—	20·1	24	0·6/56	—	Gö 652
HKS-1 (Haase/Kensche/Schmedt)	1953	19	18·3	19·7	300	520	—	28·4	37·2/80	0·56/72	200	65 215 714
HP-11 (Schreder)	1962	15·85	9·64	26	182	295	—	30·6	37/89	0·55/80	—	NACA 65-3-618
KA-6 (Schleicher)	1955	15	12·4	18·1	185	300	—	24·2	29/78	0·68/67	—	63-618 Joule 12%
LIBELLE STD. (Glasflugel)	1967	15	9·8	23	185	350	50	35·7	38/85	0·6/75	250	Wortman
MEISE/OLYMPIA (Jacobs)	1938	15	15	15	165	290	—	17	25/70	0·67/60	—	Gö 549
METEOR (Obad/Ikarus)	1956	20	16	25	405	505	—	31·5	42/90	0·6/77	250	632 616·5
MINIMOA (Hirth)	1935	17	19·5	16	200	298	—	15·3	26/72	0·6	—	Gö 535
MÜ. 13 ATALANTA (Schmidt)	1936	16	16·5	15·5	145	235	—	14·25	24/60	0·58/45	220	—
NIMBUS II (Holighaus)	1971	20·3	14·4	28·6	340	530	60/120	37	49/90	0·48/75	200	Wortman
PHOEBUS C	1967	17	14·06	20·6	269	363	—	25·8	40/90	0·5/80	262	Eppler 403
PHOENIX (Nagle/Eppler)	1957	16	14·36	17·83	165	265	—	18·5	37/80	0·53/69	185	Wortman
PIK-20 C (Eiri-Avion)	1973	15	10	22·5	210	450	140	28/45	42/117	0·69/92	206/139	NACA 43012 A
SCHEIZER 1-26	1954	12·2	14·9	10	161	230	—	17·5	23/79	0·82/56	200	—
SCHWARZER TEUFEL	1920	9·2	15	5·6	61	136	—	9	—	—	—	—
SIGMA (Operation Sigma)	1969	21	12·2/16·4	36·2/26·8	606	710	—	58/43	45/115	0·52/76	—	mod Wortman
SKYLARK 3 (Slingsby)	1955	18	16·1	20·5	253	375	—	22·2	32/74	0·56/65	210	NACA 633-620
STAKHANOVETZ (KIM 3)	1935	20·2	23	17	294	454	—	19	27/75	0·6	—	—
VAMPYR	1921	12·6	16	10	120	195	—	12·2	14	0·7	—	—
WEIHE (Jacobs)	1938	18	18·2	17·8	195	335	—	18·4	29/76	0·58/76	180	Gö 549
WIEN (Lippisch)	1929	19·1	18·6	19·5	—	248	—	13·3	—	—	—	Gö 549 mod
WINDSPIEL	1933	12	11·4	12·6	55	136	—	11·92	23	—	—	Gö 535
Motor Glider												
SCHEIBE SF 27m.	1967	15	11·96	18·7	261	386	—	31·3	30	0·7	158	
SCHEIBE SF 25c.	1968	15·3	17·5	13·4	375	580	—	30	19/70	1/75	180	
Hang-gliders												
BIRDMAN CHEROKEE	1979	10·06	18·58	5·44	25	105	—	5·65	8	—	—	
GRYPHON III	1977	9·8	15·2	7	23	82	—	5·39	10	—	—	
SIROCCO 2	1978	10·6	17·1	—	24·4	106	—	6·2	9	0·76	—	
PELZNER	1920	5·4	14·2	—	8-10	—	—	6·47	6	—	—	
Manpowered Aircraft												
GOSSAMER ALBATROSS (MacCready)	1979	28·6	44	18·6	31·7	97·5	—	2·19	—	—	—	Lissaman 7776
Birds												
CONDOR	—	3	1·14	7·9	—	11·7	—	10·26	—	—	—	

INDEX